Chicken Soup
for the Soul.

Living
Catholic
faith

D0249623

Chicken Soup for the Soul: Living Catholic Faith;
101 Stories to Offer Hope, Deepen Faith, and Spread Love
by Jack Canfield, Mark Victor Hansen & LeAnn Thieman
Published by Chicken Soup for the Soul Publishing, LLC   www.chickensoup.com

The publisher gratefully acknowledges the many publishers and individuals who
granted Chicken Soup for the Soul permission to reprint the cited material.

Cover and back cover photos courtesy of Jupiter Images/Photos.com.
Interior photo courtesy of iStockPhotos.com/©Nancy Brammer (2windspa).

Cover and Interior Design & Layout by Pneuma Books, LLC
For more info on Pneuma Books, visit www.pneumabooks.com

Distributed to the booktrade by Simon & Schuster. SAN: 200-2442

Publisher's Cataloging-in-Publication Data
(Prepared by The Donohue Group)

Chicken soup for the soul : living Catholic faith : 101 stories to offer hope,
  deepen faith, and spread love / [compiled by] Jack Canfield, Mark Victor
  Hansen & LeAnn Thieman.

  p. ; cm.

  ISBN-13: 978-1-935096-23-8
  ISBN-10: 1-935096-23-0

1. Catholics--Literary collections. 2. Catholics--Anecdotes. 3. Catholics--Conduct
of life--Anecdotes. I. Canfield, Jack, 1944- II. Hansen, Mark Victor. III. Thieman,
LeAnn. IV. Title: Living Catholic faith

PN6071.C67 C45 2008
810.8/02/09283   2008939489

PRINTED IN THE UNITED STATES OF AMERICA
on acid∞free paper
16 15 14 13 12 11 10 09   03 04 05 06 07 08

Chicken Soup for the Soul®

Living Catholic Faith

101 Stories to Offer Hope, Deepen Faith, and Spread Love

Jack Canfield
Mark Victor Hansen
& LeAnn Thieman

Chicken Soup for the Soul Publishing, LLC
Cos Cob, CT

To Berniece and Paul Duello,
who not only taught me about the Catholic faith,
but by their actions, how to truly live it.

And to all Catholics,
who change the world as real disciples of Christ,
by authentically living their faith.

Contents

❶
~On Love~

❷
~Angels Among Us~

❸
~My Brother's Keeper~

❹
~Divine Appointment~

❺
~Miracles~

❻

~Challenges~

❼

~The Power of Prayer~

~A Matter of Perspective~

9
~Lessons~

10
~Faith~

Chicken Soup for the Soul

Foreword

*J*esus Christ spoke, "And so I say to you, you are Peter, and upon this rock I will build my church" (Matt. 16:18). Beginning at that moment, Peter, Paul, Luke and other disciples began sharing their stories to build His church, proclaim their faith, and to share it with others. Now, more than 2,000 years later, nearly 1,000 Catholics did the same as they contributed stories for *Chicken Soup for the Soul: Living Catholic Faith*. These positive, powerful stories of God's unconditional love show the role the Church plays in their personal and professional lives.

This collection of humorous, poignant, faith-filled stories from people of all ages deepens the convictions of "cradle Catholics" and ignites the passion for newer members of our Church family. Heart-warming and hope-filled, these stories will lift up your spirits and nourish your souls as they express what it means to be Catholic. Savor each story and find inspiration and healing in each message. Draw strength from your fellow Catholics as you practice these lessons of faith, hope and love.

Together, we Catholics, like Peter and Paul, will continue our calling to share our stories of trust in God, to nurture and uphold one another.

It is with great joy, pride, and humility that we are privileged to share with you *Chicken Soup for the Soul: Living Catholic Faith*.

Living Catholic Faith

On Love

This is my commandment; love one another as I love you.

~John 15:12

Just One Minute, Young Man

No language can express the power and beauty and heroism and majesty of a mother's love.
~Edwin Hubbell Chapin

It's been called the $20,000 breakfast, at least that's what we'd heard.

After scrimping and saving and tweaking our budget, we had come up with the $5,000 per year tuition to send our son to St. Paul's High School, a Jesuit educational institution. On the Friday before Mother's Day of the graduation year, moms are treated to a morning of celebration. Although it was quite "hush, hush," we had heard whispers about it from other moms who had been there. We had an idea of what to expect, but still we were not prepared.

Gather 150 young men of seventeen and eighteen years on a hot and humid May day, dress them up in their finest attire, stuff them into a crowded, non-air-conditioned auditorium to sit beside their moms for more than three hours. It's bound to be interesting.

The morning began with a celebration service, a rose, and a tissue packet for each mom. Each boy—big strapping football players, small late bloomers, smart kids, challenging kids, quiet kids—crossed the archway to manhood. Each had one minute with the microphone. One minute to look into his mother's eyes and tell her what was in his heart. One minute to condense his entire lifetime into words that would last a lifetime. Just one minute to bare his soul in front of 300 others.

Some boys had been up all night searching for the perfect words, some had been working on this for months. All were stressed, nervous, and more than a little petrified.

We moms felt their anxiety and it started to rub off on us!

Everyone took pity on the poor boy who had to go first. With sweaty palms and a quivering voice, he began and set the wheel in motion. One by one each boy stood with his mother, introduced her by name and began. Many boys started with, "This is my beautiful mom." That was enough to set the waterworks flowing for most of us.

I listened intently to each boy.

"Mom, I didn't really want to go to this school, when all my friends where going to 'regular' school, but Mom I am so glad you made me come here. I will send my own son here too."

"Mom, I have worked for months on this speech and I can't stop crying long enough to read it to you."

"Mom, thank you for years and years of packing my lunches."

"Mom, thanks for not packing my lunches, for not doing everything for me, so I can be a capable adult."

"Thank you, Mom, for the thousands of miles of driving you've done."

Others went on to thank their mothers for giving up the best piece of chicken and the biggest slice of cake. Some said they were sorry for late nights and missed curfews, for not being respectful or for the bedrooms and bathrooms left in various states of disrepair. Some dug out wrinkled papers from their suit pockets, some just spoke from the heart. Some sang a song written especially for the day. Others crooned the songs their mothers had sung to them as children. One young man started to sing "You Are My Sunshine" but couldn't get through it; still he wouldn't let go of the microphone or his mom until he choked out every last word.

It was absolutely gut-wrenching to watch. I felt privy to the most intimate moment a mother and son could share. Some boys read prose, some read their own poetry expressly written for this day. Some recited quotes and some just cried and barely uttered a word.

How could it be that each moment seemed frozen in time, yet went by in such a blur? Each boy's speech was unique and beautiful, poignant and sincere. Each one perfect. Never had I heard the word "mommy" used by so many grown boys, unapologetically, unabashed, uninhibited, even surrounded by all their peers. Some draped over their moms' shoulders as they choked out the words that had been buried for so long; "I love yous" that hadn't been said and hugs too infrequently shared. Each boy-child-man who spoke was raw, honest, and genuine, and each mother listening must have felt her heart either skip a beat or stop beating altogether. The moms spoke no words that morning. Mouthing "I love you" was about the most we could muster. Besides, this was not our day to speak, it was our day to listen, just listen.

Soon you came to realize that it was not just what your son was saying to you that was important. These boys were speaking to mothers everywhere, on behalf of boys everywhere. They were speaking for the boys who could not find the words or the courage or the right time or the right place. They were speaking for those who wanted to forgive, who wanted to say "I'm sorry," who wanted to move their relationships forward, who wanted to start fresh, who wanted to tell their moms they were their mentors, their guides. It was a thank you given for things that can never, ever be repaid by boys who understood that to be God's truth.

Then my son stood. "Mom, we exchange I love yous and hugs and stuff all the time but I want to say in front of everybody how much I love you. You have always been there for me and always believed in me, and always encouraged me not to settle for less than I deserve or am capable of." He swallowed hard. "You are my rock, Mom."

I willed myself not to cradle him in my arms and rock him.

The sacrifices that each family had made to send their sons for a Catholic education, whether financial or social—most likely both—the questioning and wondering if we were doing the right thing, were unequivocally answered on this beautiful day in May. After 150 "one minutes" were up, everyone gathered in the schoolyard to pray together and plant a tree in honor of the growth and personal development these boys had experienced.

The event is over, words have been forgotten, new memories and milestones are being achieved, but the depth of feelings, the emotional and spiritual connections of that day will be remembered forever.

The $20,000 breakfast was a bargain in my book.

~Stephanie Staples

The Twinkie

Amen I say to you, unless you become like children,
you will not enter the kingdom of heaven.
~Matthew 18:3

It was my seventh year teaching first grade. I was teaching at the parochial school I had attended, associated with the church I went to my whole life.

One little girl from that class, Abby, had immigrated recently from Greece with her parents and grandparents. Abby was the only one in the family who could speak English, and she had to translate everything for her parents, including school notes, bills, and report cards. All this responsibility was obvious on Abby's shoulders and face, leaving her little time just to be a kid. She hardly smiled or laughed. Usually, no one wanted to play with her. She didn't know the rules of the games, how to be a friend, or how to engage others. She was alone in a crowd of happy people, standing on the sidelines, watching the world with her ice-blue eyes.

I worked with Abby beyond the standard curriculum. I focused on social skills, trust, and friendship. I taught her how to play, beam a friendly smile, how to be a child.

Slowly, Abby learned to trust, smile, and play. She had turned the corner that spring and was happy, instead of hunched over like a turtle ready to climb into her shell. Her schoolwork skyrocketed and she was passing every test. She even volunteered to answer questions.

One mid-March day, many exciting activities were going on at school. It was pizza day in the cafeteria, and the junior high was putting on a carnival for the younger grades. Extra recess was planned just to celebrate the warm sun.

Before the tardy bell rang, Abby stuck her cold lunch in her desk. But then something terrible happened, at least on a child's level — the kind of thing that could poison one against taking chances, trust, and friendship — someone stole the Twinkie out of Abby's desk.

I was infuriated! I was not going to allow anyone to victimize her and disrupt her progress. I stopped all morning work and had the class put away their crayons, markers, and blocks. The students' heads were down on their desks, cradled in their arms. Without letting them know how angry I was, I asked who took the Twinkie, and demanded its return. There would be no punishment if this was done right away.

No Twinkie appeared.

A few students indicated they saw Peter take it, but I felt it was up to the thief to confess. We sat in silence for fifteen minutes. No one came clean.

There would be a new plan for the day: school work would be sent home as homework. No recess; we would stay inside with heads down on desks. We would eat lunch inside in silence. And we would not be going to the carnival until the Twinkie was returned. Their little faces showed such disappointment. It broke my heart. But there were two lessons to be learned: own your mistakes with the truth, and don't pick on others. It was a teaching moment not written about in textbooks, a lesson that would be used for the rest of their lives.

Reading was supposed to start, but the class still sat with their heads down, thinking and listening to me lecture on the importance of honesty and being responsible for your mistakes.

I was really sweating it out. Was I being detrimental? Overreacting? No, my heart told me. All we needed was the truth.

The clock ticked off the seconds, minutes, and startlingly, hours.

It was almost time for the carnival. I tried another lecture, but no one flinched.

My afternoon aide arrived. A mother of four, she volunteered to take the kids one by one into the hall for questioning. I figured they might confide in someone they saw as a motherly figure rather than an authority figure. However, since there hadn't been a confession in more than four hours, I thought chances weren't good.

When the time came for Peter to be questioned, it was over within a minute. He came back into the classroom, tears welling in his eyes, hands shaking. He stood in the doorway, hanging onto it as if he'd collapse if he let go. He took deep breaths, trying not to cry. "I took the Twinkie. I'm sorry," he said in a small voice. Then he covered his face with his hands in shame.

I was livid. We had been lied to for more than five hours, with nothing accomplished. I wanted to lay into him, take out my anger through a verbal throttle. But the class had already heard my thoughts. So, I pulled a "Daniel" and threw Peter to the "lions," waiting for the attack. Let the ones who suffered throw the first stone. "Does anyone have anything they'd like to say to Peter?" I asked.

There was silence for at least a minute. I knew the kids were measuring their words, choosing their fights, remembering missed recesses. I waited.

Then, one little girl raised her hand. Maybe she'd open the kids' "anger floodgates." She pushed in her chair, stood straight and proud and said in a strong voice, "We forgive you, Peter."

The words echoed through our heads. Forgiveness... one of the last things Jesus taught us as he was dying on the cross. Forgiveness.

Suddenly, all twenty-eight kids raced to Peter and surrounded him with hugs and pats on his back, cheers, and laughter. It was like the prodigal son had returned home.

I had forgotten that God saved Daniel from the lions, and God saved little Peter. But He also saved me from a life of anger. I learned that day how forgiveness heals. How good it feels to say, "I forgive you," and how relieving it is to hear that you are forgiven.

And the contraband Twinkie? Abby never did eat it. She gave it back to Peter with a warm hug and smile.

~Holly Engel-Smothers

God Is With Us

Therefore you shall love the Lord your God with all your heart,
and with all your soul,
and with all your strength.
~Deuteronomy 6:5

"Come on Peanut," I shout. "Grab my hand!" I reach out, grasp the tips of Emily's fingers and manage to fish her out of a sea of teens, all trying to jump on one of the buses headed for downtown Rome—as in Italy.

"I've got you!" I exclaim with a grin, while pulling her through the door and safely into the bus. But what about the others? I quickly lock eyes with each exhausted, yet still wired, teen to do a head count.

"One, two three, four, five," I count, eyes darting around the bus. "And, six!" Okay. My group is all here. It's an exciting time, yet as the bus lurches away from the curb, we are so pressed together that I can't move an inch. For the hundredth time today, I think, "I must be nuts to chaperone teenagers on an overseas trip! I'm getting way too old for this!"

As the ancient ruins of the Coliseum and Roman Forum zip past our tinted windows, teens trade trinkets representing their homeland with the other passengers, while singing songs in their native tongue.

It's August 2000; our church youth group flew to Rome to join 2.5 million young people from 157 different countries—six continents—for the 15th annual World Youth Day. That's one big spiritual family reunion! Yesterday, we hooked up with everyone, in the fields next to the University of Rome Tor Vergata, for the Great Vigil. Then, we crashed for the night in sleeping bags and blankets and awakened to international contemporary choir music followed by a morning worship service.

This is the place of the early Church, a land watered with the blood of the first martyrs—the Apostles Peter and Paul and countless others who died rather than compromise their Christian beliefs. We arrived in the Jubilee year to walk in their footsteps.

Just last night we were jammed shoulder to shoulder into the Piazza del Popolo singing the World Youth Day theme song, "Emmanuel." My never-tiring teens, ever present to all the sights, sounds and smells of Rome, sang along, their hungry hearts opening wide to the gift that only "journey" can bring.

Five nights ago, as the World Youth Day's opening Rite of Welcome was about to begin, we stood full of anticipation on the square in front of St. Peter's Basilica in the Piazza de San Pietro. Various AM and FM station frequencies were dedicated to airing the message from our Pope in some twenty different languages. As our group frantically dug through their fanny packs for their radios, Kelly and Mike tugged at my shirt.

"Which station for English?" they asked.

Scanning the dial, Erin found it first and yelled out, "FM 98.5!"

"Untangle the earbuds. Share if you need to," I yelled. "Okay... good... two kids to a set... that'll work."

Pressing the headsets to our ears we heard, "May Jesus Christ, Word of God, who has called you from every continent and invites you to be converted, guide your steps, enlighten your minds and make your hearts pure, so that you may joyfully proclaim his Gospel."

"What's he saying now?" Mike whispered.

"Shhhh—listen!" hissed Emily.

"This is a time to encounter the ever-living Christ in the city of the martyrs. You are heirs to a great past. Be not afraid! Open your hearts, lives, difficulties, problems and joy to Christ. Jesus knows all that is inside you. To serve Christ is freedom. Jesus desires to enter and live in you. He knocks on the door of your heart. Christ is inviting you on a path of holiness to eternal life. Pray together, young people, with the gift of union. Jesus Christ is the same yesterday, today, and forever.

"What are you here in search of? Who have you come here to find? Search for Jesus Christ, yet understand that Jesus has first gone in search of you. Celebrate the meeting! God works mysteriously in the situations of your life. You are called to light and are a human person being called to glory. Each one of you is precious to Christ, known personally and loved tenderly, even when you don't realize it."

What beautiful, relevant and profound words, shared by the now eighty-year-old Pope John Paul II. He loves these teens deeply. And the teens could tell.

In unison, as with some invisible prompting, the crowd began chanting, "Giovanni due Paolo, Giovanni due Paolo..."

At one point, a boy darted past security and into the Pope's arms. We all watched in wonder as he embraced and consoled the young man. During this tender moment, security knew not to intervene.

"Look, he's talking to him," Peanut exclaimed, tears streaming down her cheeks. "He's hugging him like a real daddy and, and... I am, he is... I mean we are, each of us, the whole world, you, me, we came all this way and... The Pope loves me too. Right John? Just like Jesus?"

"Yes, Peanut," I whispered. "We are his family, the whole Church and He loves us." I looked around to see that everyone had tears streaming down their cheeks. We each felt the Pope's embrace and understood how united we are in this one, holy Church—God is with us.

Pressed together with teens grasping for words to encompass their feelings, I shared, "Isn't it exciting to know that God has chosen you, just like the Pope chose that boy up there, and no matter what has happened up to now, He wants to do many wonderful things in your life?"

Now, it's our last day here. As our bus weaves through the streets of Rome, words shared earlier that day by youth pastor Jim Beckman echo in my heart. Tragically, he had lost three teens from his church's youth group when they were killed in the Columbine school massacre. That morning he passionately challenged our youth to journey.

"You know the truth!" he had cried out. "Stand up and be proud of your faith! Get over yourself and be willing to risk and take the special graces from Christ in this Jubilee year out to the rest of the world."

"Hey, here's our stop," I yell as we approach the intersection near our hotel. "C'mon everyone. Kelly, Paul, Peanut—ya got everything?"

"We made it!" shouts Erin. "Get ready to get off. The pilgrimage is over."

"Is it really?" I ask. "Or is it just beginning?"

~John Crudele

Editor's note: Reaching our youth touches both the future of their souls and the Church. To learn more about World Youth Day and other remarkable conference and program opportunities for Catholic youth see, www.partnershipforyouth.org.

The Holiday Lottery from Heaven

Set me as a seal on your heart, as a seal on your arm,
for stern as death is love...
~Song of Songs 8:8

My husband grew up in a large Italian Catholic family in South Philadelphia with three families of aunts, uncles and cousins living on one block of Cross Street, and many of the other relatives just a few blocks away. Uncle Tony and Aunt Grace lived right next door to my in-laws, Philip and Rose. The two couples were especially close since Uncle Tony and Philip were brothers and Aunt Grace and Rose were sisters.

In addition to being very large, and concentrated in a three-block radius, my husband's family was unique in one particular way—the family had a category of relatives most other families do not. While the family had mothers, fathers, sisters, brothers, aunts, uncles, cousins, and grandparents, they also had a category of relatives known as "The Deads." My husband's relatives talked about the Deads as if they were still alive, especially around the holidays. A typical conversation between Rose and Grace would sound like this:

Grace: "Roe, what did you do today?"

Rose: "Oh, I went food shopping, stopped to see the Deads, and then made my gravy."

Grace: "Oh yeah? I saw the Deads yesterday."

Sure enough, whenever I went to the cemetery with my husband, all the Deads would have fresh flowers on their graves, sometimes two and three arrangements, depending on how many of the relatives had been to see the Deads that week.

My husband's family was also unique in that they had a special rule: If a Dead came to you in dream and spoke a number, you played the number the next day in the lottery.

I came to know about this rule in 1989. Uncle Tony, who had taken over his father's fruit and produce business, died unexpectedly at the end of August of that year. His death was very hard on Aunt Grace, for they had been married a long time and had been very much in love. One night, about two weeks after Uncle Tony's death, I was in Aunt Grace's kitchen with my mother-in-law when Aunt Grace said, "Tony was a great lover." The shock of this statement quickly dissipated when Aunt Grace then stated, "The week before our wedding, Tony came to my house every day and gave me a present. He was a great lover." Aunt Grace then put her head in her hands and started to cry.

As the holidays approached two months later, Aunt Grace was, understandably, a little depressed. In addition to losing her husband, money was tighter than usual and the Christmas season loomed.

At the end of November, Aunt Grace came running into my mother-in-law's kitchen one morning all excited. "Tony gave me the number last night!"

"What do you mean?" my mother-in-law asked.

"Well, last night I had a dream, and in it I dreamt that I was asleep in bed but Tony was downstairs. All of a sudden, Tony starts yelling, 'Grace, Grace, there's someone in the house! Call 911, call 911!' After that, I woke up."

My mother-in-law "remained," which is the word she used to mean that she "remained quiet and said nothing."

Aunt Grace went on. "Well that means that 911 is tonight's number! Tony just gave me tonight's number!"

The news spread through the family with the speed of sound, but because Uncle Tony had spoken such an ordinary number, only

Aunt Grace and Uncle Tony's best friend, Johnny Gerace, played the number that day.

That night, I was eating over at my in-law's house when seven o'clock rolled around. My mother-in-law looked at the clock and said, "El, it's almost seven. Go see what the number is."

As the houses in South Philly are so small, I only had to walk about thirty feet from the kitchen table, through the dining room, to reach the TV in the living room. After I turned the TV on, the familiar lottery music filled the room. The number started to be drawn right away. Turning my head to the left, I hollered, "The first number is... nine."

"You're full of soup," my mother-in-law answered.

"The second number is a one," I hollered a little louder.

By this time, my mother-in-law, father-in-law, and husband started walking quickly into the living room.

"The third number is a... 1. 911! 911!" I yelled.

Naturally, my mother-in-law started screaming, and we all ran back through the kitchen, out the back door, across the little yard, and into Aunt Grace's kitchen. Aunt Grace, seated at the kitchen table, her head bent and in her hands, was crying and hollering, "Tooonnnyyyy, Tooonnnyyyy!"

As my mother-in-law grabbed her hands and smiled into her face, Aunt Grace whispered through choked tears, "He always gave me extra money around the holidays, and he's still finding a way."

With so many relatives living so close, Aunt Grace's house filled quickly, the coffee was made and re-made, and the story told and retold. Relatives who did not live around the corner called on the phone to congratulate Aunt Grace.

Since that night, I have known that love really does transcend time and space.

~Ellen C.K. Giangiordano

VoVo's Miracle

So faith, hope, and love remain, but the greatest of these is love.
~1Corinthians 13:13

"Love is caring," VoVo told me as I sat at her bedside, holding her hand.

VoVo (the Portuguese name my family affectionately called my great-grandmother) was bedridden and receiving hospice care in the comfort of my grandparents' home. My grandma had called to let me know the doctors thought VoVo wouldn't be with us much longer. Urgently, I had set out on a twelve-hour trip to see her one last time. I was seeking wisdom. I knew VoVo held the secrets for a meaningful life.

The daughter of Portuguese Catholic immigrants, VoVo was born Mary Angel Costa in 1907. She was sixteen when she married and she and her new husband lived with her parents and six younger siblings. When she was twenty-two, she gave birth to her second daughter, my grandmother Lorraine.

The immigrant family was venturesome. First, they launched a Portuguese sausage-making business. Then, Mary partnered with her father to run a grocery store. As the Depression reared its ugly head in 1929, many families couldn't afford groceries. Mary's father insisted on helping by extending credit for numerous families. He was the first to show her that "love is caring." But, his selfless caring led to financial disaster when numerous credit extensions went unpaid.

Disaster didn't stop there. After her parents' deaths two years later, Mary assumed her father's debts, lost the business and became her brothers' mother. She fell sick from grief and spent harrowing days in bed, feeling hopeless and helpless.

In a heroic effort, Mary pulled herself together. She persuaded creditors to give her time to repay them. She found a job in a candy shop making decorative chocolates for wealthy celebrities. In time, all of her family's debts were repaid. Her determination kept the family from bankruptcy.

"Be thankful for everything, Lauren. And love others. Love is caring," VoVo repeated.

I nodded as though I understood. But, did I? I felt an uncomfortable twinge of guilt. My life had seen little hardship in comparison. Through her many losses, VoVo found the strength to give and be thankful for the smallest things. She never spoke a negative word about the families that refused to repay her even after their hardships ceased. Looking at the inner courage of a woman facing death made me realize I had so much to learn.

"My life is a simple life," she said as her rosary dangled gently between her fingers. Simple? She saw nothing heroic in her efforts to care for her family. I did.

I remembered the story VoVo had recalled many times. Her sister Olivia was going through hard times. One of her two children had died at the age of sixteen. She had gotten divorced, and suffered from her own ailments that led to the amputation of one of her legs. With a heavy heart, VoVo looked at what she could give. She only had two dollars in cash to get herself through the week. She had no bread in the house and her cupboards were almost empty. But, she realized she had flour and milk and so she determined to make her own bread. After struggling with the decision, she said a prayer to God and resolutely slipped her very last two dollars into an envelope addressed to Olivia.

As she saw the mailman approaching, she gave him the envelope and he, in turn, passed her a few. Walking back to the house, she started opening her first letter and a check fell to the ground. She picked it up, and sure enough, it was a check for $10! At that moment, VoVo felt God was blessing her for doing the right thing to help her sister.

And now, with heaven's door just a few days away, VoVo raised her pointed finger to make sure I understood her important words. "Be thankful for everything, Lauren. And love others. Love is caring."

Therein lie the secrets for a meaningful life.

~Lauren Aileen Davenport

Ave Maria

I will sing of mercy and justice;
to you O Lord, I will sing praises.
~Psalm 101:1

My father's voice was clearly singing the lead that Sunday morning in the spring of 1948. I was an eleven-year-old altar boy in a white shirt and dark robe standing with the water cruet in my hand as Dad began. His high, sweet, clear tenor voice was captivating. He led the voices of the congregation to new heights, inspired them with joy to reach notes they didn't know they had within them. Nor had they realized, when they first followed, how high my dad could go. "Ave Maria."

St. Veronica Church in East Detroit, Michigan was special that day. The other altar boys, in their black and white outfits, looked at me and smiled. I averted my eyes, but I was secretly proud and pleased that my father was singing on the other side of the sacristy.

Dad had been singing in barbershop quartets with friends, at company picnics, in beer gardens and saloons. Never in church. People turned in their pews to see the source of those glorious sounds. My father's voice had already been recognized by talent scouts who had invited him to sing in the huge cathedral in downtown Detroit. They'd tempted him with promises of heavenly acoustics and large crowds. Dad refused. He felt unworthy. He had been invited to compete on talent shows such as Ted Mack's *Amateur Hour* and locally produced radio shows during the 1930s and 1940s. Dad declined all invitations to showcase his talents. He feared that he would lose too many friends.

None of my five siblings sang with Dad, nor did our mother join in. Mom sat between her oldest daughter and Dad as he put enough energy into his singing for all of us. Another parent might have said, "You should be singing, too. Everyone in church is singing." Not Dad. He was singing for his life. "Ave Maria."

Dad was lost in his own voice and in the beauty and feeling and release of the lyrics as he celebrated the rapture of his second year of sobriety. His singing came from a deep, loving, spiritual place in his soul. And music that comes from the soul is God-like.

My siblings sat with their feet dangling off the edge of the pew, or with their little legs and feet sticking out.

Late one night, I found Dad on his knees near a chair in the living room, praying intensely, squeezing his rosary beads desperately. "Hail Mary, full of grace..." Dad changed a bead for each completed prayer. I believe now with all my heart that prayer was what gave Dad the strength he needed to avoid alcohol. He attended no meetings. He saw no counselor. He knew no sponsor. Prayer was the only recovery program my father ever used to maintain his sobriety.

Dad wasn't sick in the mornings anymore, which meant he was able to work in the car factory regularly, which resulted in his being offered a promotion. He turned it down, explaining, as usual, that he would lose too many friends. Nevertheless, the regularity of the paychecks improved our lifestyles.

As he drove us all home from church in our black 1941 Hudson that memorable day, Dad overflowed with the good feelings that come from singing with your heart and soul and he sang his personal favorite, "You are my sunshine, my only sunshine, you make me happy when skies are gray..."

During church services, I suspect Dad may have been singing his faith. Dad never said.

Three weeks before Christmas that year, in his bed, at home, Dad passed away from stomach cancer. Hundreds of his friends attended his wake and funeral.

Dad's been gone a long time now and yet both the spiritual and musical qualities of his sweet tenor voice remain with me. They are now stuff of legend with his children, grandchildren and great-grandchildren. The memory of his singing comforts me when my skies are gray. I know he is singing in that heavenly cathedral of my dreams where it won't cost him any friendships.

When my life is less than musical, I pray, "Lord, help me remember, through Dad's spirit, that You are my sunshine."

~John J. Lesjack

Passing God's Test

Then let us no longer judge one another, but rather resolve never to put a stumbling block or hindrance in the way of a brother.
~Romans 14:13

While visiting my parents in Arizona, my two daughters and I attended Mass for the Feast of the Immaculate Conception. We were driving down the road leading to the church when I saw something I'd never seen in this town before. A woman, obviously homeless, was pushing a shopping cart filled with her belongings. Where the heck did she come from? I quickly forgot about her while I settled my girls into the first pew. As the opening song started, I noticed out of the corner of my eye the homeless woman slipping into the pew next to me.

I couldn't believe it. She had a torn filthy jacket and jeans, worn-out tennis shoes, greasy hair, and a very unpleasant smell about her. As the Mass began, my mind was not intent on the word of the Lord, but only on this woman. All I could think about was the fact that I had to sit next to her, hold her hand during the Our Father, and even shake it while offering her peace.

Just as the second reading was beginning, my young daughter said she needed to use the restroom. Normally, I would insist she wait, but I took this as my chance to escape. We then slipped to the back wall to finish out the Mass. Again, I was not listening to what the priest said, but thanking my lucky stars that I was not sitting next to that woman anymore.

Then I caught the priest's words, "... all of God's children." I felt heat spreading throughout my body. I felt weak and ashamed.

This woman, no matter what she looked like or smelled like, was still one of God's children. She may have been grimy from living on the streets, but her faith was so strong she pushed her cart for miles to be at Mass. She knew that she would be welcomed in God's house no matter what.

I knew then and there that God was testing me and I was failing. I'd forgotten everything my parents and catechists spent years teaching me. Most importantly, I had forgotten God's golden rule... treat others how you would want to be treated. I had treated this woman like the plague, like she was nothing. What kind of example was I setting for my two young daughters?

Looking up, I realized that the congregation was about to sit down. I took the hands of my daughters and marched them down the aisle to the front pew. We squeezed past the homeless woman, back to our seats beside her. I said a quick prayer to God for understanding and wisdom. As my body began to cool and the knots in my stomach untwisted, my ears opened to the Word of God.

As we began to recite the Our Father, I tightly held the hand of the woman next to me. I wished her peace, as did both of my children. I stood behind her as she received the Body and Blood of Christ. I watched her kneel in prayer and reverence, as if the Holy Spirit was working inside her.

We walked out of the church and I immediately lost sight of the woman. I looked everywhere for her and her cart. She wasn't on the road leading away from the church either. It was as if she just vanished into thin air.

That day was a true spiritual awakening for me. The heat that came over me was the Holy Spirit working through me, helping me pass His test.

~Joanne Mancuso

Saying Yes

If you wish to return, O Israel, says the Lord, return to me.
~Jeremiah 4:1

y mother asked me the question she had been asking every Sunday for more than four years. "Would you like to come to Mass with me today?"

I think I was more surprised than she was when I responded with a simple "Yes."

For four years, I had been as staunch in resisting her offer as she was in making it. But it seemed that medicine, other people, and self-reliance were no longer enough. After undergoing surgery upon surgery to combat degenerating bones and soft tissue in my feet and ankles, I felt it was time to take all my feelings, confusion, and disappointment about everything—including God—and lay them right upon the altar.

Ever since my teenaged rebellion, I had come to believe that churches were full of hurting, damaged people and that religion was a crutch. But in the course of descending, step-by-step, into the world of disability, I knew that those two criteria now made me more than a viable candidate. I was a broken person—both literally and figuratively—and I had unsuspectingly become an expert on the use of crutches.

It was my mother who helped me from the car that day. When she swung open the heavy, wooden door at the front of the church, I was met by a strong musky odor and a lingering scent of incense.

With beams of multi-colored light streaming in from the stained-glass windows and the candle above the Blessed Sacrament flickering in the dim morning light, I wrapped my fingers more tightly around the plastic grips of my two, tall aluminum legs and hobbled into the church.

With a dip of my finger in the holy water, I said to myself, "Okay, God. I'm here. Have your way with me." It took more effort than I'd hoped, but I hobbled to the last row in the back of the church. When my body finally succumbed to the wooden pew, it creaked and groaned right along with me. I set down my crutches atop the kneeler and with my heart beating fiercely, I said, "Go on, God. I dare you—work a miracle in my life."

As the Mass progressed, a comforting sense of familiarity drove me to clasp my hands together. How was it that everything in my life had changed—no more running up the stairs, tennis, or walks on the beach—yet the rituals of the Mass were exactly as I had remembered? The Kyrie. The Gloria. The opening prayer. The readings. The responsorial Psalm. The Alleluia. With ease, each part came flooding back to me. Before the Gospel, as if in reflex, I took the back of my right thumb and made a small sign of the cross on my forehead and lips and then my chest. And afterward, without even relying upon the missalette, my voice commingled with those in worship around me as I recited the Apostles' Creed—word for word—a prayer that was a staple of my childhood and teens.

It was during the consecration, when the priest placed his hands over the bread and wine and every head was bowed, that I lifted my sights above the pews. I stared at the host. The priest raised it like a brilliant harvest moon over his head, up toward the crucifix that hung high above the altar.

"God, do you really love me?" I asked silently, holding my gaze upon the outstretched arms of Jesus Christ on the cross. Those arms drew me in. His answer whispered into the reaches of my soul. "I love you this much." With a catch in my throat and my eyes growing moist, I could feel my reign of rebellion finally loosening its desperate hold.

I wish I could write that by the time my mother and I left church that day, I threw away my crutches, that all of my pain suddenly vanished, that I never needed another surgery, that I was no longer disabled and I lived happily ever after, healthy and well. But I would still have a long road to travel.

But with my mother's intercession, I returned to the church into which I was baptized and in the process, I arrived at a place where I would begin to deepen my faith and my trust. God boldly answered my dare that day. He did work a miracle in my life, even though it wasn't a pat, Hollywood-style resolution. Instead, by finally welcoming God back into my heart and into my life—by visiting His house regularly to receive His Son's precious Body and Blood—He restored to me a much-needed sense of peace and wholeness and strength so I could continue on my journey.

~Kathleen Gerard

This I Know

The love of God has been poured out into our hearts
through the Holy Spirit that has been given to us.
~Romans 5:5

It happened on the first holy day following my First Communion when I was a third grade Catholic School girl.

Back then, we fasted from the night before until we received Communion the next morning. Sister Mary Madonna reminded us not to eat breakfast because we would be receiving Communion at Mass. When Sister Mary Madonna spoke, the whole class listened. She was an Audrey Hepburn version of a young beautiful nun. She walked in a golden glow of love.

Sister Mary Madonna suggested that when we got home, we should put our Oxford uniform shoes under our beds. Then, when we dressed in the morning and knelt down to get our shoes, we would remember that our morning prayers would be at Mass and that we should not eat breakfast.

I thought that was a great idea. When I got home, I changed out of my uniform and put my shoes under the bed.

I played outside, ate dinner, did homework, went to bed, woke up, washed my face, brushed my teeth, ate breakfast and got dressed. What a scramble when I couldn't find my shoes! I looked everywhere, becoming more desperate when I realized that time was running out and I was going to have to go to school out of uniform!

I finally gave up all hope and tied on my red Keds tennis shoes while my father lectured me on responsibility and organization.

Oh surely, I thought, the wrath of God would be on me today, or at least the wrath of Mother Superior.

At morning assembly, we said the Pledge of Allegiance, recited the rosary, and sang, "Holy, Holy, Holy," none of which spared me my first demerit for wearing the wrong shoes. That turned out to be only the first humiliation of the day.

The second was when Sister Mary Madonna asked if anyone had eaten breakfast. I was the only one who raised my hand. It was at that moment that I remembered where my uniform shoes were, and why!

Sister Mary Madonna merely nodded, but I was heartsick to disappoint her.

We filed into church and I had to sit in the "will not be receiving" section, taller than the first- and second-graders around me. I tried to be inconspicuous by slouching and tucking my glaring red shoes under the kneeler.

And then, the greatest heartache of all. When most everyone at Mass went forward to the banqueting table of Jesus Christ, I had to stay kneeling in my pew.

Jesus was right there. He had come in the flesh for me. I wanted Him, but I could not get to Him. He had died his agonizing death for me and all He had asked in return was for me to skip breakfast. I was distraught, unworthy and abandoned. I had failed Him. I was brought to tears.

After, we processed with song back to our classrooms and all those who had not eaten breakfast (that is, everyone but me) were given graham crackers and milk.

Justified penance, I thought. If I was not worthy enough to receive Jesus, than certainly, I was not worthy of receiving the same graham crackers and milk the worthy ones were.

I folded my hands on top of my desk and tried not to cry.

"Cindy," Sister Mary Madonna softly called my name, "will you come to my desk please?" The aisle between my desk and hers seemed longer with every step and my bright red sneakers marked my shame as surely as a Scarlet Letter.

She put her hand on my shoulder. Her long veil and full sleeve enfolded me and created a curtain between us and the rest of the class. She handed me a graham cracker and began to open a carton of milk.

"I saw you crying at Mass, Cindy."

I nodded and sobbed at the same time. The graham cracker stuck to the roof of my mouth.

"Why were you crying?" she asked, while holding the carton of milk so I could sip from the straw.

I looked up into her eyes and answered, "Because I wanted Jesus."

She took a starched hanky from deep within her sleeve and dabbed away my tears. "And Jesus wants you."

Then she handed me a holy card picture of Jesus blessing the children gathered lovingly around his lap. She said, "See how much Jesus loves you. You did receive Communion today, Cindy. A spiritual Communion. Jesus came to you because you wanted him. Jesus always hears you. He hears your heart and He answers you. Always."

At that moment, the unfathomable mystery took on utter simplicity.

Simply, completely, unquestionably, having eaten breakfast or not, Jesus loved me.

I giggled and cried at the same time. Again, Sister Mary Madonna dabbed away my tears.

"You know, don't you, Cindy?" Sister Mary Madonna hugged me.

"Yes, Sister, I do."

My heart had broken open to the sureness of His pure love and it filled me with an unspeakable joy that has stayed with me all these days.

Jesus loves me.

This I know.

~Cynthia Hamond

Living Catholic faith

Angels Among Us

*The Lord before who I walk will send his angel with you
and prosper your way.*

~Genesis 24:40

Mother's Voice

> *There never was any heart truly great and generous*
> *that was not also tender and compassionate.*
> *~Robert South*

My mother passed away quietly on an ordinary Monday night. I remember because it was so like every Monday night, no hint at all.

When we got home from grammar school, my sister and I did our homework and set it out for Dad to check over and sign. Dinner was served and cleaned up, and then we turned on the TV. I positioned the ironing board to watch *I Love Lucy* as I sprayed Niagara starch and pressed our white uniform blouses. Next I polished our regulation navy Oxfords and left them to dry on a sheet of newspaper. All was ready for Mass tomorrow. We said prayers by Mother's bedside, and then scurried up to bed.

Sometime in the night, I heard the front door open. Subdued voices did not fully rouse me, and after the door latched closed again, I fell back to sleep.

The next morning, Dad didn't just call from the bottom of the stairs as usual, he came up to our room, teasing and tugging our toes through the covers. "Wake up you sleepyheads!"

Uh oh. Why was Dad fooling around on a school morning?

The sun streaming in the window told me it was late. Dad had always gone to work by now and we'd probably miss the bus. I lifted my face to him, my question unspoken. As he stood there unshaved, uncombed, a single tear slid down his cheek.

"Her struggle is over. She's gone Home. Mother died last night."

Over? Gone? Died? There was a roaring in my ears. No. No! My mother could not be dead.

The front door I'd heard in the night! It must have been the funeral home. Sniffing, Dad tousled my hair. "Let's get dressed now." My sister, Dad, and I joined in an awful, wonderful three-way hug. He sounded positive. "Tuesday morning Mass will comfort us."

Trembling, I got up, threw up, cleaned up, and got dressed.

As students in the parish school, we always went to Tuesday morning Mass. Our mother came whenever she could. I'd always felt proud of her, taking time out like that to worship with us during the week. Few parents did. She'd be fingering her rosary, kneeling in one of the last rows. I'd quickly tap her shoulder as my class marched past her to our seats up front. I was well trained enough not to turn around after Mass started, but I always felt a deep connection just knowing Mother was back there. On those mornings I even imagined I could single out her voice as we all sang the "Tatum Ergo" or "Salve Regina."

As Dad led us into Mass, I saw my strict eighth-grade teacher sitting at her normal watchful post by the center aisle, last pew. My stomach clenched when Dad chose the seats directly in front of Sister.

Sister nodded solemnly to me as I genuflected by her elbow. In the hush, her eyes spoke—she knew.

Mass proceeded as always. Being there, surrounded by the familiar... standing, kneeling, responding, singing... I did feel calmer. My dad was right. It was comforting. I began to relax and the tightness inside subsided. Everything really was okay. I was safe.

But then, during the Prayers for the Faithful Departed, Father actually said it. He pronounced my mother's name as he prayed for the repose of her soul. It astounded me. My mother's name in the prayers for the dead! Out loud! It was horrific, surreal.

My face burned as gape-mouthed faces turned to find us...

murmurings prickled my ears. My knees shook. Subtly the organ thrummed and voices all around me rose in unison. Soft, lusty, mumbling and melodic, they blended into the well-known verses.

All but one.

Oh. No. My mother's voice. I would never again hear Mother's voice!

Sucking air as if I were smothering, I hunched, trying to be inconspicuous. My adolescent-awkward frame lurched over the pew. Sister was quick. In one silent swish, she took me by the elbows and lifted me from the kneeler. She propelled me into the narthex, pushing the swinging door closed behind us.

There I crumbled into her encircling arms. Into the fragrant cleanliness of her serge habit I sobbed. And sobbed. When I quieted, she took my face gently into her hands. Sister's earnest brown eyes held no condescension, no scolding. They shone warm and fond through the tears pooled there. Her soap-fresh face inches from mine, she whispered, eye to eye, just as if I were an adult. "Now you must be strong, dear. For your father, for your family. They need your strength."

She handed me her hanky, starched, blue-white. When I hesitated she lifted one dark eyebrow, so I used it to blow my nose and wipe my eyes.

"Now. Shoulders up." Her hand slid lightly over my shoulders as if pulling them up and back. I straightened. "God's love will get you through this." Her soft words stroked my wracked spirit. "You are okay. Go back to your seat." Her hands glided down the stiff crease of my sleeves. Almost imperceptibly, Sister squeezed my fingers. Firmly she placed her hand on my back and turned me to reenter the sanctuary side by side.

I was mortified and amazed. The nun I avoided in the halls, for whom I had the utmost respect but no real affection, had actually touched me, and hugged me. Her astonishing support was tangible in the sweet aroma still clinging to my uniform. Her tenderness was the first to penetrate my numb grief.

When I genuflected to enter the pew I did not wobble. I had no need to grab for balance. Sister believed in me. She said I had the strength to do this. It must be so. Sister said. I breathed the powdery fragrance wafting from my clothes, still warm from her aromatic hug. She was right. I was okay.

~Maryjo Faith Morgan

Reprinted by permission of Off the Mark
and Mark Parisi. ©2001 Mark Parisi.

The Miracle Doll

Whoever welcomes one of these little children in my name welcomes me.
~Mark 9:37

In the late summer of 1956, our little family farm as well as my father's furniture business were sold at auction to pay off my family's considerable debts. My father had never blinked nor considered the cost for me to overcome the crippling effects of polio. In order for me to learn to walk again, Dad totally neglected the farm and his business. He never left my side throughout all the months of my recuperation. And he never flinched at spending every spare dime we had to find the medical help available. Unfortunately, this led to our losing all the temporal things we owned, with the exception of the clothes on our backs.

My father stood with unwavering faith as we all gathered on the grounds of our little farm for the auction to begin. My mother was understandably beside herself and worried to death about where we would live and how we would survive. Suddenly, she burst into tears and blurted that it was my entire fault for getting polio. I was devastated. My dad quickly picked me up in his arms and said, "We can always find another job, and another home, but we could never replace our Christy."

And so our journey began. With no money to start over, my dad's family scraped together the money for us to move to Texas, where a Marine buddy owned a furniture store. Mr. King offered my dad the position of store manager and a small house for us to live in.

After a year, my mother was nervous and hated Texas, so once again, with the help of family and Mr. King, we scraped up the money to make the journey back home to our roots.

By the time Christmas rolled around in 1958, it didn't look like we would have a big celebration. Mom worked scrubbing floors to save up extra money for our Christmas dinner. That was one thing she missed the most... the Christmas table loaded with all the traditional Christmas foods. No matter what else might come our way, she was determined we would have a wonderful meal to celebrate the birth of the Christ Child.

Even a modest Christmas celebration was almost entirely out of the question. Of course, children never seem to give up their dreams and as the weeks of Advent arrived, I sat down and wrote a note to Santa.

Dear Santa,

Even though you stopped coming by our house, because we are so poor, maybe, just maybe you will have an extra lady doll to drop off for me this year. It's okay if you cannot bring me a new lady doll, but if you can spare a watch for my sister Peg, a slingshot for my brother Bill, and maybe a nice fire truck for my little brother, I would be very happy with that. And most of all, if you can't do that, please just leave my mommy a note, and let her know that God still loves us and everything will be okay.

Love, Christy

That Christmas morning we all gathered around the tree as usual before Mass. Wonder of wonders, besides our stockings stuffed with oranges and apples, each of us had a gift carefully wrapped and placed beneath the tree. Billy's gift was a slingshot, Mikey got a fire truck, and Peg a watch. I received the most beautiful lady doll I had ever envisioned. And Mom got a beautiful Christmas card.

Years later, I learned that Lila, one of the women my mother worked for, found her one day with my letter to Santa in her hand, sobbing that there was no way she could provide the gifts I had requested. Lila wasn't wealthy either; she and her husband Frank lived in the back of their little shoe shop. Yet Lila remade an old doll that had belonged to her daughter and sewed it an elegant silk dress using one of her own dresses. How she managed to find the tiara, I do not know. The doll was more beautiful than any I had ever seen in any toy store. The slingshot was one Frank made by hand. Peg's watch had belonged to Lila, a gift from her first husband who had died in World War II. The fire truck once belonged to Frank's son when he was a child and Frank repainted it for Mike.

The best gift of all of course, was the beautiful card to my mom, which said "God still loves you and everything will be okay."

~Christine M. Trollinger

Christ in a Stranger's Guise

> We should not forget to entertain strangers,
> lest we entertain angels unaware.
> ~Hebrews 13:2

One unseasonably snowy April in the mid-Giuliani era, my teenage daughter, Amanda, and I had the great fortune to take a whirlwind trip to New York City to see a Broadway play during her spring break from school. This was not just a trip, but a "storming" of the Big Apple, with all expenses paid by my employer for recognition of a successful project, complete with first-class airfare, two seats to *Phantom of the Opera*, dinner at Tavern on the Green, and two nights at the Plaza Hotel. Someone should have notified the unsuspecting storekeepers in Manhattan that we were converging upon their fair city to perform some serious power shopping!

Having never been to New York, we were warned by family and friends to keep purses hidden, not look anyone directly in the eye, and act as though we were hardened Brooklynites so as not to give away our true identities as two unsuspecting ladies from the Heart of America, the consummate "out-of-towners." Our strategy was to keep only minimal pocket change and cab fare handy and our purses inside our coats as we kept stride with veteran New Yorkers.

The Plaza Hotel was a contrast in extremes. Outside, the doormen greeted us at the taxi door, gesturing a welcome to the grandest hotel off Central Park. The streets were blanketed with snow and snow-white blankets from some charity covered the homeless lying atop the grates to get a bit of warmth. We nearly had to hop over them to navigate the sidewalks. What a silent but resounding statement it made about wealth and poverty.

Amanda was aghast as I hurried her up the canopied stairs, into the mahogany and crystal halls of our evening sanctuary from reality.

The next morning, after a hearty and pricey breakfast (I'd never paid $35 a plate for French toast before!), we bundled up with purses fastened securely under our coats and pockets filled with assorted one-dollar bills and coins for the homeless panhandling on what seemed to be every street corner. Off we headed on our parade down Fifth Avenue.

The pocket change and single bills were the result of hard negotiating on Amanda's part. She was determined that we would not pass even one street person without tendering some benevolence upon those who did not have the tremendous fortune of staying in such wonderful surroundings. She wore me down with my own reminders to her over the years that "there but for the grace of God" go any of us on any given day. My years of collecting Charles Dickens books and dragging my kids to our local repertory theater's *A Christmas Carol* every year had apparently impacted her in ways that were coming back to me in aces. Orphaned birds, lost dogs, "Charlie Brown" trees, and misfit toys were staples in our home. If you didn't have anywhere to go at Thanksgiving, you came to our house. My husband and I tried to raise our family to be civic-minded, law abiding and generous. It apparently worked.

What occurred next is truly unexplainable, but I swear that the events I'm about to share did happen.

We started down the street and quickly picked up the stride that swept "fellow New Yorkers" down the street in a wave of humanity that was thirty people deep. The phrase "huddled masses" had new meaning as we crowded among them at traffic lights, laughing, "We're walkin' here!" as we stood in the cold.

Amanda clinked coins into every box she saw outside the

cardboard huts shoved up against the professional buildings and glitzy storefronts. Her pockets emptied somewhere in the vicinity of Macy's. As we weaved our way in and out of stores, she hit me up for money to give, dollar by dollar, to every grate-sitter we passed. I reluctantly handed her my last single and scolded, "That's it. You're done. No more. My pockets are empty."

As we approached another crowded corner, we passed a cardboard shelter with a sign that read, "Homeless and have AIDS." A hooded figure sat motionless in the box with a blanket draped from his head down his shoulders. He never looked up. As we walked past him toward the traffic light, Amanda began to cry. I reminded her that I was out of cash and shoved my hands in my pockets in frustration. I felt the crunch of paper in my right pocket. As we waited for the world's longest light to change, I pulled out a five-dollar bill. Five dollars! No way! I looked at the money and then at my daughter's tears. "Aw, geez... here."

She beamed as she grabbed the money from my hand and started to disappear back into the crowd. I hollered, "Wait!" terrified that she'd vanish into the thin, cold air that was now cutting through my very soul.

I turned and ran toward her and the figure in the box. I watched to my amazement as he lifted his head to her in a gesture of thanks as she set the money in the box by his side. His face, almost illuminated, had nearly transparent skin and he had the palest of blue eyes. I think he may have had blond hair at the edge of the hood he wore, but I can't tell you for sure. I was just mesmerized by those eyes. He seemed to look right through me and the chill that I'd felt seconds earlier evaporated from the warmth of his expression. I felt as though I was in the presence of someone not of this world. As I wondered how I would ever explain this to anyone, a crazy thought ran through my mind. "I found Jesus... and he's in a cardboard box on a street in Manhattan."

I took hold of Amanda's hand and we turned to make our way back to the corner. We walked across the street and looked back once again toward the stranger.

There was no one there.

No box. No sign. No silent figure.

Amanda and I just looked at each other. Neither of us spoke for several blocks.

Finally, we said in unison, "Did you see Him?"

Soon we found ourselves climbing the steps of St. Patrick's Cathedral. "Let's go light candles, Momma," Amanda said. "It's Good Friday."

So it was, and so we did.

~Marla Bernard

13

A Gift to Die For

See, I am sending an angel before you,
to guard you on the way and bring you to the place I have prepared.
~Exodus 23:20

As we stared sadly out the hospital room window, the bare trees were skeletons looking blankly back at us. Green grass and budding flowers hid below the frozen old dirty snow. The gray March sky loomed as a harsh blanket overhead. It seemed nature was feeling the same sadness we were. Life both outside and inside that room was struggling to remain.

Grandma had been sick several years before. She had multiple myeloma and the doctors did not give us much hope. This was back in the days when there were not many options. Though she received treatment in the form of pills, positive results were not quick to appear. So we continued to pray for her fervently.

Our prayers were granted, and one day we were told that Grandma was in remission! My oldest sister, who was very close to her, was getting married soon and desperately wanted her grandmother at the wedding. Her prayers were answered, and the day of the wedding Grandma proudly strode down the aisle in her pink flowing dress as she was escorted to her seat, as well as into the reception.

Some years passed and Grandma wasn't feeling well again. The diagnosis: leukemia. At this point, there wasn't much hope, and she was hospitalized quite often. But this time was different. This time would be the last.

I visited her each day after work. I was in college at the time and worked part-time as well. I tried to be positive for her, as I could tell she was scared and sad.

"Soon it'll be spring," I had said to her one day, "and you'll feel better. It'll be cheerier outside."

She turned to me, and it seemed she was about to say something, but she looked away instead. I knew what the expression on her face meant. She felt she'd be lucky if she was still here come spring.

On this dreary March day, most of the family was there. My mother, my sisters, and my godparents were present. Oddly, my father, who was the most perfect example of what it means to be a Catholic Christian, was not there because he worked two full-time jobs to support his family, one of them as a Catholic School teacher and the other as a custodian. I've often wondered why God did not allow him to experience what happened next. But then, God knew he didn't need to experience it, because he already had faith enough to move mountains. What transpired next was witnessed by those of us who needed an increase in faith.

My grandmother was quite agitated as she was slipping away. But she looked out the dismal window and said, "Look. Look at the beautiful flowers and trees."

We thought she was delirious. But she persisted. "Look how beautiful!" she kept exclaiming. "I never expected it to be so beautiful!"

Had she been on any medication, we might've thought it was the meds talking, but she was not. She was giving us a special gift. She was on her way to heaven and sharing the experience with us!

"Look at all the beautiful roses!" she continued in amazement. As we all have strong devotions to St. Therese the Little Flower, this specific mention of roses touched our hearts in a special way. "Wow, there's a trellis covered with roses! Such beautiful flowers and trees! I never expected it to be so beautiful!"

She continued for quite awhile with vivid descriptions of the wonder she was seeing as she traveled home. Then she put her hand up as if to cover her eyes from a bright light. She seemed to be focused on someone we could not see, and listening intently and nodding.

"Do you see anyone, Grandma?" my sister asked.

Grandma nodded. "I see the Blessed Virgin, and she is beautiful!"

"Do you see anyone else?"

"I see Louie," she said, smiling. Louie was my grandfather, who she'd fallen in love with when she was fourteen.

"I'm so peaceful," she sighed. "I'm so peaceful."

Following in my father's footsteps, I too am a Catholic school teacher. Every year I tell my fourth-grade students this story of my grandmother's journey home to heaven. They listen in awe and amazement. I've been told by several of their parents years later that their children never forgot this story, and it really helped to instill in them a strong spiritual sense. My hope is that it does the same for you as well.

~Debra Scipioni

14

Home for Christmas

Earth has no sorrow that heaven cannot heal.
~Thomas Moore

"I'm not ready to die," my dad said tearfully.

"It's unfair. You're full of life. I need you," I shouted angrily.

In June, my dad had been diagnosed with terminal stomach cancer. The doctors expected him to live two months.

Dad always smiled and joked whenever anyone was around him. He started reading the Bible daily, saying he had to make up for lost time. He prayed continually and told us how much he loved the Lord. Dad dared to ask God for several things—to see his son get married and for quality time with his children. The Lord granted Dad's wishes.

As the Christmas holidays approached, Dad grew weaker and spent more time sleeping. He wished to spend his last days at home and with the aid of hospice, his wish came true. My mother, sister-in-law, and I shared caring for him. We learned how to be his nurses, controlling the machine that checked his vital signs, administering medications, and supplying nourishment.

Christmas had always been our favorite time of the year. This holiday season was different; we just went through the motions. My thoughts were troubling me. What gift could I give Dad to treasure in his last moments? I tried to think of things to give him great comfort. I couldn't bear for Christmas to come and not have something special for him. Would he even be here for Christmas? I wandered through malls in tears and left disappointed. Nothing seemed appropriate. Standing on my faith, I prayed that God would direct me to the right gift.

One morning, my answer came while I was driving. I visited our priest and asked him to perform a service on Christmas Day at my parents' home. Reluctantly, the priest stated that day was the busiest of the year for him. I stressed that the service was truly the only gift that would comfort Dad. I suggested doing the service early on Christmas Eve day. The priest agreed to have the service at two o'clock on Christmas Eve afternoon. I was delighted and felt ready for Christmas. I had peace of mind; I knew it was the right gift. Dad was pleased to hear about having his own special Christmas service.

On December 24th, at 4:00 A.M., my phone rang. My mother was calling to tell me to hurry to their home. Dad was dying. Living an hour away, my husband and I raced to put our clothes on and headed out. On the way we picked up my brother, Jamie. When we arrived, my dad was propped up in bed. He was going in and out of trances. He was having a deep conversation with an invisible someone and speaking in an unknown language. We had never experienced anything like it. With my arms around him in a tight embrace, I told him how much I loved him. He shook his head, came out of the trance and muttered, "I love you, too."

"Thanks for waiting for me, Dad," I cried as tears flooded.

Sternly he said, "There was no need to hurry. I'm not ready yet," as though he knew exactly when the right time would be. I sat on the bed next to my dad, hugging him tightly as though I could prevent him from leaving me. I never left his side that day. Christmas music was playing in the background as we read the Bible together.

At two o'clock, the priest arrived along with a nun. My mother informed them that Dad was near death. As the priest came into the bedroom, Dad's eyes sparkled. He smiled and held the priest's hands. He'd been waiting for him. The priest began Mass with all of us crowded around Dad. My brother, husband, and I sat on his bed. Other family members, including my mom and Dad's brother, stood in the small room. We all held hands. Throughout most of the service my dad was speaking in tongues again. Then when the priest came to Our Lord's Prayer, my dad joined in and recited the prayer out loud. After we all received Communion, the Last Rites were given.

When the service was over, Dad smiled and nodded to say thank you. Some family members left the bedroom and my mother walked the priest and nun out of the house. We turned the Christmas music back on softly.

Dad stared at the top of the dresser directly in front of his bed and shouted "Mom!"

We called my mother to come into the room. After a long pause, he said, "I'm ready." Dad raised his hands as if reaching for someone. His eyes stayed focused on his vision. His body shook, and then his soul left. We realized it was his mother he was calling. She'd come to meet him for his journey to heaven.

The Lord asked Dad to spend Christmas with Him. And Dad had received the perfect, comforting Christmas gift... for all of us.

~Julienne Mascitti

15

The Rocking Chair

At the time it comes to pass, I am present:
"Now the Lord has sent me and his spirit."
~Isaiah 48:16

When their pregnant daughter, Joyce, and her husband, Ed, moved from out of state, Flo and Bob welcomed them into their home.

Ed soon found a well-paying electrician's job, and the couple was happy to be in their hometown again, awaiting the birth of their first child. Flo enjoyed cooking for them and helping them, and as she did she reminisced about her mother, who had passed away when Joyce was only two years old. Oh how she would have loved cuddling her first great-granddaughter!

Joyce went into labor in the early morning hours. Nichole Marie Mitchell was born a healthy, happy baby. As Flo watched her daughter cradle her own daughter, she missed her mother even more.

Flo helped Joyce take care of Nichole; she bathed her, rocked her, fed her, and enjoyed her the three months they lived with them. Nikki was a beautiful baby who slept well most nights.

One night, when Nikki was about a month old, she went on a crying jag. Flo knew Joyce was exhausted that day, so Flo started getting out of bed to take care of the baby. As she put on her robe, the crying stopped; she heard the rocking chair squeaking loudly on the hardwood floor.

In the morning, as Flo was making breakfast, Joyce said, "Thanks so much, Mom, for getting up last night to take care of Nikki."

"I didn't get up last night, Joyce. I heard the rocking chair and assumed you rocked Nikki until she quit crying. Are you saying you didn't rock her, either?"

Joyce shook her head in disbelief. "This is impossible. If it wasn't me or Ed or you or Dad, who was rocking my baby last night?"

Flo smiled. "I think it was her great-grandmother."

~Floriana Hall

A Thanksgiving to Remember

To this very hour we go hungry and thirsty,
we are poorly clad and roughly treated, we wander about homeless.
~1 Corinthians 4:11

My husband had taken the car to see about a job and I stayed at the rest area with our six children. I kept them busy playing games and reading books. I prayed as hard as I could that my husband would get the job and this madness would all come to an end. When he came back and slammed the car door, I knew the news was not good.

My heart fell to my knees when he told me twenty people had showed up for the job and it was given to someone else.

That night, one of the churches in Portland had a free dinner, so we hurried and had the children wash up in the bathrooms. We all loaded up in our run-down car, with the muffler held up by a coat hanger, and filled the radiator with water again. I thought how good it would be to have a hot meal instead of bologna sandwiches every night. No one would get this thrilled about a hot meal, but being homeless, we all knew what a treat this would be. We all just kept eating the soup, chicken, potatoes and biscuits as if we could store them up for later use. When we were ready to leave, I asked for the leftover biscuits, as did many others who were homeless. They only served one meal a week and I wished it were every day.

That night, as we did every night, we read the Bible by flashlight. I don't think we would have been able to hang on if not for the Word of God that we read before we went to sleep. Words like, "I will never leave you nor forsake you." When you're homeless, it's as if you become invisible to the rest of the world. You do begin to feel as if you're all alone in such a big world.

In the morning, we were all just as tired as when we went to bed. It's not easy at all to sleep eight people in one car. It's hard to stay warm with only the few blankets we had to share among us. We got in the car and left to make a garbage dump run. We drove around to the back of the grocery stores and went through the Dumpsters in search of food. We found fruit that was bruised, some bread that had not all turned green. Many times on a good day, we found doughnuts and other kinds of sweets. However, standing there I could not help feeling overwhelmed at the fact that we were fighting the flies and maggots for our next meal. "God give me strength," I would say time and time again.

As my husband looked for work every day, my children and I would walk around the city picking up cans and bottles to return for the deposit. Sometimes we collected enough to get some juice and a sack of cookies to go with our bologna.

When nothing else worked, my husband and I would stand with a sign that read, "will work for food." It was an embarrassment and we felt so ashamed. I never looked up at anyone, pretending that I was elsewhere and this was not happening. Some people threw food at us and screamed horrible names. But we had to survive, and for the sake of our kids we would do whatever it took to get them food to eat.

Thanksgiving was drawing near. It was turning colder at night and we had a difficult time staying warm. My husband had not found work and we were at a loss as how to gather up enough money for a first and last month's rent as well as the deposit that all places wanted. It looked so hopeless.

We planned to go to the only place having Thanksgiving dinner for the homeless, but our car stopped running. My husband worked on it, but it was no use. We were stuck at the rest area. I wanted to give up and felt I could just not go on another day.

The night before Thanksgiving, I put my children to bed and I went and sat on the bench with my Bible and flashlight. At first, it was hard to read because I was crying and my mind was busy with what we were going to do now. I prayed for help and must have talked to God for a couple of hours before I joined my family sleeping in the car.

The next morning, Thanksgiving Day, as my husband again tried to fix the car, a truck driver who had been watching him just came over and asked if he could help. My husband told him the battery was shot and the plugs were fouled and something about the radiator. The man informed us that we couldn't get parts today, so it would have to wait till tomorrow. My husband swallowed his pride and said right now we can't afford to fix it. He said that was okay and he'd be back at 10 A.M. tomorrow with the parts.

That was the beginning of what I call a Thanksgiving of miracles.

People stopped by with food and blankets as well as some clothes. A woman brought a patchwork quilt that she had made and just gave it to us. A family brought a ham and some biscuits and a gallon of milk. Two elderly women brought some homemade fudge and two apple pies. I don't know to this day how so many people knew we were there. We just could not believe the way they were all so willing to share with strangers who were homeless. My husband and I thanked everyone as best we could but our words did not seem like much to offer them all in return for their great compassion showered upon us.

After we ate, a man talked to my husband about a job he had heard about and told him to go over there after the holiday. What a miracle this day had been, I said to myself.

That night it was hard to sleep, we were all just so thankful. I prayed and thanked God because I knew he had answered my prayer and sent each and every one of those people to help us. That next day the truck driver did come back and got our car running again. He hugged us and again off he went.

This Thanksgiving we can share what we have with others. We will be the ones to fill that void.

Now we can join you in reaching out to each other with love and kindness.

~Judy Ann Eichstedt

17

Angel on the Line

*The angels may have wider spheres of action and nobler forms of duty
than ourselves, but truth and right to them and us
are one and the same thing.*
~E.H. Chapin

Looking back, I'm not quite sure all these years later whether or not my telephone counselor was, or rather is, an angel. Whatever her official angelic status, she was certainly an angel to me. I can recall distinctly the circumstances of, and the details surrounding, our first telephone conversation....

I had recently returned home after nearly six months at a rehabilitation hospital following two spinal cord surgeries. The surgeries were supposed to repair three disks in my neck, but had left me paralyzed from the shoulders down for a number of months. I was still improving but progress was slow; I was undergoing physical therapy five days a week.

Along with my husband, Walter, I was trying my hardest to get things back to normal, or as normal as I could. I was finding this was not as easy as I had hoped or planned it would be. I was especially concerned that I do the right things for our five-year-old son, Jeffrey. He was so young and had been through so much already. I wanted to do the "right" things—I was just not sure what that was. This led to my phone call to the county mental health center, which happened to be located in my town, but on the opposite side of town. Without being able to drive yet, I would be unable to get to any appointments with a counselor. I was desperate for help, so I called anyway, ready for all the obstacles ahead.

I dialed the main telephone number, anticipating the endless rounds of being put on hold or transferred to "someone who can help" me. So, imagine my surprise, when after just a ring or two, a warm, friendly voice answered:

"County Mental Health... can I help you?"

"I hope so," I said, "I need to speak to someone about how I can help my little son." I didn't give too much detail, figuring that I would have to repeat it endless times during the course of finding a counselor. I thought I'd save the facts for then.

"I can help you," said the voice, kindly. "Tell me your name."

"My name is Donna." I started off slowly, almost disbelieving that I could find help this quickly, without dialing even one extension, without being put on hold or transferred even one time.

"My name is Norma," came the reply.

"That's easy to remember—that's my mother's name." I was even more incredulous with each passing moment. It had never occurred to me that Norma didn't then, or in any of our subsequent phone conversations, ever give me her last name. She was simply "Norma."

I then told her about my spinal surgeries. I told her quite frankly that while my medical condition was still improving, it was not anywhere near where I thought it should be, and that this was depressing me. I didn't know how to protect Jeffrey from feeling those fears as well.

"I'm glad you called," Norma said. "You have been through a lot. I understand what you are saying about your spinal surgery—I am an RN."

Finally! I found someone who was not only willing to listen to my words, but who could also understand the emotional as well as the medical side of my concerns. This was a rare find, indeed!

I remember Norma saying during that first call: "Remember that despite everything going on, you must stay steady and grounded for Jeffrey. Show him that you are working hard to get better for him and for you. He loves you and needs you."

"Thank you, Norma, thank you for listening. I appreciate it so very much!"

"You're welcome, Donna."

I hung up the phone, and thanked God that I had found such a warm, kindly counselor with whom I could easily discuss very personal issues.

One moment that stands out in my mind is one day when I confessed to Norma that I couldn't understand how God had allowed this to happen to me, and, as a result, to my family, especially little Jeffrey. And how guilty I felt for having those feelings. I was so confused!

I will never forget Norma's words to me that day: "Don't worry, Donna. God gets blamed for a lot of things. He is used to being blamed for things that happen on earth. He understands your frustration—and your anger, too."

Those were the words I needed to hear, and just when I needed to hear them! What comfort it gave me to know that He wasn't angry with me! I was able to overcome those feelings eventually because of Norma's personal counsel. She was my friend and she sounded as though she knew just how God felt about me.

Then, the inevitable day came.

It had been a month or so since I had last spoken to Norma—the longest time that had elapsed between any of our phone calls. I wanted to call her to let her know I was still working hard and still making progress in my therapy. As I made progress, my anxiety and depression were diminishing, just as Norma had told me they would. Having Norma to talk to me was also a major factor in the decline of my concerns for Jeffrey. He was helping Walter and me cope (mainly by being himself) and was growing into a sensitive little boy who liked to help people. Things looked brighter for my whole family.

I wanted Norma to know the full impact she had, not only on me, but on Walter and little Jeffrey, as well. Her influence was nothing short of miraculous—just as miraculous as our initial telephone contact had been.

I dialed the number that linked me to the one person who had helped me without ever telling me her last name, someone who never charged me for her counsel, or for taking the time to listen to me. This time, however, Norma didn't answer. A new voice answered my call.

"County Mental Health... how can I help you?"

I asked to speak to Norma, expecting to be transferred to her extension. I was stunned by what I heard next.

"I'm sorry, but there is no Norma here. Is there a last name?"

"Uh, no. She never gave me her last name. But I've talked to her at this number several times."

"I'm sorry, there is no one by the name of Norma here, and there hasn't been, at least since I've been working here."

I thanked the receptionist for her time and hung up the phone, still trying to sort the latest turn of events out in my mind. I was a bit confused, but this certainly convinced me that Norma is an angel. I don't know where she is, but I am quite sure that she is helping someone in their time of need this very minute.

~Donna Lowich

Living Catholic faith

My Brother's Keeper

And the king will say to them in reply,
"Amen I say to you, whatever you did for one of
these least brothers of mine, you did for me."

~Matthew 25:40

18

"Buddy, Can You Spare a Prayer?"

Rejoice in hope, endure in affliction,
and persevere in prayer.
~Romans 12:12

I was feeling sorry for myself. I was going through a divorce and had moved from my home by the ocean in Southern California, back east to be near my family. I had only returned a couple of months when my mother had a massive heart attack and died. "How could she have picked now to do this when I needed her so much?"

I felt only darkness, even while soaking up the full sunshine of the morning as I walked toward the library building. My father, devastated by her death, now needed me more than ever. In desperation, I began taking care of other elderly people in the area by starting my own business and working six days a week.

As I approached the front door of the building, I saw a man sitting on a stone bench outside the library. He was smoking a cigarette. His clothes were filthy, his faced unwashed and unshaven, and there was a stench of stale nicotine in the air around him. As I got closer, he spoke to me. "Can you give me a dollar, lady?" he asked rather gently. I stopped, not wanting to just walk by without answering. Emotions came up in me after months of my own losses and I fired back a quick reply. "I'll give you a dollar, but you are going to have to earn it."

He stared at me as if I had said something rather crazy. I didn't give him a chance to ask what he was supposed to do.

While trying not to drop the books, I fumbled in my purse and pulled out a one-dollar bill. Handing it to him I said, "I've had a really bad day, and you're going to have to pray for me."

A tender expression came over his weathered face. "Okay, but will you say one for me too?"

What's wrong with the world? He had his dollar. I didn't feel like I had anything left to give to anyone, and here someone else was asking.

"Alright," I replied. "I'll pray for you." I thought this would now settle the issue as I turned my back and started to walk away from him.

"Will you pray for me now?"

His soft words floated in the air, stopping my world. The books in my arms almost fell to the ground as I heard him say it. What was this turning into? Inside, though, I heard the quiet voice of God speak to my heart. I knew I had just said I would pray, and now I was being put to the test.

"Alright," I told him as I went to sit on the bench. "I'll pray for you."

Without another word he took the cigarette from his mouth, and reaching down, crushed the lit part into the dirt around the bench. He then put what was left of the cigarette into the front pocket of his shabby shirt. Removing the dirty cap from his head, he got off the bench and knelt down beside me. He closed his eyes and waited for me to pray.

To this day I will never know what people thought as they came in and out of the library, observing me praying for this humble man in his tattered clothes who knelt before me. In my eyes, he was no longer homeless, but God's helper sent to me. In his asking me, daring me, to stop and pray, something happened. He gave far more to me than I could have ever given him.

The years have gone and the hurts have healed. New ones come and go, but the lesson I learned that day was forever sewn into my soul. Many wonderful things in life do not come wrapped in the packages we think they should. God used a carpenter, not a king, to save the world.

Maybe if I could go back in time and be a wiser young woman than I was, it would have been me asking this raggedly clothed man, "Buddy, can you spare a prayer?"

~Kate Prado

The Least of My Brothers

*Children are God's apostles, sent forth, day by day,
to preach of love and hope and peace.*
~J.R. Lowell

A Guatemalan and I traveled on foot in the mountains. Because of our loads and the steep incline, we stopped under a mango tree to rest amid the cane houses of a tiny village. Soon curious children approached, innocent of the world of television, cartoons, and swing sets. They were the barefoot children of the cane houses with dirt floors. I sensed the expectation of a story... so I told them the "Big Mouth Frog" story, to which they reacted with unusual joy.

We peeled and divided oranges from our backpacks for the two dozen kids, until only a half orange remained for us. Then we saw her, the bashful one, the round-eyed girl of seven, half-hidden behind a crumbling adobe wall. We gave her the remaining half of the orange.

She said thanks, took the half orange, broke it into two parts, and gave half to her little brother and the other half to her little sister who was even more shy and hidden. She thanked us again and went off with nothing for herself... and we stood there with nothing left to give her.

A year later in the same area, I found myself with a family where the father was gravely ill. Sitting on the dirt floor of their smoky cornstalk house, we prayed together for their father. I stayed with the mother and half dozen kids and we talked and prayed until the darkness came.

I hadn't noticed when she crawled into my lap, but I remember wanting to tell the child that she needn't worry because things would get better. But I knew it would not get better. The truth was that things would probably get worse. I wanted to tell her brothers and sisters that they would go to school, and their father would live, and there would be plenty to eat, and...

That made me remember the wheat buns I had in my backpack. I knew that often these families went without eating, so I handed some of the buns to the mother and gave the last of them to the child in my lap. To my surprise, the child said thanks, took the bread, broke it, and gave it to her smaller brother and sister sitting beside us, and, although she had none left for herself, she expected nothing more.

That's how I recognized her... in the way she said thanks, took the bread, broke it, and shared it.

~Dave Huebsch

I Spent the Night at a Homeless Shelter

*Jesus throws down the dividing prejudices of nationality
and teaches universal love, without distinction of race, merit or rank.
A man's neighbor is everyone who needs help.*

~J.C. Geikie

Father Henry has a way of getting people to sign up for projects they don't want to do. And I really didn't want to do this one. Reluctantly, I agreed to work the temporary shelter in our church hall.

Pictures of dirty derelicts with filthy fingernails flashed in my head. Visions of jittery drug addicts danced before me. Images of drunks drinking from brown paper bags entered my mind.

However, what I found at the homeless shelter was much more unsettling.

Before I even entered the shelter, the glowing tip of a cigarette caught my attention in the darkness near the entrance. A man was hunched over against the cold, smoking. He took a deep drag, threw the butt on the sidewalk, and crushed it with his grimy tennis shoe.

Oh brother, I thought, here we go.

The man said in a cheery voice, "Oh good, you must be my night relief. I can go home." He was the evening shift volunteer.

Inside, Charles, the head volunteer, said, "We have ten guests tonight, the men on this side and the women on that."

Women? What are women doing here?

In my mind, the homeless would be easier to disregard if they were different from me. If I could dismiss them as being responsible for their own fate, then they would be easier to ignore. I reasoned, if that man would go to drug rehab, lay off the booze, or take his psych medicine, he would not be on the street. Any illusions that all homeless people were addicts, drunks, or mentally ill men, were about to be shattered.

While our guests slept, Charlie and I talked, made coffee, and read. In the wee hours of the morning, Charlie nodded off, still holding his newspaper.

Two groggy guests went to the bathroom and back to bed.

About four in the morning, I heard a shuffling noise and saw a man headed toward the freshly brewed coffee. At first, he seemed to be what I was expecting... a drooped, sluggish man who walked unsteadily.

The man sidled up to me and flashed a beautiful smile. "I'm George and if I live four more days, I'll make it," he announced.

"To what?" I inquired, imagining some sobriety milestone.

"To my seventy-fourth birthday!" he beamed.

He's not much older than Hal. I thought of my husband who didn't look, move, or act anything like George. Hard living must age you.

George saw playing cards on a table. Sounding like a kid looking for a playmate, he said, "I know a game if you feel like playing. It's real easy. You pick five and make six."

This crazy old coot isn't making sense. How can you pick five and make six? I surprised myself by saying, "Deal."

He dealt five cards, then told me to draw from the deck or discard pile to get the sixth. "The first one to gather three pairs wins," he explained. "I still wake up at four because I worked on the farm and then on a garbage truck all my life. Try as I might, I just can't sleep late."

"I know what you mean. I worked day shift for twenty years. Now I work evening shift but I still can't sleep late, either," I related.

As we played cards, he seemed more like my dear Uncle Paul than one of "those homeless people." He sheepishly grinned as he picked up my discard and won a hand. Then, he covered his face in mock remorse as I won. We chuckled and nudged each other as Lady Luck took turns sitting on our shoulders.

George checked his watch often. He said a young man asked him to wake him up for work. Homeless people work? George woke the man at five on the dot.

The young, well-groomed man tiptoed from a cubicle and hustled to get washed and dressed.

When he came back, I offered him a cup of coffee. "No thank you ma'am, never did like coffee."

"Tea?" I offered.

"Oh, yes ma'am. That would be nice. Thank you."

Next, a young woman scurried toward the bathroom with a pile of neatly folded, clean clothes in her arms. Where do homeless people get clean clothes? I wondered.

I handed the young man the brown-bag lunch other volunteers had prepared.

"This is sooo nice. Thank you," he said, with the gratitude of a kidney recipient.

"When she comes out, tell her I am heating up the car," he said. Homeless people have cars?

After they left, a surly young woman marched out of the sleeping quarters, grumbling to herself.

I chirped "Good Morning" twice but got no reply.

Well, this was what I was expecting... misfits, with no social skills, whose families wouldn't take them in because they were so difficult.

She sat there slurping coffee and glancing at me sideways. Suddenly, she bellowed, "Were you out here awake all night while we were asleep?"

"Yes," I answered carefully. "I got here at midnight."

She said with deep appreciation, "That's wonderful. Thank you for being here and watching out for us."

As the other guests awoke, they acted like any guests who visit my house. Some were engrossed in the morning news. Others sleepily sipped their coffee in silence. The rest gathered around the table, eating, and talking.

A teenager came out of the men's quarters. What's a teenager doing here? I wondered but never got a chance to ask. The teen came over and patted my card partner on the back. "Goodbye Pops. I leave today."

George struggled to stand and extended his arthritic hand to the boy, then went out and stood in the cold, waving until the boy's bus was out of sight.

People at the table exchanged quiet chats, good-natured bantering, and serious discussions about the morning news. They praised the cooks for the delicious pancakes and homemade oatmeal cranberry cereal.

The day shift volunteers arrived and joined us for breakfast. The homeless woman opposite me bowed and prayed before eating. I hadn't said grace.

As I looked around the table, the last myth melted like the butter on my silver dollar pancakes. There was not a familiar face left in the group. I could no longer tell who were the volunteers and who were the homeless. Sitting there, looking for clues, I was struck with a notion. There were none of "those people" at the table. It was just a table with "us" around it.

The only thing that makes me any different from "those homeless people" is a home.

~Joyce Seabolt

21

Brothers at Ground Zero

There is not brotherhood of man without the fatherhood of God.
~H. M. Field

ighting exhaustion and impending nausea, I stumbled from the examination room of the field morgue next to the rubble of the World Trade Center. It had been a long day and I desperately needed rest.

There in an adjacent tent, two young freshly-arrived Catholic priests sat, looking very intimidated. Hardly into their twenties, it was an easy assumption that they were newly ordained, and like all of us, extremely uncomfortable with what was happening in that tent of unspeakable horrors. I felt sorry for them. Such places cruelly rip out whatever might remain of youthful innocence. I'd lost mine in Vietnam more than thirty years before, and compassion welled up within me for them. We were in the middle of a waking nightmare.

I shuffled over to them. "Hi Fathers. How are you?"

Looking at each other, one said nervously, "We were sent to administer the Sacrament of Last Rites and bring what comfort we may."

Searching their eyes, I could see that these young men were overwhelmed, and understandably so. We all were.

Glancing back into the exam room, I shuddered as I thought about what they were about to walk into. They were about the same age as my own son, and I wished I could protect them. What was in that room was something for which no seminary could ever prepare them.

I had been laboring several days among the forensic and Medical Examiner teams. The putrid air inside the morgue was sticky with the heat and humidity of a late New York City summer. In spite of my biohazard mask, the stench of death assaulted my senses, and my mind recoiled at the sight of the decomposing body parts of my fellow Americans on the stainless steel tables.

A firefighter had stood next to me one day sobbed softly, and I reached over and put a gloved hand on his grimy shoulder. Glancing up and seeing "Chaplain" on my helmet, he nodded his thanks wordlessly through bloodshot, tear-filled eyes. He had just brought in the fragmentary remains of a fellow firefighter from the smoking ruins outside. Few words exchanged—few required.

The examination ended and the remains were tenderly slid into a small biohazard bag. The Medical Examiner looked at me and said softly, "Chaplain?" Her eyes, peering over her mask, seemed to say; "We've done all we humanly can. Now we look to God." Glancing around for a priest to give Last Rites, or a rabbi to say Kaddish, we would each participate in ministering. Without forensic evidence to determine religion, we tried to cover every possibility for the sake of the family.

In a repeated ritual, a U.S. flag was unfurled, and gloved hands reached out to help cover the stretcher holding our brother. Tenderly, we tucked the edges of the flag around the stretcher like a mother lovingly tucking a child into bed. I prayed. "Thank you Father, for a life given while saving others. There is no greater love than to lay down your life..."

Firefighters and officers carefully lifted the stretcher. Leading the small procession, I exited into the street toward a waiting ambulance. As the flag-draped bier came into view, hundreds of people working outside instantly stopped everything, formed lines, and snapped to attention. Only the sound of electrical generators broke the silence. "Hand salute!" someone barked. Tearfully, I saluted and stood at attention to one side as they placed the stretcher into the ambulance.

Everyone stood silently, holding their salute to their fallen comrade. The doors closed, and the ambulance slowly slipped away into the darkened streets. Finally someone shouted, "Order salute!" and everyone returned to their work.

I turned back to the two priests before me. My heart broke for them. "Fathers," I said, "your service to our Lord Jesus in this terrible place is honorable." Glancing at each other again, they seemed to relax a bit as I continued. "With your permission, I would like to pray for you." Their eyes widened a bit at this, for I suspect it is rare that anyone offers to pray for a priest. They are, after all, assumed to be the ones who do the heavy lifting in ministry. Tonight, the ministers needed encouragement.

"Well, thank you, yes, that would be very kind of you," they said tentatively.

Kneeling down in front of where they were sitting, I clasped their hands and began to pray. "For their strength to face the challenges of service here, we are asking You, our Father in Heaven, to protect and give the assurance of Your love for them as they reach out to bring the comfort of Christ to others. We pray for their empowerment as instruments of Your grace far beyond all they can ask or imagine. Jesus, let Your face be seen in theirs as they minister for You."

God's presence seemed to fill the room. I began to sob with the pent-up pain of the previous days. Looking up, both of the priests were also weeping. Spontaneously we stood and hugged in an embrace of Christian fellowship in the Spirit. In this place of suffering, we stood together in Christ. These brave young priests—willing to walk into the bowels of hell to minister to their flock—became true heroes in my eyes that night. So were they also in the Heavenly Father's eyes.

Walking out into the deep darkness before dawn, I tried to glimpse the stars, whose twinkling orbs often give me comfort. Finding none in the glare of search lights, I gazed at the mountain of smoking, twisted steel, and the billowing clouds of smoke rising from the "pile." Steelworkers cut away the rubble with torches, making bright fountains of sparks. I whispered a prayer of thanks that the stars still shone brightly somewhere far above. A new day would soon dawn for us all.

Come quickly, Lord Jesus.

~Bruce R. Porter

22

The Church in Juarez

If God is our father, man is our brother.
~Alphonse de Lamartine

We arrived in the border town of El Paso, Texas on a hot June afternoon. The sun and cement made the downtown bus station feel like an oven. I looked at the bridge one block away that would take us over the border into Juarez. We had come to build two houses for two families who lived in ramshackle *casas de cartas*, cardboard houses.

That week, my group of thirty people, including our parish priest, would suffer each day in the terrible heat, sweating and working, laying block and mortar. Although we were physically building the house for two homeless families, it felt like these warm Mexicans were welcoming us home. They gave us lodging, they cooked all our meals, they kept us safe, and they made sure we had what we needed during the day. In short, they did what Christ called all of us to do in Matthew 25:35: "I was a stranger and you welcomed me."

The father of one of the families was off working somewhere in the city, and the mom and four kids watched us shyly as we worked. The oldest boy had a withered arm and some kind of brain injury. He couldn't speak, and the younger children looked out for him and took care of him. We could sense the excitement in all their faces as they watched their houses take shape. They helped us with the important tasks of fetching tools, bringing us water, and giving us words of encouragement in Spanish that only a few of us could understand.

I looked across from the dry mountainside on which we were building to the other side of the Rio Grande. I could see the sparkling buildings of glass, the busy interstate, the wide streets and large houses, the bustle of a booming economy that stood in such stark contrast to the dusty slum in which we labored. But I could also see that these Juarezians were rich too—rich in community, sustained by the deep, abiding faith that each day they were in the hands of God, who would deliver them and work miracles for them. In the slums of Juarez, there were no secular thoughts or accidental, random beginnings to anything. The grace of God is in everything that happens each day, and our little group was the miracle of that day.

At one point, some of the neighborhood kids came by and invited us to join them in a friendly game of soccer. Ha! We blithely went down to the dirt playground, lambs to the slaughter, while the world's best soccer players plotted our demise. We lasted about an hour before we begged for mercy and retreated to our safe house, with its warm showers and television, to lick our wounds and assure each other that, after all, they had the home court advantage.

We continued to work on building the walls, installing the windows, forming the cement crown that would tie everything together, and finally, on the fifth day, we put on the roof.

On the last day, we incorporated the handing over the keys to the houses into a short liturgy. We sang songs and placed at the feet of the two families the gifts we had brought—the image of the Virgin of Guadalupe, a Bible, and a crucifix. We also gave food staples—oil, flour, sugar—then toys for the children, and hugs to embrace those who would never be the same... that was us. The love between our two groups was palpable, and tears flowed from everyone. As I looked into the eyes of the smiling boy with the withered hand and wordless lips, I saw the very eyes of Christ looking back at me. I felt such a warmth in my heart that all the painful days of work, sore muscles, and thirst were forgotten.

At the end of the ceremony, we prayed and asked God's blessing on the houses. I looked around at these gentle new friends and I heard Jesus say, "This is My Body." And when I read that night of the terrible violence and gang murders over the weekend in Juarez, I heard Jesus say, "And this is My Blood."

We went back to the place where we were staying and had our own last supper. Most of us were anxious to return home to our families and lives we had left behind. Some of us really did not want to leave at all.

In the morning, we gathered our things and left for the border. It would be a two-hour wait to get through the long lines of people trying to cross over into the United States. As we were waiting, a man selling newspapers said to us in Spanish as we were passing by, "Bien gente!" "Good people." What a wonderful thing to say and hear.

We crossed over into the United States, where the return to our own culture seemed to be more of a shock than going into the slums of Juarez. Everyone was busy, going fast, with very little time. I looked back at the border and the fence, and I reflected that there would be no walls in the kingdom of God. In fact, the two little houses that we built had already brought down the wall just a bit.

~Ben Lager

23

A Brother's Love

The way we came to love was that he laid down his life for us;
so we ought to lay down our lives for our brothers.
~1John 4:16

One spring morning in 1967, my parents received a telegram from the State Department reporting that my younger brother Tom was missing in action in Vietnam. A second telegram stated that Tom had been located, but was in critical condition. Shortly thereafter, a Marine officer and a chaplain arrived on my parents' doorstep to inform us that Tom had perished from his wounds.

For the next twenty-four hours, our world fell apart. The phone lines across the country began buzzing with the news. We notified my brother Bill, who had served his time in the Marines and was in his second year at Texas A&M University, where he was studying to be an engineer. Long distance, we shared our unimaginable mournful grief.

Early the following day, my parents received a call from Japan. "It's me, Tom!" My little brother went on to explain that his death was a clerical error and that he was very much alive and on the mend. When his wounds healed, he would soon be returning to the war front.

It was at this point that my older brother Bill decided to postpone college and rejoin the Marines. He asked for duty in Vietnam to be with my younger brother Tom and hoped to convince him to file for a transfer under the Sullivan ruling. This ruling allows military family members to ask for relief from hazardous duty if more than one family member is serving in the war zone. Bill had always looked out for his younger siblings, and he was determined to do so again. Bill wanted Tom out of harm's way while he served in Vietnam himself.

Of course, Tom would have no part of it. He was determined to stay the course and finish his tour of duty. Even though Bill could not persuade Tom to leave Nam, he went forward with his reenlistment so that they could at least be close to one another and he could watch out for our younger brother.

On the day Bill left, just before he walked out the door, Dad handed him his own Sacred Heart Badge and said, "Son, it might not stop a bullet, but it can keep you safe along the way. Just remember, it is only as good as the faith you put with it. If you wear it as a scrap of material and you don't follow Christ, it will be no help at all. Remember what is important... trust Christ and follow Him. He will get you safely home. That is all the protection you really need."

After retraining, Bill landed in Vietnam on August the 21st. Sadly, that very day, Tom was again wounded, this time much more seriously. His amphibious mobile unit struck a land mine and Tom was badly burned in the explosion. Bill managed to track Tom down in a hospital in Dong Hoa within a couple of days of his arrival. Unfortunately, because Tom's wounds were so severe and infection was a danger, Bill was not allowed in to see Tom before the medics transported him for treatment. All Bill could do was stand outside Tom's room and say a quick prayer for his little brother's recovery. Then he reported for his own duty in Da Nang.

In order not to worry the rest of us, Bill wrote letters home telling us that he was assigned to an office in Da Nang as a clerk. He jokingly referred to his great quest to serve as being reduced to shuffling papers. That was our Bill—always protecting others from worry or fear. His ploy worked, and we believed that he was fairly safe there. We focused our worry and prayers on Tom's healing and support during his recovery.

On September the 28th, the Marines again paid a visit to my parents' home. This time there would be no follow-up phone call saying it was a mistake. The Marines reported that on September 21st, while on night patrol, Bill's entire unit was caught in an ambush. They were trapped in crossfire of rocket and mortar fire, which claimed the life of every man in Bill's unit. Bill managed to survive long enough for another unit to find him. He had received the Last Rites and was able to make his last confession before he expired from his wounds. Bill's Sacred Heart Badge was enclosed with the letter.

Dad was right. Even deep in the jungles of Vietnam, Christ kept His Sacred Heart Promise and came to take our Bill safely home.

~Christine M. Trollinger

"What If..."

We must love men ere they will seem to us unworthy of our love.
~William Shakespeare

I was working in the high tech sector of Ottawa when I was sent to a one-week database course downtown.

Each day that week, I enjoyed a nice casual walk downtown during my lunch hour to unwind from the complexity of the program. Two days before the end of my course, while on my walk, I noticed a terrible unavoidable stench of urine coming from a homeless man who had just walked by me. My first reaction was of repugnance as I walked away farther from him. Then, for some inexplicable reason, I decided to sit nearby and observe this man. Downtown Ottawa had plenty of homeless people, but something told me to keep my eyes on this particular one.

What I saw next truly shocked me. He stood near a storefront and simply let the urine run down his pants. First I was appalled, then a compassionate thought came to me with the reality that he most likely had been kicked out of every establishment and was not welcomed anywhere in such condition.

How sad, I thought, to see a grown man get to the point where he no longer cared for his own presence, who probably had nobody caring for him. How low and rejected he must have felt. Still, with perceptible pessimism, he had enough strength to go on one more day.

I went from feeling disgusted and numb, to feeling overwhelmed by sadness.

Realizing that this man was probably hungry and cold, I rushed to the nearest fast food restaurant, where I purchased a warm bowl of chicken soup, a sandwich, and a warm cup of coffee. With hesitation, I approached him, wondering how he would react. As I offered him the meal, my fear dissipated when he gently reached to take the free lunch. His eyes hardly rose to meet mine. Then, he gave me a humble "thank you" and a grateful smile.

I looked at my watch and realized that my afternoon class was about to start. I ran to the building where my course was taking place, just a couple of blocks away.

That afternoon, all the sophisticated database tools and lectures seemed quite irrelevant. I found myself drifting and thinking about the man and the mystery of his life. This was not the first time I had offered food to a homeless person, but something about this man truly captured me in a deep and puzzling way.

That night I had a very vivid dream. I saw my own dad as the one being rejected by his family and society. In my dream, my dad was the one now living in the streets and looking and smelling just like the man I had seen the day before. The dream felt truly real, and so was my frustration and feeling of helplessness to get him back on his feet, back to his family and feeling of self-worth.

Waking up from this terrible nightmare gave me great relief. It had all just been a dream! However, as the day unfolded, I kept wondering,

What if that had really happened to my dad, or someone else I loved dearly. What if the man I saw the day before had lost someone who he loved and missed dearly?

I felt the urge to do something. Something that would help him believe that he could have a fresh new start, something that would give him a sense of self-worth.

In a flash I had a very clear vision of what I was going to do next.

During my lunch hour, on the last day of my course, I bought this man a "Caring Kit" containing a new comb, mirror, shaver, soap, nail clippers, aftershave, a towel, underwear, socks, pants, shirt, some food and snacks, and a specially chosen card. Feeling an unbelievable boost, I carefully packed them all together in a zippered bag and included the card I picked for him. It had a quote from the Bible with a reassuring message that God is never too far and His love is eternal.

I eagerly anticipated the end of my course. I kept checking the time and wondering if I was going to find this man again. During rush hour? Who was I kidding? What were the odds? He could be anywhere!

Regardless, I knew I had to try. If I could not find him, I would just find someone else who could still make use of all this stuff.

An inexplicable sense of being guided took over me. Without resistance, I started to walk in a totally opposite direction from the area where I had seen the man the previous day. I went down a few blocks and walked briskly, filled with purpose, while mentally questioning if indeed I was heading in the right direction. Regardless, I continued to walk farther and farther away. I was now quite a few blocks from where I had started and at this point I told myself that when I reached the next corner, if I did not see him there, I would simply turn around and take the bus home.

When I reached that corner, I felt shivers down my spine.

The man I was looking for was standing at that intersection.

I found myself quickly searching for the right words to say. I paused for a moment. Then I walked toward him and asked, "Excuse me, what is your name?"

He looked up and with a faint voice he said, "My name is Danny."

I took a pen from my bag and wrote his name on the envelope holding the card I had carefully chosen for him. As I handed the card and the bag with the gifts I said, "Danny, your guardian angel has sent me to you. This is for you."

His eyes lit up, and the smile on his face said it all. "Thank you, thank you, thank you," he said as he anxiously looked inside the bag like a kid opening a present on his birthday. Then he briskly walked away.

I felt blessed and filled with incredible joy.

I never saw Danny in the streets of downtown Ottawa again. I often wonder how he is. I pray for him and wish him a better life with dignity, self-respect, and love for God.

And I wonder, "What if..."

~Miriam Mas

Thanksgiving in Romania

*First of all, then, I ask that supplications, prayers, petitions, and
thanksgivings be offered for everyone.*
~1 Timothy 2:1

I braced myself to feel especially homesick as the holiday season approached. It had only been a few months since I had moved to Bucharest, Romania, and only eleven months since the 1989 revolution that ended the Communist regime there. Nine of us Americans served together in the capital city as missionaries. We had come to bring the message of hope to university students.

As a team, we had to intentionally plan how to make the holidays fun. We would build new memories. After all, we were family now.

The days had grown colder and the grayness outside matched my mood. Life was rustic here. We had no heat, water only one hour per day, and an abundance of rats. We had only received mail once since we arrived. I had worn those letters thin from reading them so often. I missed my family and friends. I missed America.

Our team made plans to celebrate Thanksgiving on Saturday, two days after the American festivities. Wendy had tucked cans of pumpkin, corn, and peas into her suitcase when she came, earmarked for Thanksgiving. Marian bought already-kneaded dough from the bread store to make dinner rolls and crust for Wendy's pumpkin pie. Vicki and I found wrinkled potatoes with long eyes at the meager outdoor market. None of us could find the one remaining dish anywhere. When I made "gobble, gobble" noises in the outdoor market, I learned the word for turkey is *curcan*. Everyone we asked agreed there were no *curcans* in Bucharest. If fortunate enough to have meat, it would be pork.

We contemplated substituting a chicken, but the chickens were so scrawny. We often joked that Romanians killed their chickens by starving them to death. Only a turkey would do for our Thanksgiving feast.

My roommate, Vicki, and I prayed every day for a couple of weeks before Thanksgiving. "Father, we know this is not anything important, but we also know that you love us and you love to give us good gifts. You tell us in your Word to ask, so that's what we're doing. We are asking you to please provide a turkey."

In the evenings, international students from Arab countries made their way door-to-door through the Foreign Student Dorms selling everything from warm-up suits to demitasse cups. Every time they came, they peddled an entirely different stock. We referred to it as the Home Shopping Hour.

The night before our Thanksgiving, we heard a knock at our door. Vicki jumped up expectantly. Two young Arab men stood there with a bulging duffle bag.

I asked what they had to sell, in my broken Romanian.

One of them answered. The word didn't sound like *curcan*, but I couldn't understand what he said with his thick accent. It didn't matter, because I knew what they had brought to sell us. I knew God's ways and had experienced these kinds of coincidences so many times before that I had grown to anticipate them.

The other guy reached into the duffel bag and my heart did a flutter kick. He pulled out... a soccer ball.

"Is that all?" I asked, stunned.

Yes, that was all they had.

I pushed back hot tears. My hopes had screeched to a halt.

I made my way to the bathroom to cry alone. "Lord, was this too much to ask? We've given up so much to be here. Do we have to give up a turkey, too?"

The next day, the group began to assemble in Mark and Wendy's room for our Thanksgiving meal. Besides the Americans on our team, we had invited several Romanian students, all newly serious about following Christ.

A vase of mums stood in the center of the lace-covered serving table. One by one, we added our food offerings, in chipped enamel pans. No one had pretty serving dishes. No one minded.

Only Daniel and Marian had not arrived yet. Suddenly the sound of a kazoo trumpeting a processional tune wafted in. Scurrying to the door, I got there as Daniel marched in carrying a pan spilled over with a plump turkey! Even Santa with a sack would not have been a more welcome sight.

We bombarded Daniel with questions. He had bartered for a turkey the night before with one of his many connections. He and Marian had decided to surprise us. They succeeded.

Our turkey did not come the way I had expected it. It didn't matter. We had a turkey. My immediate response of discouragement the night before did not stop God from giving.

As we gathered around, John explained to the Romanians about the original Thanksgiving. He said the Pilgrims wanted to thank God for bringing them through the first winter in their new land, and to share their bounty with their new friends. We did too. He went on to say that the Bible tells us to remember what God has done for us in the past and to thank him for his blessings. John gave us an opportunity to remember aloud.

"I'm grateful for this turkey," someone said. "It shows that God cares about the smallest details that touch our lives."

The Romanians chimed in. "I have new life in Christ."

"I thank God for sending you to tell us about Jesus."

"Finally we have freedom, and it is a precious thing."

Their joy reminded me, once again, of my purpose in being there, worth every sacrifice in my Spartan lifestyle.

We grasped each other's hands and thanked God together for His goodness to us.

The small dorm room overflowed with hard-backed chairs

scattered about. Many of us sat cross-legged on the double bed as we ate from mismatched plates and tin-tasting flatware.

I had never experienced a better Thanksgiving. Our turkey, a gift from God's hands, tasted divine. I had expected a crummy holiday and instead, created new memories.

I have returned to the States now, and I am homesick for Romania. Even now, many years later, no other Thanksgiving has compared to that first one in Bucharest.

~Taryn R. Hutchinson

*Living
Catholic
faith*

Divine Appointment

*May the God of peace, who brought up from the dead,
the great shepherd of the sheep by the blood of the eternal covenant,
Jesus our Lord, furnish you with all this is good,
that you may do his will.*

~Hebrews 13: 20-21

The Accident

Your ways, O Lord, make known to me; teach me your paths.
~Psalm 25:4

It was, after all, a mistake. It had been one of the worse nights of my residency. There had been so many admissions that I had virtually lost count, and I barely was able to keep up with the needs of my own patients, much less all the other ones I was cross covering. I was desperately rushing to finish checking labs and ordering tests before hurrying off to morning report.

Later that day, I was struggling to fight back fatigue and finish rounds when I received a page to report to Radiology immediately.

"Oh great" I thought. "Now what's wrong?" However, upon my arrival I was the sudden focus of congratulations and pats on the back.

"Great pickup!" they said. "Look at that," one of the radiologists said, pointing to films from an upper GI series hanging on the view box.

"A small bowel tumor, classic appearance!" I stood there dumbfounded; I had no idea what they were talking about. I picked up the chart and leafed through it. Yes, I had ordered the upper GI, but it wasn't my patient. Then I realized what had happened. In my haste to keep up with everything the prior evening, I had ordered an upper GI on the wrong patient!

Looking closer at the chart I learned that the patient was a priest, and director of a local Catholic college. He had been complaining of cough and fever, as well as nonspecific malaise and therefore, as was common in those bygone days, was admitted to the hospital for an evaluation. After the upper GI revealed a cancer of the bowel, he was operated on the very next day. The surgeon had paged me to the operating room to show me, saying, "You really saved this guy. I've never caught one of these this early before." I was too embarrassed to say anything, so I nodded my head politely and walked out. I didn't tell a soul what had happened.

The hectic pace of residency quickly resumed and the incident was soon forgotten.

About a week later, I was paged to the surgical floor. When I returned the call, a nurse informed me that one of the patients wanted to speak with me. I told her that I didn't have any patients there. She replied, "It's a priest, and he's quite insistent on speaking with you." I froze and felt a deep sinking feeling in the pit of my stomach.

In a near trancelike state, I slowly made my way to his room. As I entered, I had a sudden urge to throw myself at his feet saying, "Forgive me, Father, for I have sinned," but instead I quietly introduced myself and took a seat by his bed. A distinguished-looking man in his late fifties, he had piercing eyes that seemed to stare directly into my soul.

"Were you the one who ordered the test on me?"

I nodded my head and said nothing.

"Why?" he asked.

"It was... an accident," I stammered. I told him everything, the words almost pouring out of me, a relief to finally tell someone. He appeared pale and said nothing for a long time, the two of us sitting in utter silence. After a while he finally spoke. "The last several months have been something of a spiritual crisis for me. I had begun to question how I had spent my life, and the very core of my beliefs. I was offered a new and important position, but I didn't feel capable or worthy of it. Then, I began to feel ill and I was going to turn the offer down." He paused, "Since the surgery my symptoms seem to have disappeared. I now know what I should do. You see, my son, I believe there are no accidents. When they came to take me for that

GI test, I knew that something was amiss, yet at the very same time I felt deeply that I had to go."

He seemed to sit more erect in bed and his voice gathered force. "The day before I had prayed for some sort of sign to guide me, and now I understand that you were chosen to be its instrument."

As he spoke, I felt the hairs on the back of my neck rise and a strange sensation came over me.

I sat there stunned, not knowing what to say or think. The priest smiled. "Such talk troubles you, doesn't it?"

I told him of my own inner struggles trying to reconcile reason and faith in the context of my own religious tradition. "Ah," he replied, "one of your people grappled with such questions long ago. I will introduce you to him."

My beeper summoned me. As I rose to leave he asked that I wait for a moment and sit on his bed. He placed his hand upon my head and said, "I offer you my thanks in the words your people once taught us. May the Lord bless you and keep you, may His face shine upon you and be gracious unto you, may He lift up his countenance upon you and give you peace..."

Several months later, I was called to the hospital's mailroom to sign for a package that had just arrived for me from Europe. I was shocked to see that it had come from the Vatican. Opening it I found it was from the same priest, except instead of Father his title was now Monsignor, a special assistant to the Pope. Inside was a short note that said, "As you once helped me through my spiritual turmoil, may this aid you through yours." Enclosed was a beautiful bound English translation of the great physician/philosopher Moses Maimonides' monumental work on the struggle between faith and reason, *The Guide of the Perplexed*.

I walked to the small patient garden next to the hospital entrance, sat, and heard the soft songs of the birds and caught the smell of the spring blossoms in the clean air.

I sat holding the book and was lost in thought for a long time.

Maybe there are no mistakes.

~Blair P. Grubb

Something About Tessa

Thus says the Lord of hosts:
Render true judgment and show kindness and compassion
toward each other.
~Zechariah 7:9

n second grade I attended a private Catholic school. Discipline in the 1960s was strict to say the least.

Corporal punishment along with trips to the principal and stints in the corner were a pretty familiar regimen to me. The nun told my mom at conferences, "Your daughter is just like a marble in a coffee can, rattle, rattle, rattle!" In today's world I might have been labeled an attention deficit disorder child. Although I seemed to have difficulty with focus, I was not a disrespectful child, nor did I harbor any ill will towards authority.

There was another girl in my class who seemed to have greater difficulty than I. She, like me, was somewhat a tomboy with a strong willfulness about her. Her name was Tessa. She even topped me in punishments, and the other children shunned her. I heard whispers behind her back that she was, "just off the boat, so to say, and very poor." I did not know how they could tell this, since we all wore uniforms and clothes were not a status symbol. I guess they heard things from their parents, but my parents were not prone to gossip. So at the time it was a mystery to me how the others knew she was poor and why that would affect their opinions of her.

One day, Tessa came to school with invitations to her birthday party. I was always excited to go to a party, and this was no exception. I went home and talked to my parents about attending, and they agreed. The following weekend, my father took me to the store to look for a gift. I insisted to my dad that it be something special.

In those times, gifts from other kids at birthday parties usually were small, like a jump rope or jacks. We had a family of seven and were pretty well off, but we were not extravagant in the gift area. We only received presents twice a year, at Christmas and on our birthdays, and they were usually something we needed, not wanted. Things that were wanted were earned.

That said, when my father and I were shopping, I spied a small, beautiful, real porcelain china tea set. It was out of character for me, but I fell in love with it and knew I had to have it for Tessa. Somehow I convinced my dad to purchase it. I made a card, wrapped the gift, and the big day came.

My dad followed the directions on the invitation; Tessa's home was downtown, not far from the school. My dad dropped me off at the door. He told me to have fun and that he would pick me up in an hour and a half.

I knocked on the door and as it opened to Tessa's smiling face, I was drenched with wonderful baking odors. Then, as I stepped through the door I was shocked at the stark nakedness of the room. In our neighborhood a popular trend was wall-to-wall carpeting. Tessa's floor was wood with only one worn rug in the middle of the room. There was no television and very little furniture. The only decorative item hanging was a crucifix on the wall. The large dining table was made from plywood and a couple of sawhorses. It was beautifully set, though, with what looked like a handmade crocheted cloth.

Only her siblings and parents were there. As I looked around, I realized that I was the first arrival. Tessa and I talked and joked for a little while until it became apparent that I was the only one who had accepted her invitation. I was amazed how well she took it. Then we all sat down to a feast of homemade delights.

The mood was light as we all shared our birthday wishes for Tessa, and as I looked at the lone present sitting in the middle of the table, I silently thanked God for the insight to make it a good one. Tears of joy sprung from Tessa's eyes as she opened her tea set. Her family gasped.

"Thank you," she said. "No one has ever given me so fine a gift."

All at once, tears sprang from my eyes too, because never had I seen someone clothed in something so beautiful as gratitude. But when we returned to school, Tessa kept her propensity for the corner. Others still shunned her, and to this day, I cannot figure out why.

~Therese Guy

Just Listen

Not everyone who says, "Lord, Lord," will enter the kingdom of heaven, but only those on who do the will of my Father in heaven.
~Matthew 7:21

I blew a gusty sigh from my lips as I watched my eight-year-old son Paul race outside to catch our dog. Cringing inwardly, I pictured our ninety-pound black Lab romping through the neighborhood at full speed, scaring little old ladies and innocent children.

Stirring my boys' supper on the stove again, I turned the heat up a little, hoping to speed the process along. I glanced at the kitchen clock for the umpteenth time, and realized I was running just as late as the last time I'd looked. Feeling more than a little guilty, I grimaced as I pictured my always-punctual husband waiting for me to finish getting ready... again. We were due to arrive at a dinner banquet in less than an hour and I was still dressed in my robe, with my just-shampooed hair wrapped in a towel. To soothe my conscience, I reminded myself that the phone had been ringing at a near constant rate all afternoon, which definitely added to my tardiness. Having a home-based candle business was a great way of earning extra money, but it certainly created extra commotion during the holiday season, which was now well under way.

If I could just get those noodles simmering, I could put on the lid and go get ready. I turned the heat under the skillet a little higher. Just then, my eldest son, Jerome signed for the delivery of ten cases of candles that the UPS man was getting ready to unload on my kitchen floor. I released yet another full-cheeked sigh and rolled my eyes, knowing all ten cases would have to be tagged and marked before they could be put away. "It'll have to get done tomorrow," I thought. "The customers will just have to wait."

So as not to embarrass myself and shock the UPS man, I escaped from the kitchen and began to look for the dog out the bedroom window. As I stood there impatiently scanning the backyard, a tiny voice crept into my head. "Call Laura." With a small shake of my head, I ignored the thought, gave up the window search, and proceeded to lay my clothes out on the bed.

"Call Laura." This time I argued with the thought. Laura? Who's Laura?

Ryan's mother. Ryan was the new kid in my son Paul's class. The boys had played together once, but I had actually spoken to Laura very little... mostly just short, friendly conversations while we passed each other in the school parking lot. As I reached for my pantyhose, I remembered why I had let Paul go home with Laura the first time I met her... it was her smile and friendly face. That sounds naïve, but true. I just knew, by way of a deep and peaceful instinct, that she was a good lady. I remembered chatting with her briefly in the hall at school several days earlier. "We'll have to get together sometime. I'll call you," I had said, as we shuffled along with the after-school rush.

"Call Laura," the voice in my head repeated. I yanked on my pantyhose, and vowed to call Laura soon and set up a lunch date or something fun. "Call Laura."

"Okay, Lord, I'll call Laura later. Right now, I'm late!" I spoke aloud.

Just then, a waft of burning spaghetti sauce filled my nostrils. "Oh, noooo!" I exclaimed, as I envisioned the Hamburger Helper on its way to becoming "hamburger flambé." I rushed to the kitchen and stumbled through the maze of boxes. After quickly turning the burner to low, I scraped at the gummy noodles, now adhered to the bottom of the pan.

"What next?" I mumbled, as my two-year-old son, Roy, tugged on my robe. "Mommy, read me a book?"

I managed a weak smile and answered, "I can't right now, sweetie. Mommy's very busy right now."

"Call Laura."

"Please, Lord... I'll call her tomorrow... I promise." Yet even as the words slipped from my lips, I knew the truth. God was trying to tell me something. This sort of inner-calling had happened before, and I knew I should not ignore it.

With dinner under control, I hoisted Roy onto my hip and went to look for the cordless phone. When I found it, I just stared at it. What would I say to her? "Uh, Laura, this is Liz... yeah, Paul's mom. Remember me? Well... the strangest thing just happened... God told me to call you." She'll think I'm loony or something.

I sighed, and then looked up the number while popping a Barney video in the VCR for Roy to watch. One hand began applying my mascara, while the other dialed her number. As I listened to the ringing, I became apprehensive about what I would say. Maybe I should hang up.

"Hello."

The mascara wand stopped and I swallowed hard before saying, "Hi, Laura. This is Liz... Paul's mom. How are you?"

I don't recall what she answered, since it took me just a split second to realize she was crying. I asked her what was wrong, and she explained that she had just found out that she had been pregnant for the very first time, and had lost the baby. (They'd been blessed with Ryan through adoption.) To make matters worse, she had just been informed that she had developed an uncommon, possibly life-threatening, cancerous condition in her uterus.

Suddenly, my predicament seemed petty. Suddenly, it didn't matter whether we would be late for dinner, or whether someone would call the dogcatcher before we could lasso the dog. Suddenly, I cared very little if all the candles were put away before the customers arrived. I gripped the phone tightly and closed my eyes in a silent prayer.

When it was my turn to reply to her tearful declaration, I said, "I am so sorry for what you are going through, but I want you to know, you can stop crying because God has taken special care to have me call you tonight. I believe He wants you to know that He is present and in control of your situation. He cares about you very much and will not abandon you."

I then proceeded to tell her about the chaos through which I'd just ventured to call her. We laughed a little, and then talked with all seriousness about the truth... God had definitely placed her in my heart for a reason. I knew it... but more importantly, she knew it.

From then on we became good friends and prayer buddies. Like most people who are dealing with an illness or crisis, Laura went through some difficult times when she felt afraid. Sometimes I felt afraid for her. It was during these times that we would remind each other of the day that God whispered her name into my heart.

In case you're wondering... the dinner tasted fine, the dog came back on his own, and I actually was ready to go within minutes of my husband's arrival.

And Laura's condition was healed completely.

~Elizabeth Schmeidler

29

Our Season of Faith

Do not conform yourself to this age,
but be transformed by the renewal
of your mind,
that you may discern what is the will of God,
what is good and pleasing and perfect.
~Romans 12:2

Though my career as a banker was financially rewarding, I was never content with the work. Compliance regulations, qualification formulas and credit declinations seemed always so cold and, well... calculating. It was no wonder that, after only my fourth year on the job, I began to look with envy at the teaching career my wife, Julie, had chosen. Still, to make a career move so late in my life was absolutely out of the question. To leave a secure position and return to school was something that would take more faith than I possessed.

Yet God continued to speak to me through an odd feeling of longing. I'd find myself watching Julie as she graded papers, smiling, until late at night.

Then one winter's evening I found her fretting over a student's worsening academic performance. "Baxter began the year doing so well, but now his work has dropped to nearly nothing."

The next evening as I arrived home, Julie met me at the doorway. "Will you drive me to Baxter's house?"

Reluctantly, I agreed and together we began our journey. Baxter's home was at least twenty miles from where we lived and hard to find in the dark. We turned off the highway, then rumbled down a county roadway onto a narrow dirt path.

Before us stood an old run-down trailer-house, unlit and barely visible in the mid-winter darkness. In what might have been called a front yard, which was really only a cleared spot in the woods, four elementary-aged children busily gathered firewood. One poured kerosene into a lantern and another was petting a mangy old dog. A chubby kid in overalls hurried toward the car and enthusiastically greeted Julie. "My mom's not home yet, Mrs. Chapman, so you can't come in. But we can visit out here."

My wife happily chatted for ten minutes, but there was no need to go inside. She had seen what she had come to see. On the quiet drive home, Julie batted back a tear. "His work was good in the early fall when the days were longer. But now, in the dark, he can't see to do his homework."

As I drove through the Arkansas night, I realized I had discovered what God was calling me to do.

By the end of the month, I said farewell to my friends at the bank. Then, for two and a half years, we struggled to make ends meet while I attended college.

Eventually, our perseverance paid off, and I was offered my first teaching contract. After my first day, I proudly brought forth my new class roster for Julie to see. There among the list of seventh-graders was a name that we both recognized: Baxter. He had found the strength to hang on, and had finally made it into junior high... and so had I.

Baxter and I became fast friends. He was a big friendly kid with a permanently fixed smile, and though his ability was well below many of his classmates, he always gave his very best.

Then something strange happened. It was nearing Christmastime and I assigned an essay; "What Christmas Means to Me."

Baxter surprised me with his composition. In large block-printed letters and with a jumble of spelling and punctuation errors, the sincerity of his work shone through.

Some wise men heard that a new king would be born in Bethlehem, and they made their way through the woods to find him and they followed a star and they came to a barn where the baby was already born. And when they saw him, they knew it was Jesus, and they bowed down and worshipped Him, because they knew that the new baby lying in a manger, would be the King of all kings.

When I paused, Baxter quickly pointed out, "There's more on the back."

The wise men were amazed at all they had seen that night, and while they were walking back to their homes, they talked about all the great things they had seen. Then, when they got about halfway home, one of the wise men turned to the others and said, "Hey, do you know what? This ought to be a holiday." And from then on, it was.

Baxter smiled his simple friendly smile.

"Baxter, do you believe that? Do you believe that Jesus is the Son of God and that He was sent here to be our Savior?"

Baxter seemed uncomfortable and shifted his weight from one foot to another. "I'm not sure, Mr. Chapman. I go to church sometimes, and that's what they say. But how can you know something like that for sure?"

"You have to have faith that it's true, Bax," I said, pointing to my chest. "And when you have faith, you'll know, because you'll feel it deep inside your heart."

As Baxter walked away that day, I experienced a new feeling of purpose, one that I had not known before that moment. And from my own heart, I knew that I was exactly where God intended for me to be.

Six weeks later, shortly after Christmas vacation, Baxter approached my desk. This time he held a small New Testament, open to a well-marked page with a single underlined verse: "For God so loved the world that He gave his only begotten Son, that whosoever believes in Him, should not perish, but have everlasting life."

Excitedly he whispered, "They gave this to me at church, Mr. Chapman, on the day I was saved. They say I can keep it for my own."

Though I shook Baxter's hand and patted his back, there was no way I could express the happiness I felt.

More than a decade has passed since Baxter entered my first classroom. As a now-seasoned teacher, I've learned that students come suddenly into our care, share a part of our lives, and through our time together, our lives are altered forever.

Two years ago, I grieved when I received word that Baxter had died in an automobile accident.

Sometimes in the quiet of an early winter's evening, when I'm driving along winding country roads, I recall how a boy named Baxter, through his own faith, found the courage to exchange a broken-down trailer-house for a mansion on high.

And from deep within my heart I hold to my own faith, the assurance that I will see him again one day; only this time it will be in the company of the King of kings.

And you know what?

A day like that just ought to be a holiday.

~Hugh Chapman

30

The Man behind the Game Plan

The brotherhood of man is an integral part of Christianity,
no less than the Fatherhood of God.
~Lyman Abbott

On Holy Saturday evening, a bonfire's glow illuminated the faces of those gathered outside Blessed John XXIII for the Sacrament of Initiation. Sonny Lubick wiped his eyes and watched James Ward, his defensive backs coach, lean toward the bonfire and light a candle. Sonny, along with all the other sponsors, families and supporters, followed the candidates whose candlelight spread the light of Jesus into the darkened church.

James Ward had watched Sonny Lubick for three years, admiring the head coach's commitment to faith, character, academics and football, in that order. So when James decided to become a Catholic, he asked Sonny to be his sponsor.

Sonny, the winningest football coach in Colorado State University history, couldn't often attend the candidate's evening training sessions since they fell during the busiest part of the season. However, he and James often met before lunch. Then Sonny shared his own faith and background.

"I guess I'm a habitual Catholic," he said. "My religion was ingrained in me by my parents, my grandmother and the nuns."

Sonny grew up in a small suburb of Butte, Montana, which

supported nine Catholic elementary schools and twelve Catholic churches. Even so, with his father a copper mine laborer and his mother a waitress, a Catholic education seemed impossible. His mother talked an elementary school into accepting Sonny at $2.50 a month rather than the normal $5.00 monthly tuition.

He chose, against his father's wishes, the smaller Catholic high school over the 2,000-student public school. Of the eighty graduates in his class, at least ten became priests or brothers. Many others were doctors. "The dumb guys became coaches," Sonny teased.

As a football coach, Mass attendance wasn't always easy, yet Sonny missed Mass only once in ten years.

In his fifteen years as CSU coach, Sonny met every Monday morning with the team chaplain at 7:00 A.M. during the season, rain, snow or sun. They discussed problems and then prayed together.

On Wednesday mornings at 7:00, Sonny, the chaplain and six or seven of his fifteen coaches got together for Bible study. The coaches took turns providing their homes for Thursday evening non-denominational chapel time. Usually twenty to thirty players of the sixty-member squad participated. The coaches' wives provided cookies or other goodies.

Another chapel time, held before boarding the bus on game day, enlisted many more players. "The bigger the game, the larger the number of players that came to pray," said Sonny. "I guess they thought they could handle the smaller games on their own."

"But," Sonny insisted, "we never prayed for victory. We asked for safety... that no one would be hurt."

The chapel meetings were the "glue that held the team together whether we won or lost," Sonny said. The attitudes of those players who attended spread over onto players who didn't participate.

Sundays involved hard work for both team and coaches. Sonny arranged schedules to coincide with religious services. If a player couldn't get to practice on time because of church, he could come late with no consequences.

Sonny's coaching concentrated on getting the best from a player. Talent was important but so is character. Given the choice of a recruit with good character or one with little character but better talent, he chose the one with character. He taught team play and stressed academics. He very seldom lost a player because of poor grades, and that was without the academic helpers most universities employ.

Sonny visited each recruit's home and often reminded them, "I promised your parents I'd take care of you so I want to eliminate problems before they occur. I can't do that if I have to monitor drug use or bail a player out of jail."

"When I become a head coach," James Ward said, "I hope to display the same faith, compassion and love for my neighbors, players and coaches as, you, Sonny."

The Holy Saturday Easter Vigil proceeded and with moist eyes Sonny watched each member of the congregation light a candle. Then he joined James in front of the assembly. Amid the smell of incense and the soft glow of candlelight, Sonny placed a cross around James's neck. He laid his hand on his shoulder as the priest anointed James with oil.

Sonny Lubick had coached many teams, won and lost bowl games, conferences and border wars. He'd been accorded honors like Coach of the Year and Father of the Year.

But his best honor came, he claimed, when he served as a part of the game plan which led his friend and fellow coach to the Catholic faith.

~Linda L. Osmundson

Get Out of the Boat!

Jesus said to them, "My food is to do the will of the one who sent me, and to finish his will."
~John 4:34

I opened my Bible to the passage I was seeking: "As Jesus was walking beside the Sea of Galilee... he saw two other brothers, James son of Zebedee and his brother John. They were in a boat with their father Zebedee, preparing their nets. Jesus called them, and immediately they left the boat and their father and followed him" (Matt. 4:18-22).

I wished I could be as decisive as James and John. "At once they left their nets and followed him." I wished I could be as sure as them... "Immediately they left the boat..."

Once I had put my leg over the side of my boat, but the first thing I thought about was if I was going to sink or not.

My decision to answer God's call to become a deacon wasn't a glorious triumph in my life but rather an awkward, desperate attempt to find solid ground before jumping in and swimming for shore. I wanted answers. I wanted a concrete definition of what my role of deacon would be.

After four years of Diaconate formation and parallel tracks for a master's degree in Catholic studies at the University of St. Thomas in St. Paul, I could not find the concrete definition I so desperately sought.

I wrote my resignation letter from the program.

Before putting it in the mail, I made a lunch appointment with Deacon Riordan, the Director of Clergy for the diocese, to explain my frustration. After thirty-plus years as a professional speaker and business strategist helping executives of large companies define their futures, I found it incongruent to take this next step without knowing exactly where the coming days would take me. I had never gone into a program, never spoken before an audience without knowing precisely what I was doing. This unknowing about where I would be and what I would be doing as a deacon was unsettling beyond measure.

What was God calling me to do once I got out of the boat?

But there I sat at the lunch table, with Deacon Riordan, ready to give up after four long years of study and commitment.

I poured out my lack of confidence, my need to define the role Christ had for me after ordination, my need for a concrete definition. Deacon Riordan respectfully listened to it all, encouraged me with questions, then took a long pause. "Thom," he said, "the question is not one of having a concrete definition of what Christ is calling you to do or be. The question is one of trust. Your trust in Him, your trust in being called, your trust in His design for your life." He wiped his chin with his napkin. "You think about that and call me in a couple of weeks and let me know what you decide."

We got up from the table without another word spoken.

It was no coincidence that my speaking colleague and friend in Christ, Naomi, called me then. Somehow she always knew when I needed encouragement and support. Although we came from different denominations, we shared the same commonality of faith. Partners linked by our professions, but disciples linked by our Savior, we encouraged and challenged each other many times over the years. Repeatedly she had challenged me, "Thom, what are you going to do with your faith?"

I poured my heart and soul and confusion out to her. She listened compassionately as always. "Thom," she began, "Jesus said, 'Follow me, and I will make you fishers of men.' We're supposed to follow, He does the making, the empowering. And indeed He did! With Peter the fisherman, too. Remember how Peter was upset because he'd fished all night and caught no fish? Then he encountered Jesus, the Master Fisherman and the miracle was performed... the boats nearly sank from the lavish outpouring of God's blessing!"

I was beginning to understand her message to me.

She concluded, "When Jesus called James and John and they stepped out of the boat, they had no idea what lay ahead for them, but they followed anyway... they trusted His plan for them."

She was right. Deacon Riordan was right. It all came down to trust in our Lord. I knew all along that He was calling me to serve His purpose in His Church. Why was I demanding to know the particulars rather than just trusting in Him?

Trusting that He would make me what I needed to be for Him, I resumed my studies and was ordained on September 29, 2006.

Yet that was only the beginning of the next phase of formation.

Interestingly enough, I found myself assigned to a parish much different than what I expected. Yet, it was a great gift to me because it drew me through to the next layer of formation, the longer walk with Christ. For soon another assignment came... along with sleepless nights in prayer and the strains and stretching of yet deeper trust and deeper faith. I was assigned to a church in downtown Minneapolis. Only then did I begin to see how God was drawing me to the gifts He gave me rather than all the skills I'd developed in my practice all those years. God brought all my life experiences together there as I explored scripture with the homeless, the successful, the worker and the executive. My wonderful community is serving as Christ in the center of the city, to all God's people: the lost and found.

God has a purpose for me... and all of us... in His plan. When I finally trusted Him and quit trying to design it myself, it turned out to be far bigger than I could have imagined.

Once I got out of the boat.

~Rev. Mr. Thomas J. Winninger

© 2006 Jonny Hawkins

Lassoed by the Rosary

> *We know that all things work for the good for those who love God,*
> *who are called according to his purpose.*
> *~Romans 8:28*

avid Twellman, a forty-something pastor, headed a thriving suburban Methodist church just outside Dallas. He had accomplished two master's degrees, a stint in the Navy, a doctorate in ministry, and eventually, marriage and a couple of children. Knowledgeable and devout, with a dry wit and a studious temperament, he was well schooled in the Bible and spent long hours immersed in study and preparation for his Sunday sermons.

The mid-90s found Dr. Twellman at the peak of his career, busy with preaching, teaching, counseling, and being all things to all people. To be "all things" to the youth group, he swallowed a goldfish, making good on a promise for record high attendance. He went to endless meetings and sampled every potluck dish imaginable. His congregation loved him and he loved them. Well respected among the leaders of his denomination, Dr. Twellman was rising quickly in the church ranks.

It was a good life, except for one little problem... Pastor Twellman had begun to suspect he might be Catholic.

This was an unsettling thought for a man who had spent much of his life in the "Bible Belt" and had heard his share of anti-Catholic rhetoric. He thought he knew all the reasons to reject Catholic doctrine—the claims about the "Real Presence," the authority of the

Pope, and the curious devotion to Mary were just a few. But he found that the harder he tried to turn off the thoughts about Catholicism, the more they persisted. Over time, he found himself guiltily poking through Catholic books and on some surprising occasions, even defending Catholic positions in theological discussions. Theoretically, of course. No harm in playing devil's advocate, was there? Still, he wondered what was happening. Why the restlessness? Why the mental wrestling match over issues of truth? Where was the increasing pull toward all things Catholic coming from? Could it be that God was trying to tell him something?

One evening, he left work and drove the usual route home, which took him past a Catholic church. This night, instead of driving by, he was drawn magnetically to the church; his car seemed to turn into the parking lot itself. It was dusk when Pastor Twellman approached the church and despite the lateness of the hour, he found it unlocked. He pulled open the heavy door and stepped into the quiet fragrant space. Near the altar, he noticed the sanctuary lamp burning beside the tabernacle. He felt himself being drawn to it and immediately fell to his knees. Time stood still. Only God and David Twellman know what exactly took place in the quiet of the man's heart that day, but it was deep and real and unforgettable. He knew all about the Catholic teaching on the Real Presence of Jesus Christ in the Blessed Sacrament, but at that moment, he experienced it. He knew he was in the presence of God.

How much time elapsed, he was not sure, but when he finally rose to his feet, he made his way to the rectory next door and knocked. An elderly priest opened the door. He was obviously fixing his dinner. David introduced himself and confessed sheepishly, "I think I might be Catholic."

At this, the kindly priest reached into his pocket and pressed a rosary into his visitor's hand. "Pray the rosary," he said. "Mary will lead you to her son."

The pastor left and got into his car. "Must be a Catholic thing," David mused to himself as he regarded the black beads. Still, he stopped at a Catholic store on the way home and bought instructions on how to pray the rosary. Soon he began to make it part of his daily prayer life. He learned that the Hail Mary is a prayer with deeply biblical roots. He learned that to pray the rosary is to enter into a profound meditation on the life of Christ. He prayed and he prayed. And along the way, a nearly miraculous thing happened. The rosary became like a lasso that took hold of him and pulled him into the heart of Christ... and toward the Catholic Church.

A conversation with a Catholic theologian followed and soon Pastor Twellman was sitting in a classroom being introduced to Ecclesiology, the study of the origins, the meaning and the structures of the Catholic Church. Things were falling into place. From there, David continued to learn more about his new faith and on a glorious Sunday morning in 1999 the formerly Protestant pastor declared, "I finally stop protesting!"

He entered into the Catholic Church and received Our Lord in Holy Communion for the first time. He gazed at the nearby statue of the Blessed Mother, reminding him he was home. The rosary, forever in his pocket, had done exactly what the priest had promised.

Mary led another soul to her son.

~Eileen Love

Editor's note: Today Dr. Twellman is a faithful, practicing Catholic and a professor of Biblical Studies at the Institute for Pastoral Theology, part of Ave Maria University. His wife and their children are converts too.

Mama's Orchid Corsage

He gives no best who gives most;
but he gives most who gives best.
~Arthur Warwick

The town of Canon City, Colorado, boasts such a large Catholic population that several alcoves in the old bank building on Main Street there bear religious statues. One of those statues is of the Virgin Mary. Years ago, something very special happened concerning that statue.

It all started because, as a child of a sick father and a mother who'd worked hard at menial jobs to support us, I'd always dreamed of buying my mother the beautiful orchid corsage that she deserved for Mother's Day. But it was only after I grew up and became a nurse that I could afford even carnation ones.

By the Mother's Day after my first promotion, I was living in Arizona and I bought Mama the corsage of my childhood dreams... a huge Cattleya Orchid whose velvet rose-purple petals cascaded like a fountain into white netting and purple ribbon. Okay. So it was a bit overboard for a tiny woman like Mama, but I didn't even think of that then. All I thought about was getting it delivered to her little apartment overlooking Main, and how delighted she'd be when she saw it.

Only she didn't sound as delighted as she did dismayed. She did say it was the most beautiful corsage she'd ever seen and she thanked me, but I knew something was wrong. When I asked her what, I couldn't hear her answer for a loud clanking noise on her end of the phone. She'd have to close her door to the hall stairway, she said. When she came back to the phone, she said, "That's Jack, my neighbor's, empty booze bottles he's taking down to the Dumpster," she sighed. "That dear old cowboy is becoming a drunk since his wife died and he moved to town. It's terrible and no one can do anything about it. We've all tried."

When I got Mama's attention back on the corsage, her voice sounded strained. "You really shouldn't have done it," she said. "It's too elegant and beautiful to be worn by a pudgy old work horse like me; I wouldn't feel right wearing it."

I felt so hurt I fought tears.

"Mama!" I cut in. "That orchid is exactly like the wonderful person you are! That's why I've always wanted you to have one. Now, promise me that my dream corsage will be worn tomorrow by the greatest mother in the whole world." A long silence. "Mama?"

"All right, dear," she finally agreed. "I promise. I appreciate the thought, honey, and I feel good that you love me so much."

After we hung up, it finally dawned on me that my childish dream for Mama was something for my benefit more than hers. I felt ashamed that I was forcing her to complete my childhood dream. I called her back to tell her she didn't have to wear that corsage, but she wasn't home.

Nor did I manage to catch her before Mass the next day. After lunch, she called me. Her voice was bubbly. "Honey," she said, "that orchid is so beautiful that it's heavenly! Thank you!"

"Then you did wear it and enjoy it?" A long silence. "Mama?"

"Jeanne, the truth is... I didn't wear it. But before you get upset, I did keep my promise. That orchid is being worn by the greatest mother in the whole world... Our Lord's Blessed Mother! Remember the statue of Mary in the alcove just across the street? Well, I went over in the wee hours this morning and taped that orchid on Mary's shoulder, dear. I can see it from here and it's exactly where it belongs. I honestly tried to put it on last night... my shoulder is just too narrow for it, honey. But I can't tell you how much joy that orchid is giving me as it rests beautifully on Our Holy Mother's shoulder. Okay?"

"Of course," I managed to say.

Neither of us mentioned it again during those next months of phone conversations between Colorado and Arizona. Mama was always full of news, including the report that her neighbor Jack was staying sober. We both wondered what had changed him.

When I was in Canon City for an August visit, Jack was taking his garbage downstairs as Mama and I were carrying up groceries. As he doffed his old scuffed cowboy hat, we paused on the stairs to speak. His face flushing a bit, he said, "I forget that, these days, I don't have to sneak my garbage down the stairs. I don't have those clankin' bottles to hide anymore."

Mama said that was wonderful, and Jack replied, "It really is! Mrs. Murray, did I ever tell you about the sign I got that stopped my drinkin'?"

"Why, no, you didn't," Mama said. "What happened?"

"It was this spring... on Mother's Day. Now I know it sounds plumb loco, Mrs. Murray, but I swear to you that I saw it. That statue of the Holy Mother, right across the street, was wearin' a great big orchid corsage for Mother's Day! I knowed it was a sign to me to quit drinkin' and I ain't had a drop since." He smiled sheepishly. "Now tell me, do you think I'm daft?"

Mama, who, along with me, had been struck open-mouthed silent and still posed holding a bag of groceries, suddenly came alive. "I know you're not daft, Jack," she said, "and you must be right about it being a sign because I can see the miraculous change in you."

He smiled, satisfied, as he walked past us and on down the stairs.

Both Mama and Jack are dead now. But what a fond memory that orchid corsage always brings to mind... the memory of a mother who graciously accepted a gift she really didn't want and turned it into a miracle.

~Jeanne Hill

Go With the Fear!

Sarah said, "God had given me cause to laugh and all who hear it will laugh with me."
~Genesis 21:6

"If God gives you a gift you should share it with others. Never let fear keep you from sharing God's gift!"

What? I jolted back to reality as I heard Father Greg delivering the rest of his homily with conviction. The mother of three grade-school children, I often fell into a state of semi-exhaustion during Mass as soon as I heard the words, "Please be seated."

I was alert now as Father proclaimed, "I want to repeat this so everyone understands. If God gives you a gift, you use that gift to the best of your abilities. Never let fear stand in the way of accepting God's gift and sharing it with others!"

I knew this was God's way of talking to me, but how did He know I was still in hiding? I had left the field of standup comedy over a year ago. I couldn't stand the performance anxiety. I thought I could camouflage myself next to the other soccer moms and pretend it all never happened. I was in denial that it was one of the true joys of my life. Seventeen years of performances across the country were full of adventure and good times, but I let fear win. I had quit the business. I was hiding and keeping quiet. But now, in church today, God caught up with me and He jolted me back to reality and He was talking really loud!

"Never let fear stand in the way of accepting God's gift and sharing it with others!"

God was talking to me about my comedic gift. I find humor in everything. Humor is my way of dealing with the hurt and pain rampant in our world today, as well as the stress involved in raising a family. Humor = pain + time. I know the formula well. Humor is all around us if we give it a chance. In my high school speech class, I shared my perceptions of life at every opportunity. My fellow classmates at Woodlands Academy of the Sacred Heart gave me the title of "Class Clown" in our high school yearbook. I considered this a true honor because I was very quiet and shy.

In college, I kept my dreams at bay. My father had warned me that pursuing drama would make it difficult to find "real" work. It wasn't until I graduated from college and discovered improvisation through Chicago's Second City training classes that I knew I found my true destiny. It was exciting to be surrounded by other creative souls who enjoyed finding the funny in everyday life. I listened to the lectures and grew as a comedic actor. Two years later I took on yet another challenge, solo performing. I walked down the street to Zanies Comedy Club and stood on stage alone for the first time. I was terrified yet I knew I was home. Secretly I felt consumed by incredible performance anxiety. It was nearly paralyzing.

Seventeen years of performances and the nervousness did not abate. Because I knew how to carry myself, no one ever suspected my insecurities. The night that I filmed my segment of Showtime's Comedy Club Network at Zanies in Chicago, I felt overwhelmed. In the past six months, my weight had dropped significantly and I looked gaunt. I studied my reflection in the mirror. "This cannot be a healthy way to live," I thought. "Why am I doing this to myself?" And the answer was always the same. "This is what makes me tick." In my self-questioning, I held onto a vision of the performer I could become.

The Showtime taping went well but at a cost. I was emotionally drained and I continued to lose weight. I grew weary and gave up the fight. I let fear win. I quit. I hid from my dreams.

Nobody could understand why I ran away from something I

loved so much. No one understood. But today God had found me hiding in His church. He had a voice in Father Greg and He was using it. There was no denying the seriousness of this message. I knew I'd better listen.

I began to pray that God would ease my fear. I asked Him for the courage to find comedy again. Incredibly, my fear gradually lessened. Finally I gathered the courage to return to the stage. This time, however, my topics would gain a new focus. I would joke about the craziness of raising a family. Talking about my children comforted me.

It was a Saturday night and I was about to go on stage at St. Mary's Parish in Buffalo Grove, Illinois. I couldn't wait for the show to start. I felt so happy knowing that the spirit in the room was about to go up, up, up. I noticed that the woman who scheduled my appearance was full of anxiety as she attended to details... name tags, announcements, last minute arrivals. It was her first time booking a comic for a parish event. Would the audience approve? Would anyone be offended? Is she funny?

I couldn't help but chuckle because I was there to do good. These dear parishioners would laugh, sing and tell their own personal stories before the evening ended.

The intro music started and immediately energized the room. I hit the stage dancing. Picking up a laundry basket, I ran into the audience handing out shirts, sweaters and pants, asking my new friends to help fold. "We're in this together!" I shouted. A pregnant mom held up a neatly folded bloused and proclaimed, "I ought to be pretty good at this by now."

The party was just getting started!

Having faced my fears, I'd found fulfillment in sharing God's gift of comedy and laughter. I'd discovered my niche and my anxiety was only a memory.

My show at St. Mary's came to an end on a great high note. I was aware and thankful that I was living my dream. A senior citizen approached me as I walked across the room and she stretched out her fragile hand. Her eyes were filled with tears, though she had the grin of a young child returning from a birthday party.

"Since my husband passed, I've kept to myself and haven't been out much. Tonight I felt compelled to take a chance. I'm so happy I came to your show. Thank you so much; I haven't laughed this hard in years."

With these words, I felt complete. I thanked God for the courage to "never let fear stand in the way of accepting God's gift and sharing it with others."

~Sally Edwards

Living Catholic Faith

Miracles

*There are only two ways to live your life.
One is as though nothing is a miracle.
The other is as everything is.*

~Albert Einstein

35

Medjugorje Miracle

*Miracles — whether prophetically or of other sorts —
always occur in connection with some message from heaven,
and are intended by God as a seal or endorsement
of the messenger and his word.*
~Aloysius McDonough

For all of my ninety years, I've had a great devotion to the Virgin Mary. I didn't believe that Mary could answer prayers, but that she was an intercessor to her son, Jesus. While I was raising eight children, I needed all the interceding I could get! I turned to her often, mother to mother. A statue of the Blessed Virgin sat prominently on our buffet and fresh flowers adorned her, especially in May.

I knew Mary had appeared to youngsters in Lourdes, France, and to children in Guadelupe, Mexico. Then in the 1980s, I read new accounts of Mary appearing to youngsters in Medjugorje, Bosnia. Intrigued by the modern-day miracle, I bought books about it, subscribed to the *Medjugorje Magazine*, attended seminars on the topic... and bought a ticket to Bosnia.

At eighty years old, with back problems and a mild heart condition, I didn't know if I could climb the mountain, but I just knew I was supposed to go... to be there... to see where Mary had appeared.

I didn't go planning to see a miracle, but many who had been there did. There were hundreds of accounts of miraculous healings and faith conversions.

Our tour group arrived in Medjugorje late one damp November

night. The next morning we learned our scheduled trek had been postponed, due to the rain and slippery slopes. One younger man who had made the trip twice before, said he could wait no longer... he was climbing the mile-long mountain path right then.

I said, "Me too."

So with more determination than strength, I set off for the climb. I was surprised to see the trail was only jagged rocks. Step by cautious step, I slowly hiked upward, past a woman even older than I kneeling in prayerful meditation... past a half-dozen rowdy ten-year-old boys running and yelping with joy. They raced ahead of me; later I came upon them again, kneeling in quiet prayer.

Within two hours, I stood in breathless wonder and awe at the top of the mountain, on the very site the Virgin had appeared. I knelt in the sprinkling rain and did what I always do... I prayed for her children.

The trek down was even more difficult than the ascent. Each step on the rugged rocks jarred me as I struggled to find stable footing. The rain intensified as we wound our way through the foreign streets of the city. I returned to the group, soaking wet but marveling that, not only had I made the climb, I had done so without my usual pain. "Maybe that was the miracle," I mused.

The next day was just another day in war-torn Bosnia, but it was Thanksgiving Day in the States... and the tour guide had a plan to make it a day of Thanksgiving in Medjugorje too. On every tour the staff purchased and distributed groceries and supplies to the most needy in the community. All of the dozen members of our tour group readily offered to contribute to the fund and help with the deliveries.

Our large bus stopped at the grocery store where the ordered bags of goods were loaded into the back. Carefully, we counted the twenty-four garbage-size bags. Local church and government officials had made a list of the twenty-four families in most desperate need, and the bus headed off to share Thanksgiving with them.

The first stop was a shanty with the roof partly blown off. My new friends and I filed past damaged household furniture sitting on the dirt lawn and entered the one room the family of four occupied. Laughing, smiling, and crying, the old couple accepted the food and supplies. Two young boys in clean ragged clothes chattered their gratitude while their toddler brother clung to the grandma's leg, whining and fussing. Their parents were tortured and killed by the enemy, the tour guide had explained. Yet the family jubilantly hugged us goodbye and we headed off to the next stop.

The bus driver seemed to have the route and stops memorized from the many trips before. At the next run-down house, a wrinkled old woman in a headscarf stood waving from her cluttered front porch. As our group entered, she placed her hands on each of our faces and kissed us, one by one, thanking us in her native tongue. Inside we gathered in one of the two rooms left standing in her once three-bedroom home. There she prayed, not for herself, but for us, her guests.

The driver stopped next at a ramshackle house at the end of a lane, and before the tour guide could say, "They aren't on our list this time," a man and two young boys raced toward the bus clapping for joy. At the directive of the tour guide, the bus pulled away, leaving them looking forlorn and rejected.

"Can't we please leave them some food?" I politely protested as I looked back at the family waving sadly.

"We only have twenty-four bags," the guide explained, her voice thick with sorrow. "We have other families waiting for these. We promised them."

The team sat, despondent, until the driver stopped at yet another war-damaged home. There, a couple who looked even older than I cared for two grown sons, both suffering from a wasting muscular disease. Yet their faith and joy exceeded ours as they crowded the entire group into their tiny kitchen to pray... and share food the old woman had prepared for us.

And so went the day, house after house, family after family, each physically destitute and spiritually wealthy.

"That's twenty-four!" the guide said as she checked the last name off the list after the final stop.

"No, twenty-three," someone corrected. "There is one bag of food left."

Dumbfounded, the group looked in the back of the bus to see one lone bag of food.

"We all counted the bags and the people on the list three times," one member said.

"There was no error," our guide said, then beamed. "Are there loaves and fishes in that bag?"

The entire team stared at each other first in confusion, then in awe, then in elation. We cheered, "Let's go!"

The bus returned to the ramshackle house at the end of the lane and the man and two boys raced out, as if they were expecting us.

~Berniece Duello

The White Rosary

Every believer is God's miracle.
~Gamaliel Bailey

My father died on a day of "holy expectations," the first day of Advent, a day he would have attended church to prepare for the coming of Christ. Father always attended Mass on Sundays and Holy Days of Obligation, obeyed the Ten Commandments, and led a humble and honest life. Before he died he received the Sacrament of Anointing of the Sick, and that's when he confided to the priest his concern for his "fallen away" daughter. Me.

On the Feast Day of the Immaculate Conception, we held a prayer vigil for him at the funeral home. In an intimate, warmly-lit viewing room, a dozen family members gathered together in a circle around Dad's open casket. He was dressed in a gray suit, white shirt, and burgundy tie. The wood bead rosary I'd given him when Mom died was twined through his folded hands.

My cousin Gayle from North Dakota—the "devoted" Catholic everyone called her—came prepared to lead us in the rosary. She offered us two extra rosaries, a white one and a brown one, and placed them on the table in front of us. "After we're finished," she explained, "I'll put the white rosary in your father's pocket. When it comes back to you... and I trust that it will... you'll know that your dad is in heaven."

I hadn't held a Catholic rosary for a long time, but under the spell of her unshakeable faith, and certain now that the white rosary was imbued with Divine potential, I grabbed it off the table and felt its tiny beads between my fingers.

Gayle chose to recite the Joyful Mysteries, reflections meant to help us "enter into the ultimate causes and the deepest meaning of Christian joy."

"Hail Mary, full of grace..." she began.

"... Holy Mary, Mother of God," we responded, "pray for us sinners, now and at the hour of our death."

As we sat in the quiet serenity of the funeral home reciting the rosary, I recalled the night he passed away. My sisters and brother and I were staying at the hospice center where Dad had been transferred three days earlier. It was my night to be with him, though by now he had lost consciousness and no longer responded to our presence. By 10:00 P.M., my siblings had gone home. I was alone with Dad in the quiet hospice room listening to his labored breathing and the gurgling sounds coming from his throat. Occasionally his arms twitched or his head jerked. Sometimes he furrowed his brow, a sign, according to the hospice literature, that he might be working out unresolved mental or spiritual conflicts.

Standing by my father's bedside, I thought about the conversation he'd had with the priest at the hospital, the one about my leaving Catholicism for Buddhism. Afterwards, I had told Dad not to worry, that Buddhists and Catholics went to the same place. "I hope so," he'd said, "because I want to see you again."

I wanted to see him again too, in a place beyond religious differences and misunderstandings, beyond the suffering of aging, sickness and death.

While I watched the tightness gather in my father's face, I feared that he might be grappling with the implications of our differing religious views in some deep region of his psyche. So I took out my Buddhist rosary, a strand of 108 crystal beads, and even though I felt awkward and self-conscious, I leaned in close and began to recite the Hail Mary out loud.

They say that our sense of hearing is the last to go, and that in an unconscious state a person can still hear. I hoped they were right. I didn't see any visible signs that Dad heard my prayers. He died five hours later.

Gayle concluded the five Joyful Mysteries and I gave the white rosary back to her. As promised, she put it in my father's pocket. We buried him the following day, next to Mom.

The Sunday after the funeral, my cousins went back to North Dakota. On Monday, my siblings and I went back to the grim task of going through our parents' belongings to decide what to take, give away, or store. My mother was a collector, and among her many treasures was a large box of costume jewelry that she'd intended to use for craft projects... plastic bead trays, bead kits, old candy boxes, shoe boxes, all filled with earrings, bracelets, necklaces and ropes of beads. As I held up each pair of old clip earrings, each brooch, necklace and bracelet, I called out to my siblings, "Does anybody want this?"

After an hour of sorting, the weariness of making irretrievable life decisions prompted my sister to say, "Let's keep it all and worry about it later."

On the Feast Day of Our Lady of Guadalupe, "the Lady we prayed to the night of the Prayer Vigil," my cousin would tell me later, I went back to our parents' apartment and once again began to open every bead box, candy box and shoe box. I separated the nice brooches from the ugly ones, the semi-precious gemstones from the plastic ones, the chains with usable clasps from the broken ones.

Finally, I came to the last shoe box. I lifted the lid and found one more pile of tangled necklaces. I stuck my fingers into the mound and grabbed a handful, to examine if any of them were worth keeping. In the bottom, under a jumbled strand of black rhinestones and strings of fake pearls, something familiar shone through... the whitish color, the tiny little beads strung on a cotton cord, the cross... it was identical to the one my cousin had put in Dad's pocket!

I pulled the white rosary out from under the heap and held it in my palm like a priceless jewel. Through tears of joy, I stared out the window and reveled in the wonder of sacred signs.

By the end of Advent, I had told the "white rosary" story to all my friends, relatives and acquaintances. The rosary's magic was beginning to work its way into my own deep psychic regions. Christmas Eve, as I left my sister's party and headed home, I thought about midnight Mass, the sacredness of the coming hours and my dad's Catholic faith. He would have wanted me to celebrate the real Christmas. "Do Buddhists believe in Jesus Christ?" he always asked me.

I exited the freeway and headed for St. James Cathedral. If I could find parking then I would go, if not, well...

The church had arranged plenty of parking. My destination was set. For the next three hours I feasted on choral groups, brass ensembles, pipe organs and operatic solos, all heralding the divine birth of Jesus. After the Archbishop held up the host and blessed the wine, the procession of worshippers rose to receive the Body and Blood of Christ, choirs sang "Silent Night," and I "entered into the deepest meaning of Christian joy."

By the time I got home, it was 2:00 A.M. but I wasn't at all tired. The celebration of Christ's birth filled me with energy and the possibility of new beginnings. I looked over at my Buddhist shrine where I had put the white rosary and a picture of Dad. The white rosary encircled my father's photo like a ring of protection.

My process of reconciliation had begun.

~Joan D. Stamm

37

Jennifer's Angel

If the world is really the medium of God's personal action,
miracle is wholly normal.
~D.E. Trueblood

After giving birth, our daughter, Jennifer, was alone and in severe pain in the hospital's intensive care unit. Following an emergency caesarean, she was suffering from life-threatening toxemia, eclampsia and her kidneys were failing. Her three-pound baby boy, named Jake, was rushed to a prenatal unit in a hospital three hours away. The doctor requested that Jake's father go with the baby.

Later that evening, the night nurse came into Jennifer's room to let her know her brother had come by to check on her condition.

"He told me he couldn't stay, but had to move on," she said. "Jennifer, I can see that you are feeling pretty groggy. I'll tell you about his visit later, when you are more alert."

As the pain medication took effect, the throbbing in Jennifer's abdomen subsided and she fell asleep. Three hours later, the same nurse strode into Jennifer's room with a portable telephone tucked under her arm.

"Jennifer, I wanted to bring you a telephone so you can call your brother. I would like you to let him know that you are doing okay before I leave for the day. I promised him I would remember to tell you."

"I don't have a brother."

"Your maiden name is Harris, isn't it?"

"Well yes..."

"Jennifer, maybe you don't remember me coming in earlier. Last night, a man about your age walked in around midnight and asked to see you. He looked just like you and said he was John Harris. He wanted to make sure that you were doing okay." Patting Jennifer's hand, she continued, "I explained that you were in Intensive Care and no visitors were allowed. I assured him that you were stable and told him that his new nephew had been transported to a special unit for premature babies. Mr. Harris told me that he understood and that he couldn't stay. He just wanted his sister to know that she was not alone."

"Now I remember!" Jennifer exclaimed, as she tried to sit up in bed. "I did have a brother, but he died in childbirth! My parents named him John."

Jennifer felt her stomach tighten with pain. She smiled weakly, and laying back down on her bed, she began to drift off again.

Confused, the nurse shook her head. While she checked Jennifer's pulse, she told her she would leave the phone with her in case she changed her mind and wanted to call her brother later.

My husband and I finally got to California two days after Jake was born. Jennifer told us what happened... that her "angel-brother" watched over her until her father and I arrived.

Our family rejoiced at how God protected Jennifer when she felt most alone by sending our John to her.

~Paulette L. Harris

38

The Pretty Lady

Holy Mary, Mother of God,
pray for us sinners, now and at the hour of our death.
Amen.
~From the Hail Mary

The drone of the HEPA filter and the beeping of the six infusion pumps hooked up to my son's heart almost made me miss his whisper. "Mom. Did you see the pretty lady? Did you see her?"

Cameron had been diagnosed with Acute Myeloblastic Leukemia in June of 1997, one month after graduating high school. Two cord blood transplants and one lung resection later, we were sitting on Ward 9200 at Duke University Hospital. Two days before, the doctors had given me the horrific news that my son was going to die. There was nothing more all the doctors in the world could do, except relieve his pain with morphine.

I had heard that with narcotics some patients have hallucinations. Indeed, Cameron had tried to call his dog Sebastian, who had died the previous year, to his side. Once I caught him eating an imaginary ice cream cone, his tongue flicking out to catch the drips of mint chocolate chip on his arm.

Today seemed different.

I thought Cameron was napping, when he suddenly opened his eyes, and began to smooth the crisp white hospital sheets.

Ever vigilant, I had jumped up from the recliner/chair/bed that had been my mainstay, to rush to his side. He kept smoothing the sheets.

"Cameron, is everything alright? Do you need something?"

"She's beautiful. Don't you see her?"

I looked all around the room, but saw nothing.

"See who, Cameron?"

"That lady... Mary."

"Mary? Your grandmother? Nana?" My mother's name is Mary, and they had always been close, but she was in Wisconsin, as it was my father's turn to visit and stay until the end. "Do you see Nana?"

"No." Cameron was still insistent on smoothing out the sheets, but almost in a patting motion now.

"She said her name is Mary. She said everything is okay. She's beautiful. She's wearing a white dress, and it's really long. It takes up the whole bed."

Cameron kept smoothing the sheets as his face relaxed and he leaned back against the hospital pillows.

"Mom. Did you see the pretty lady? Did you see her?" he whispered.

I nodded my head in affirmation, a pure reflex at this point. Anything to bring Cameron a moment's peace.

I've heard that the Virgin Mary appears to those about to die, and gives them a glimpse of heaven so they will be comforted. I've even heard that she accompanies them on their journey. I'm not Catholic, so I wouldn't know about the traditions and doctrine, but I hope she likes dogs... and mint chocolate chip ice cream.

~Dawn Holt

The Fish, the Knife and Saint Jude

Every child born into the world is a new thought of God,
an ever-fresh and radiant possibility.
~Kate Douglas Wiggin

It had been a perfect afternoon. The sun was slowly descending in the west, casting a rosy glow on the dusky foothills as it cut through the haze of early evening. The river was winding noiselessly by as I cast my fishing line in for the last few times.

James, my six-year-old son, had long since tired of fishing and was leap-frogging over the ash-colored boulders that lined the river. "Dad, look what I found!" I heard him squeal with delight. I carefully placed my rod and reel down on the riverbank and went to see what was causing his excitement.

"Look Dad, I found the greatest pocket knife!" He clutched his treasure in a clenched little fist as he stumbled over the boulders to meet me. It was a handsome little knife, with two shiny silver blades that folded within an imitation wood handle; it was just the right size for a boy to slip into his blue-jeans pocket. "Isn't it terrific?" he asked, his eyes sparkling.

"Yes. You take good care of this knife, Son, and you'll be able to use it for a long time."

I went back to my fishing pole and started to reel it in. I felt a sharp tug... then another! The tip of my pole bent almost to the water's edge and the line stripped from the reel with a high-pitched whine.

"James, quick, I've got one!" I hollered. "Get over here and help me!"

James grabbed onto the pole and together we struggled to reel in a large rainbow trout. It burst from the water as we were bringing it in and we could see the myriad of colors. The trout dove into the murky water again, snaking more line, and we played it, my hands over James's, waiting for the fish to tire.

Finally, we began to reel it in towards the shore. James reached down with our net as I pulled the fish in close to the riverbank. He scooped the immense fish into the net, and with my help, hauled it up onto the bank. "What a fish! It must weigh six pounds!" I exclaimed as I put it on the stringer.

I cast one more time while out of the corner of my eye I saw James playing with the fish on the stringer. "Well, it's about time to call it a day," I told him as I reeled in my line a final time.

"Dad! Oh, no! Dad, I've lost my knife!" James turned his panic-stricken little face towards me; tears welled up in his eyes and threatened to spill down his freckled cheeks.

We began to look for the little knife, but the sun was down and the boulders on the lakeshore had taken on the ghostly appearance of large black shadows. We couldn't see well enough to find our noses, much less a tiny pocketknife. "Looks like it's a lost cause, James," I told him sadly.

"I know what. Let's ask Saint Jude to help us. Maybe then we'll find it," he said with a glint of hope in his eye. I recalled that his godmother had told him that Saint Jude was the patron saint of lost causes or hopeless cases.

"All right," I replied doubtfully, "you never know."

James prayed with the refreshing faith and earnestness found only in young children. "Saint Jude, please help me find my knife."

We got down on our hands and knees, our vision limited by the lack of daylight, and scratched around in the dirt and between the boulders, looking one last time for the elusive little knife. No luck.

Sadly, James conceded we were not going to find his knife. We picked up our gear and headed for home, a somber feeling casting a pall over what had been an almost-perfect afternoon.

When we got home, hoping to ease his sadness, I said it was time to clean the trout we'd worked so hard to catch. James wandered over, still a little distraught over having lost his knife. He clambered up onto a tall stool so that he could see everything I was about to do.

James watched with fascination as I slit the trout from head to tail. With a sharp knife, I slowly, carefully cut the stomach open. Suddenly, a sharp "clank" sounded, as something fell from the trout's innards and hit the bottom of our stainless steel sink. I picked it up and washed it off. There, in my hand, was a little imitation wood-handled pocketknife, its two shiny blades tucked safely within its handle.

James nearly plunked right off the chair he was perched upon. "I knew Saint Jude would help me find my knife!" He shrieked with joy. "Ya gotta have faith!"

~Mike O'Boyle as told to Sherry O'Boyle

Roses from Heaven

Lovely flowers are the smiles of God's goodness.
~William Wilberforce

"What do you think I should do?" my seventy-seven-year-old mother asked me again during our nightly chat on the phone. I sighed. I had heard the same question from her for more than ten months and I still did not know how to answer.

Through a series of medical tests, it had been discovered that my mother had a blockage in the carotid artery on the right side of her neck. Now she was faced with a dilemma. Was it riskier to have surgery, considering all her other health problems, or do without surgery and have a higher risk of having a stroke? The doctors had left the decision completely up to her. My two sisters, brother, and I struggled with the choice along with our mother.

Finally, after nearly a year of worry, she told us, "I've decided to have the surgery. I don't want to be a burden if I should have a stroke."

"We would never consider you a burden," we told her. But we supported her in whatever she chose.

Now we knew what we had to do.

We made our annual October pilgrimage to the shrine of Our Lady of Consolation in Carey, Ohio. The shrine was witness to many miracles of healing. People leave prayer requests and letters of thanksgiving there. We have always had a special devotion to St.

Therese of Lisieux, known as "the Little Flower." When we go to the shrine, we write our petitions asking St. Therese to intercede for us in asking Our Lord to grant our requests. We know the strength of the Little Flower, for she has interceded for us many times before. In her autobiography, *The Story of a Soul*, she stated that she would spend an eternity showering the world with flowers for all who ask for her help. Many people say they smell roses or receive roses unexpectedly after they have prayed to her.

When my family gathered there, I wrote, "Dear St. Therese, please ask Our Lord to protect my mother as she undergoes her operation. Grant that it may be successful. Thank you for your intercession."

I'm sure that my siblings wrote similar petitions, which we left in the overflowing basket at the feet of the statue of St. Therese.

The chilly October morning of the surgery arrived and we all gathered in the hospital waiting room. As the tedious waiting began, I held my rosary and prayed. The surgery was to last nearly three hours and we were told that a nurse would take phone calls from the operating room and report the progress to us.

The friendly nurse introduced herself and, as promised, updated us. At 10:15 A.M., she said, "Surgery is just beginning." It seemed all of us took a collective breath and prayed.

Then, fifteen minutes later, an astounding thing happened. The same nurse came to us with a beautiful bouquet of roses in her arms. She smiled and handed one to each of us. Amazed, I knew at that moment that the surgery would be successful.

Curiously, I asked the nurse, "Why are you giving us roses?"

"My boss told me to," she replied as she left us and passed out the rest of the roses to others in the waiting area.

The surgery was successful and my mother completely recovered. We are still grateful for the roses and the gentle message from the Little Flower.

~Carol J. Douglas

A Gate to a Miracle

How little do they see what is, who frame their hasty judgments upon that which seems.
~Robert Southey

I don't know what made me go into the doctor's office that afternoon when I noticed a dent and a bruise on my left breast. After all, I had just been to see him three weeks earlier and left with a clean bill of health. He'd told me my mammograms were normal and he would see me again next year. I thanked him and went back to a temporary teaching assignment I had accepted just a few days earlier.

And now, here, I was sitting on an exam table, facing a young surgeon I had never met before. He said that the bruise looked like the result of a sharp blow, that I must have hit myself very hard on something.

"But I don't remember hitting myself anywhere," I said, bewildered. "Am I to worry about this?"

"As the wall of the breast heals, it will go back to normal," he responded. "However, I do feel a thickness in the breast."

"A thickness?" I repeated, echoing his words. "It wasn't there three weeks ago."

He said he wanted to do a biopsy just to be sure it was nothing more than a bruise.

"Biopsy?" I felt chills run up and down my spine.

"To err on the side of caution," he assured me.

I went home that night confused and a little scared. Where could I have possibly bumped myself? And not remembered?

The next day I went shopping with my daughter. I was sitting outside the fitting room while she was trying on clothes when I suddenly recalled everything. Since this was a Saturday, I had to wait until Monday to call my surgeon.

"Yes!" I said, as soon as I heard his voice. "Yes. I did hit myself! I was hurrying onto the school playground and hit myself on the steel handle of the entry gate."

"Did you hit yourself in the spot of the bruise?" he asked.

"Yes. In the exact spot."

A sense of relief washed over me, certain that I would not have to have a biopsy now. "So, what do you think the thickness was?"

"It was probably the scar tissue that formed from the bruise where you hit yourself. But," he continued, "I would still like to go ahead with the biopsy to be certain there's nothing there."

That Thursday I had the biopsy. The surgeon found a lump in the scar tissue that had formed from the bruise. As I opened the gate, I had hit myself in the exact spot where a malignant tumor had been growing for about two years.

That night, I sat my children down on the couch and told them I had breast cancer. I'll never forget the looks on their faces. Confusion. Fear. Concern. Their expressions are etched in my soul forever.

My surgery was scheduled for the only day that the operating room had an opening—Good Friday. And it was good indeed. The surgery revealed that all my lymph nodes were clean, as well as the marginal tissue around the tumor.

"What are the chances of that?" I asked over and over again, thinking about the gate hitting me in the exact spot of the tumor.

But this I knew for sure—God had opened a gate to a miracle.

~Lola DeJulio DeMaci

42

Our Lady's Crown

*Flowers are God's thoughts of beauty
taking form to gladden moral gaze.*
~William Wilberforce

Mother's Day has always been a special day for my family and the Portuguese communities throughout the world. Mother's Day falls on or near May 13th, the day Our Lady of the Rosary first appeared to Lucia, Francisco and Jacinta in Fatima, Portugal, in 1917.

All my life, I remember going with my family and participating in the festivities honoring Our Lady of Fatima in California. Daddy was always so proud to be a part of the "festa" celebration committees. All five of us girls had been a part of the celebrations. In fact, two of my sisters were asked to be queens and crown the statue of Our Lady of Fatima at church.

When we moved to Washington State, we felt blessed to find the Catholic Church there was called Our Lady of Fatima. They did not practice the annual devotion, but it didn't take long for us to get a novena and crowning in May, as close to the 13th as possible.

We started out with crowning a small statue. Then Daddy and a friend built an altar, which could be carried in procession by four men. On the altar was a statue of Our Lady of Fatima, surrounded by fresh flowers. For a few years, we tried to get our entire congregation to join in this labor of love, but all we would get was the few Portuguese and Hispanic families who knew that constant prayer and devotion is what Our Lady asked of the three shepherd children in 1917.

When our new church was built a few years ago, my sister, brother-in-law and their family had a breathtakingly beautiful statue built on a platform, complete with the shepherd children and sheep, like in Portugal.

Our Lady was crowned at all three of the masses on Mother's Day. I had been asked to make the crown of flowers and, as always, I used pink sweetheart roses, my favorite flower. When we went to Mass the following weekend, I was shocked to see the pink roses had turned a beautiful shade of deep red! Father Alejandro, also surprised, told me we had received a special blessing. Interestingly, there was one rose missing from the crown, nowhere to be found.

Three months after the May crowning, the flowers on Our Lady's crown were still dark red and as soft as velvet. I stood in front of Our Lady and asked, "I know I have no right to ask, but can I have a sign that this is a blessing or miracle of some sort?"

I looked down and saw under one of the lamb statues, the pink rose, missing since May. I picked it up. It was still soft, light pink, with a little brown on the tip.

To this day, that rose has a special place in the cabinet in the gathering area, where it remains, soft and pink, with the original crown.

~Delores Fraga-Carvalho

The Heart of a Mother

Hear and let it penetrate into your heart, my dear little child:
let nothing discourage you, nothing depress you.
Let nothing alter your heart or your countenance.
Also do not fear any illness or vexation, anxiety or pain.
~Our Lady of Guadalupe to Juan Diego

In January of 2006 I began praying that my son Ryan and his wife Jocelyn would have a baby before Christmas of that year. They had been trying to get pregnant for most of their six-year marriage.

About this time, a friend of mine gave me the prayer that Our Lady of Guadalupe said to an Aztec named Juan Diego, in 1531, in Mexico. "Hear and let it penetrate into your heart, my dear little child: let nothing discourage you, nothing depress you. Let nothing alter your heart or your countenance. Also do not fear any illness or vexation, anxiety or pain."

I decided that would be my prayer for the year. I wouldn't let my heart ache, be discouraged, or depressed, but I would ask Our Blessed Mother to pray to her son for my children.

The last week of September, my friend who works in a dental office was working on a patient who mentioned that she worked for Catholic Charities and that they were really short on couples wanting to adopt a baby. My friend left the patient and called me right away. I called Jocelyn at work.

Jocelyn called Catholic Charities the next day and got the

information about an orientation that they were having in October. Ryan and Jocelyn attended the classes and filled out the forms to begin the process of adoption. They quickly put together five photo albums with pictures and information about themselves for birth mothers to look at, plus they completed their home study and more forms. On October 31st, Ryan took their photo albums to Catholic Charities.

On November 26th, I was selling tickets for a church event in the back of the church where several people stood visiting. A young Hispanic man who I had not seen before approached me and motioned me to follow him down the center aisle of the church. He didn't speak English very well but pointed for me to look on the wall where the light was shining up. He asked me in broken English, "Do you see Our Lady of Guadalupe?"

I said, "I'm sorry but I can't."

"I do!" he beamed.

"You are blessed to see her," I simply said.

Four days later, Ryan and Jocelyn came to our house and told us wonderful news. They had gotten a call from Catholic Charities that a sixteen-year-old girl had picked them to be the parents of her baby boy, due on January 28th. They were scheduled to meet the birth mother on December 18th.

I thanked God that night and told Him January 28, 2007, would work just fine for having a baby for Ryan and Jocelyn.

On December 9th, I was sitting in another church with Ryan, waiting for the ceremony to begin. While I was telling him my story of the young Hispanic man, I looked up to see Our Lady of Guadalupe featured on the stained-glass window at the end of our row. I pointed her out to Ryan. During the Mass, the bishop said, "Today is the feast of St. Juan Diego, the man Our Lady of Guadalupe appeared to."

Ryan and I looked at each other, stunned. He whispered, "Mom, you better go to Mass in three days... December 12th is Our Lady of Guadalupe's feast day."

I seldom go to Mass during the week unless it's Tuesday, when I lead a Bible Study. December 12th was on Tuesday.

I went to Mass that day and prayed to Our Lady of Guadalupe all the prayers that were in my heart and thanked our Heavenly Father for hearing my prayers.

At midnight, two days later, the birth mother had an emergency caesarean. The baby was born at 12:45 A.M., weighing four pounds, twelve ounces.

On December 15th, Ryan and Jocelyn held their baby, John Paul, for the first time.

On December 23rd, they brought him home.

There really is no way to describe what I felt as I was at Mass on Christmas Eve. We were there to celebrate the first Christmas gift, a Baby wrapped in swaddling clothes. As I looked at John Paul swaddled in a blanket, my heart was so full of thanks for this most wonderful Christmas gift... through the intercession of Our Lady of Guadelupe.

~Linda Mainard

Lost and Found

And I tell you, ask and you will receive;
seek and you will find;
knock and the door will be opened to you.
For everyone who asks, receives;
and the one who seeks, finds;
and to the one who knocks, the door will be opened.
~Luke 11:9-10

We had waited nearly two years to get a Chesapeake Bay Retriever puppy. I daydreamed of names, felt the brown puppy fur between my fingers, and smelled a young warm-bellied pup. The breeder called with a possible dog for us; he was four months old, had no training, and could not be AKC registered. I explained he would be our family dog and accompany my husband and son hunting. I assured her that his age and lack of early attention was okay with us. For some reason unbeknownst to me, I was determined to have this dog, no matter what. Thus, on a windy day, in late December, we met him. He was shy and afraid of us, of everything really, but I just knew he was my dog. We named him Kenai after our favorite river in Alaska, where my parents lived.

Less than one month later, our only child, our sixteen-year-old son, died. As I grieved, whimpering and crying in my pain, Kenai sat at attention at his fence, listening for my movements in the house. He watched and waited, 24/7. I spent more than an hour each day sitting cross-legged on a railroad tie in the yard, Kenai lying across my lap. His fur became a prayer blanket to me, his eyes a healing solace. I sometimes wondered if he was an angel, sent to companion me in my grief.

On April 1st, a little more than two months after Justin died, I made a business trip to California. It was a mistake for me to travel so soon. I didn't realize how exhausted I was and how little energy I had to expend. I couldn't wait to get home. On a Sunday evening, I called to check in with Jim, my husband. He sounded awful and told me he had some very bad news. While at the fire station on Interstate 80 in Wyoming where he volunteers, a train passed, blowing its whistle. Kenai, standing next to him, had bolted in fear, simply disappearing into the stark barren landscape. Jim searched for hours and finally drove the forty-five minutes home, bereft. He knew how much Kenai mattered to me, and couldn't believe this loss.

When I got home, we drove to Wyoming and searched and searched. No one had seen him. On Holy Thursday, a friend and I drove to every house, every ranch, and posted lost dog signs. I berated myself for seeking a lost dog, while there were places in the world with people searching for missing family and friends. Yet I knew the loss of our son had left us hopeless. We could do nothing to change it. I had to do something now to try to find Kenai, to ease our loss. I had to believe again.

Kenai was only seven months old—a shy, frightened dog. But I had to try, to hope for a miracle. I posted a missing dog report on dogdetective.com.

The summer passed. Whenever we went to our cabin, ten miles south of where we lost Kenai, I scoured the landscape. I knew that perhaps someone had found him and kept him, or he had been eaten by a predator, or killed by a car. But I still looked. Something inside me believed in hope. I stopped telling my husband what I was doing. He felt bad enough.

Nearly nine months passed. Christmas was coming and we planned to visit my parents in Alaska. It had been the worst year of our lives, and we needed a respite. On December 23rd, we left Colorado in a snowstorm. Two feet of snow had fallen; cattle were dying on the plains. Arriving in Alaska, the serenity and beauty welcomed us. My parent's cozy lodge was a comforting place to spend Christmas.

The morning of December 24th, my husband was on the telephone. I heard snippets of the conversation. "In a dead cow carcass? Brown dog? Skinny? Can't get near him?" He hung up, shaken, and explained. A rancher out with her cows had spotted a small animal on a distant ridge. She determined it was a dog. She could see it had a collar and flash of silver around its neck. When she approached the animal, it ran. Searching the Internet for lost dogs, Brenda found my notice I'd long given up on but never deleted. She promised to leave food near the cow carcass the dog used for shelter, and warned there was another big storm coming.

At Christmas Mass, I couldn't concentrate. Images of shepherds, ranchers, sheep, dogs, mangers, cradles, and cow carcasses traversed my mind. Was it possible that Kenai had survived all this time, alone? Did I dare I believe he was alive?

I asked myself, as I do every Christmas, "How is the Christ-child birthed within me this year?" Might the birthing be hope in a dog that was lost and found? That what seemed to be dead could live? Dare I believe and hope for a miracle?

Brenda promised to keep feeding him until we returned on December 31st and could meet her at the ranch. She was certain the skittish dog was Kenai. Though he wouldn't let her within twenty-five yards of him, the kibble she left on the snowy ground was wolfed down each morning.

January 1st dawned clear and sunny and we drove to Wyoming. Entering the ranch, we stopped to scan the landscape with binoculars. On a distant ridge we saw him. There was no doubt now. My stomach started to churn. Within a few minutes, we met Brenda. I could barely breathe. There was only room for one of us in her tractor cab. Jim stared at me and whispered, "Go."

Maneuvering to the ridge top seemed longer than ten minutes. Cows followed as we lurched through icy snow drifts. The sun radiated brilliance against snow and rock. We stopped where Brenda had left food for Kenai. Heart pounding, I stepped from the cab.

Brenda backed the tractor away. I walked forward. Suddenly I saw a flash of brown on the other ridge. Clapping my hands, I called, "Kenai, Kenai, Kenaiii," over and over and over. Could he hear me, would he remember?

Kenai stopped and sniffed the air. Instantly wiggling with recognition from nose to tail, he raced through snowdrifts toward me. Whimpers and cries erupted from both of us. I fell to my knees in the snow, arms wide open, calling him. I could see his puppy collar! A solid, furry hay-smelling body launched into my embrace. He was undersized, but unharmed. We jumped up, tumbled around each other, playing, touching, petting, tears pouring forth. I can't believe he remembers! He's safe!

When Jim was within one hundred yards of us, I knelt, presenting to him Kenai. Kenai looked to me, then rushed to Jim as I watched, sobbing with joy.

Oh yes, I hope. I believe.

~Pegge Bernecker

Living Catholic faith

Challenges

We must take our troubles to the Lord,
but more than that, we must leave them there.

~Hannah Whittall Smith

45

Playing Catch

Grief knits two hearts in closer bonds than happiness ever can;
common sufferings are far stronger links than common joys.
~Alphonse de Lamartine

On a stormy August night, my father and I went out to walk the dog. I was six at the time and did everything with my dad, my best friend. As we walked, we talked about baseball and I soaked in every word my father had to say. We got all wet in the rain and he joked that Mom would be worried about us. Being with my dad was always fun, no matter what we were doing.

Shortly after we returned home, Dad and I lay down in bed and tuned into the ballgame on his portable TV. He said he wasn't feeling well and before I knew what was happening he had a massive heart attack. Time seemed to stand still as he died right there in front of me, an image that forty-one years later is still as vivid as if it happened yesterday.

Soon after the police and ambulance arrived, our parish priest came to the house to give my father the Last Rites. He stayed with my family as the undertaker came and took my father away. There were many people in the house. The scene was chaotic. I was confused and scared.

The priest, Father Michael Judge, came and sat by me. I was crying and overwhelmed with grief. He told me that it was okay to be sad but offered that he was sure that my father was in heaven with God. I sobbed, "I don't want him to be in heaven, I want him to be with me!" He understood and just kept holding me as I wept. I tried to put my feelings of despair into words, but being so young it was hard. "Now I have no one to play catch with in the yard all the time!" He just listened and assured me everything would be okay.

Those were the last things I can remember until after my father was buried and all the family and friends left. It was then that I realized that my dad was never coming home again. I was so lonely. My mom seemed depressed and really could not do much to comfort me, although I am sure she wanted to. My sister was handling her grief the best she could. It was just hard for me to make sense of what was happening.

One day, the doorbell rang and I heard my mom talking to a familiar voice. Father Michael had stopped by to see how we were doing. My mom called to me and when I came down, he stood in the living room with his baseball glove. "Want to play catch?"

At first I resisted his efforts to fill the void in my life, but he persisted and returned every chance he could to play catch and spend time. Soon we became friends and he helped me sort my feelings and get my life going in a positive direction. He taught me how to accept what had happened and to find hope in God that someday my dad and I would be reunited. He checked in on me all the time.

I grew older and Father Michael got transferred to another parish, and although we kept in touch, I saw him less and less. Throughout the years he kept in touch with my mother inquiring about how my sister and I were doing. He was pleased to hear that I had a family of my own and three kids that I did everything with.

On September 11th I sat in front of my TV watching the horrors unfold at the World Trade Center. I couldn't believe what was happening. Then the news broke, "Father Michael Judge, the New York City Fire Department Chaplain, has been killed at the site while trying to bring comfort to victims, firefighters and police."

As Father Michael's picture flashed on the screen, the news reporter described, "This beloved priest was carried by the firefighters he served to a local church." I was stunned at the news and was instantly overcome with emotion.

In the weeks that followed, I attended a memorial service for him at a parish near where I grew up. One by one, people came forward with story after story of how Father Michael brought comfort to them in times of need. I could not believe how one man could have had the time to serve so many with so much love and caring. After the ceremony I talked to an elderly woman who told a story quite similar to mine. I asked her why she thought he had taken such an interest in people like us who were dealing with the loss of a parent. She told me that when he was young, his father passed away unexpectedly and that he made helping those in this situation a priority in his life. It all started to make sense to me.

When I returned home, I was sitting around feeling blue. My oldest son was seven at the time and asked me why I was so sad. I told him that Father Michael was a very old friend who died during the attack two weeks before, how he had helped me and so many others like me, and how he always came to play catch with me to help make me feel better. I explained, "Father Michael is in heaven now, but I'm sad to lose a friend."

My little boy thought about this for a moment and then reasoned with the simple and beautiful logic that only a child could have. "Don't worry Dad. I think he is probably happy to be there because don't all priests want to be with God?"

Then he grabbed his glove and said, "Want to play catch?"

~Tom Calabrese

St. Elmer

Nature is but a name for an effect whose cause is God.
~William Cowper

When I was a little girl, my dad told me stories about Elmer, a misbehaving grasshopper. Dad could spin a yarn a mile long and keep me spellbound with Elmer's antics. I didn't realize it at the time but Dad was telling parables, a story with a moral, and his stories always had a consequence for Elmer's misbehavior. Fifty years later, I can still hear the floorboards creek as I recall how Elmer tried to sneak past his mom and get away with some infraction. I'd hold my breath waiting to see if Elmer got caught, and sometimes just when I thought he'd pulled one over on his parents, they'd wake him up and make him take his "medicine." His punishment was doled out with a heaping helping of love and consequences for his actions.

Whenever we visited our cousins who lived in the country, Dad and I would chase grasshoppers through open fields in search of Elmer. He told me that if I ever did catch Elmer, I'd recognize him by his antics; he would spit tobacco juice into my hand. I must have caught a million grasshoppers during my childhood. They all stained the palms of my hands brown, but none completely fit the description of Elmer. They were too small, too long, too brown, or the wrong shade of green. I was always in search of the real Elmer.

As I grew up, Elmer the grasshopper faded into a happy childhood memory. I thought I had put him to rest when my dad died, but five years later, I was reminded of Elmer once again. I had been a preschool teacher in an inner-city school district for seventeen years. In the beginning, my classes always filled rapidly and sometimes even had a waiting list. As the years went by, though, the neighborhood changed; gang members took over. When a drug bust occurred across the street from school as I was taking children on a field trip, I decided it was time to leave. Enrollment had dwindled so low that my teacher's aide and I had to advertise for students. We'd ride around the neighborhood and post fliers on street lampposts. My coworker's mother-in-law taught in a Catholic elementary school for decades, and I would often say to my colleague, "Why don't you approach her principal and we'll offer to set up a preschool in the parish?"

Each year the answer was the same. The parochial school was too small and there was no space available. Summer was drawing to a close and a new school year was about to begin, but enrollment had declined so much that it appeared we would not have an afternoon class. I drove all over the neighborhood with neon-pink advertisements and a roll of adhesive tape. I posted notices on telephone poles, at park playgrounds and in store windows. I was despondent and worried that perhaps posting the papers constituted some municipal misdemeanor, defacing property or something. And here my name and phone number were posted all over town. I drove home in tears, and prayed aloud, "Lord, show me the way. You know my love of teaching and You know that I have a lot to offer children and their families. Guide me. Give me a sign, and not a neon pink one to post!"

I pulled into my driveway convinced that I didn't even know how to pray. I wiped my tears with the back of my hand, and when I got out of the car, I couldn't believe my eyes. As I inserted the key into my door, I saw the biggest, fattest greenest, granddaddy of a grasshopper perched to the left of the doorknob. It did not move. I did not move. I smiled and I said, "Well hello Elmer. Hello Dad."

A sense of peace and calm washed over me. I knew somehow that my prayers would be answered and there was a plan for me. I was home a half hour when the phone rang. A lady introduced herself and told me that she was a member of the parish where my coworker's mother taught. She explained that she had a preschool child with severe food allergies and was unable to locate a school that would eliminate certain foods, thus providing a safe environment for him. She was at her wit's end and decided to start her own preschool, but she was in need of a good teacher. She said she had sent questionnaires to her fellow parishioners and inquired about the viability and need for a neighborhood parish preschool. She told me that my name was mentioned on half of the returned questionnaires. I was a veteran teacher with twenty-five years experience and well known in the community. She asked if I'd be interested in an interview. I could hardly answer, I was ecstatic and shocked and relieved.

"Of course. I'll bring my resume."

After I hung up, I slowly opened the door. There sat the grasshopper, still roosting. I swear he winked at me before he flew away. "Goodbye St. Elmer!" I laughed. "Thank you, Heavenly Father."

The Catholic school still had no room for a preschool, but their enrollment was so low the school was in danger of closing. The founder located an empty storefront a block away which was owned by the local Protestant church. Together the two denominations collaborated to refurbish the old building. Parishioners and congregants volunteered time, money and effort. Everyone from high school students to the elderly assisted in some capacity. The Catholic Church sanctioned the preschool and the founder adopted the church's name. St. Stephen Protomartyr Early Childhood Development Center opened its doors five years ago—the only food allergy-friendly preschool in the nation. Our tiny little preschool was one of the contributing factors in keeping the elementary school open and definitely a deciding factor for many parents of children who have life-threatening food allergies.

The Catholic faith teaches us to put our trust in God and allow Him to work out our problems. I teach my little students prayers. One of our favorite ways to honor the Lord is to take a nature walk. When we spy a butterfly or grasshopper, we stop in our tracks and say aloud, "Thank you God for our eyes so that we can see your beautiful creature." I silently say, "Hello St. Elmer. Hi Dad," and I thank our Heavenly Father for His goodness.

~Linda O'Connell

Mother's Way

An ounce of mother is worth a pound of clergy.
~Spanish Proverb

As we drove to her first appointment, Mom, always a talker, chattered incessantly about whatever came to mind. She spoke of neighbors old and new; some were dead, others still alive. She seemed resigned to the fact that she wouldn't have a garden that summer. She asked if we could stop at Extra Foods for some of the weekly specials on our way home. Her chatter seemed so irrelevant and hollow. The only thought that kept running through my mind was, "My mother might die."

Fat raindrops fell as we pulled into the parking lot of the Dauphin Regional Hospital. Mom patiently waited in the front seat while I hunched over the trunk, fighting with a wheelchair that seemed to have a life of its own. Once she was in it, the wind chased us to the front doors... and into the next chapter of our lives.

Moments later, a surgeon asked Mom numerous questions. My pen wrote serious words such as, "inoperable lung cancer, aggressive chemotherapy." Each letter became a blend of blue ink and warm tears.

"Oh dear, that's not what I wanted to hear," Mom said, her frail hands clasped on her lap.

What seemed like an eternity later, we headed back to the comforts of her home. Mom continued out loud with her thoughts as I drove along the drenched streets.

"The weather sure has been miserable the last couple of weeks," Mom continued. "I certainly hope it clears up soon for the farmers."

With numb fingers, I unlocked the apartment door and rolled the wheelchair inside. Mom asked me, "What do you want for lunch? Soup, salad or kasha?"

It was then that my built-up fear hit. My gasp of grief escaped as I searched for comforting arms. I, at forty-seven years of age, felt like a frightened child walking the last twenty steps by myself on the first day of school. I was alone and I couldn't turn back.

My mom found the strength to hold on tight to a quivering woman who was grasping her as if for the last time. "My little girl, you have to be strong for me and for everyone else in the family." Her arms brushed my back and controlled my sobs but did not ease the heaviness in my heart. As my mom's body rocked against mine, she whispered, "Did you think I was going to live forever?"

"No," I thought, "I only hoped you would."

Long months passed and with each visit, a different person greeted me. She wasn't the same mom I grew up with but if I looked deep into her sunken face while she was telling me a story, I could still see her and reflect, "Oh there you are."

I would check on her in bed and hear her praying, in Polish. Then she would lie back and sleep until early morning while I knelt in the room next to hers, praying in English.

Six months after her first chemotherapy treatment, Mom was placed in the Palliative Care Unit. Her days were a jumble of heavy sedation, moments of pain, and periods of alertness.

On her last day, my mom was in a coma. I laid my hand on the crisp sheet beside her and placed her hand on top of mine. It was my self-satisfying way of her letting me know that everything was going to be all right.

It was her final breath that drew me to her chest. My knees buckled beneath me, as I clutched for one last attempt at being safe in my mother's arms.

Two days after the funeral I woke up from a sound sleep and

felt content for the first time in weeks. It was then I remembered the dream I'd had the night before.

A car was stuck in a snow bank and the tires were being rocked back and forth in an attempt to escape the slush. Mom was sitting in the passenger seat, writing something on a piece of paper. I couldn't see the driver. As the vehicle emerged from the snow, Mom handed me the note through the open window and said, "I guess we'd better be going."

I stared at the unfinished sentence on the paper: "I just wanted to thank you...."

I looked up with questioning eyes and was faced with my mom excitedly blowing me a loving kiss goodbye. It was then that I noticed the driver... my dad... who had passed away twenty years before, after forty-three years of marriage.

I had to smile as I considered all of the biblical versions portraying death mixed with the stairway to the pearly gates, glistening stars, and kind angels. None of that happened. My dad simply picked Mom up in their green 1974 Oldsmobile and drove her to heaven himself.

I can only imagine that Mom talked nonstop the entire way, telling him stories he already knew.

And if I know Dad, with his light foot on the gas pedal, knuckles wrapped firmly around the steering wheel and head peering over the dashboard, they arrived at their destination safely together.

~Judy Stoddart

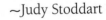

"Catholic families believe in holy acrimony."

48

Sacred Silence

Silence, when nothing need be said, is the eloquence of discretion.
~Christian Nestall Bovee

My husband and I went on a short vacation in Taos, New Mexico, to watch the hot air balloon rally, and then we drove fifty minutes to Chimayo to visit the old mission church, El Santuario de Chimayo. Many people have claimed miraculous healing over the years, supposedly from the dirt found in a grotto. Some scoop it up to take with them. Some eat it. Outside the grotto is a room filled with crutches, braces, pictures of people, and rosaries from those who claim healing from the dirt.

On this particular day we arrived at the church mid-morning and entered the mission church. I wanted to pray and gaze at the paintings that detail the life of Jesus in vivid colors. I had barely begun my meditation when I heard a muffled sobbing. I did my best to stay with my meditation prayer and quiet myself to "be still and know God." The sobbing got louder and then softer, but it was constant. I looked to see who was crying so hard and saw a woman, alone, about my age. She did not seem to be in physical danger or pain. I decided to wait until the woman left the church, then I would be able to pray better. The woman eventually left and I settled in to meditate in sacred silence.

When I moved to the grotto, the sobbing woman was just coming out. The entrance was small and only one person at a time could use it. I waited for her to exit and we met, face to face, eye to eye. I entered the grotto to continue my pilgrimage. As I looked at the icons, statues, and prayers of thanksgiving that lined the walls, I could hear the woman still crying in the outer room. I was not the only person who seemed uncomfortable with it. Several people whispered, "I wonder what is wrong with her?"

She was not in the outer room when I exited the grotto. I was amazed again at the many visible signs of healing on display. There was a lot of faith wrapped up in each one of the crutches, braces, or pictures. Those who put their story of healing on display with much gratitude made the outer room a sanctuary of deep faith—a faith that transcends what mankind says can't be done, and trusts in a God that can do it.

Next, I went to the outdoor chapel, behind the mission church and down a slight hill. As I slowly made my way down, I knew that I hadn't quite been still enough to let God know why I needed to be there, what I thought needed to be healed in me. There, near the altar, on one of the rows of benches, sat the sobbing woman, the only person at the outdoor chapel. She was still weeping from the bottom of her heart and soul. She'd been crying for at least an hour.

I sat across the aisle from her looking at the simple altar and once again seeking to open my heart and let out my own needs and the needs of people I was praying for. But I could not focus on my prayer. I had an active meditative prayer practice and thought I should have been able to pray anywhere, no matter what other activity might be going on in the area. At this point, God or Jesus or Mary stepped in to my prayer saying, "How long are you going to wait before you comfort the sobbing woman? You have followed her all morning without acknowledging her or her sorrow. Are you my faithful servant? Do as I have done."

Immediately, all sorts of reasons went through my mind about why I couldn't comfort her. I didn't know her. Maybe she wanted to be left alone. What would other people think if they saw me with her? And then I knew the healing I sought would come in the way Jesus taught us... by loving my neighbor, or a sobbing woman, as I loved myself.

I rose from the bench and walked across the aisle and sat next to the woman. Taking a big breath, I touched her shoulder lightly. "I don't know why you are in so much sorrow and pain, and I want you to know that I care and I will be praying for you."

The woman turned and reached her arms around me and held on tight. I hugged her back and she continued to cry on my shoulder. She tried to speak a few times and couldn't. I simply held her, patted her, and gently massaged her back.

I don't know how long we sat that way. Finally, she let go. She thanked me many times and when we looked in each others' eyes I knew I saw God in hers.

I thought about the sacred silence for which I had been searching and realized sacred silence sometimes comes with noise, when you, "Do as I have done."

~Kerrie Weitzel

49

My Saturday Starfish

Be mindful of prisoners, as if sharing their imprisonment,
and of the ill-treated as of yourselves, for you also are in the body.
~Hebrews 13:3

After living and working in the entertainment industry in Los Angeles for nearly a decade, surrounded by a sea of superficiality, I was starting to lose perspective. I didn't care who was on the cover of "x" magazine or who wore what designer's dress to the latest awards show. I was the girl who returned a flashy $400 purse my boss gave me and went and bought a $10 one-of-a-kind bag at the flea market instead. I was always more of a "one-of-a-kind" girl. Being an un-superficial girl living in a superficial town, I decided I needed to do something more fulfilling... but what? A few days later, my Catholic church announced that a local juvenile prison needed volunteers. Convinced it was a sign from God, I signed up.

I started going to the prison camp every Saturday morning. We'd first have Mass with the boys, given by one of the priests from my church, followed by an hour of socializing. The boys were fourteen to seventeen years old; most grew up without their fathers, and almost all were gang members (identified by their many tattoos that they liked to show off to me). I believed they could turn their lives around. All they needed was a little faith. A little encouragement.

The people who ran the program told us to talk to the same boys every week, to establish a rapport with them, something they weren't used to from their parents. I eventually learned that most of the boys were not religious; some did not even believe in God, but they attended the Mass and social hour afterward since they were starved for outside human contact.

When I first entered the prison camp, I stood in awe of the boys. They were all so cute and young and innocent-looking; any one of them could have been my younger brother. These boys couldn't have possibly robbed or killed anybody... right? Luckily, I did not know which boy had committed which crime, or else I might have run back to my car. One of the volunteer rules was to never ask what crime they had committed; if they wanted to tell you, they would (and most did, as I'd soon find out).

Fernando immediately befriended me. Fernie, as he preferred to be called, was sixteen and had joined the same gang that his two brothers had belonged to. One was now in jail for life, and the other had left town to escape the gang. Fernie had been arrested for having a firearm. He had huge dimples; even when he wasn't smiling, it looked like he was. And I was supposed to believe that this kid might have killed someone?

At first, the boys did not open up too much. The most they divulged would be about their limited three-minute showers, the food they were sick of eating, and not being allowed to have coffee. But soon we talked about everything... their families, their girlfriends, their babies' mothers, the kinds of crimes they'd committed. But, often, they'd want to know more about me. Did I ever get into trouble? Did I believe in God? Did I have a boyfriend? Did I have a baby?

I asked Fernie what he wanted to do once he got out of the camp. "Eat my mom's spaghetti," he said. "And tell my girlfriend I love her. Being in here really makes you realize you miss people, you appreciate them." So poignant for a sixteen-year-old, I thought. I then asked if he was going to go back to gang life. He said he didn't want to, but it was tough. "You can't just get out... they'll kill you." He explained that you have to basically flee town to get out. One of his brothers did and now had a family and kids in Utah. The other was in prison for life for manslaughter. Fernie was at an impasse.

"It's like my other family," he said. "A lot of good comes from being in the gang."

"What kind of good?" I asked.

"We're there for each other. We party and have fun; it's not all about violence. It's about protecting the neighborhood from bad guys and robbers. Plus, we help the homeless."

"How?"

"We drink a lot of beer and give the empty bottles to the homeless who cash them in, then come buy drugs from me and my homies."

At the end of the hour, we always held hands and prayed. Week after week, Fernie didn't want to pray for anything. One Saturday, I told him there must be someone to pray for, like families or friends. He insisted there wasn't. So I prayed the same prayer I did every week: for the boys, that they'd have the strength to stay off the streets and out of these camps, once they got out. I prayed they'd beat the statistics. "I know you can turn your lives around," I said.

I thought Fernie believed me until a couple Saturdays later. He would be out in a week or two and told me, "I don't want to go back to gang life, but I will."

And here I thought I'd been making progress with him. Frustrated, I said, "There are other, non-gang ways of life for you. God can help you if only you have some faith." Desperate, I added, "Besides, God says to 'Love your enemy.'"

"Why?" he asked. "Then they'll hurt or kill me instead of me doing it to them."

I was speechless. I looked up to the sky and hoped Fernie wouldn't see me cry.

I felt helpless, wondering if anything I told him and the boys even sunk in. I felt disheartened, questioning if I was making the least bit of difference in these boys' lives. I decided my days of volunteering there were over—this was too hard. After all, what was the point?

The next day at church, the priest told a beautiful story about a boy at the ocean at low tide, when all the starfish are stranded in the sand, about to die. The boy tossed as many as he could back into the water. A man came up and asked him what the point was, why it mattered, when there are millions of starfish along the miles of the ocean and he couldn't possibly save them all. The boy picked up another starfish and tossed it back into the water and said, "It matters to that one."

As we exited Mass, little starfish were given to everyone. I put it in my wallet, to remind myself that I was helping those boys, after all. Even if just a little kernel of what I said seeped into their brains, I was grateful. How could I not go back and keep trying?

Just like my $10 flea market purse, I soon realized these boys were all one-of-a-kind. They were each a starfish, waiting to be tossed back into the water. And I needed to be there to help as many as I could... or at least one... back in.

Fernie phoned me months later to say he moved to Utah to live with his "good" brother, to turn his life around. He enrolled in high school and found a job as a dishwasher. He said he was happy even to just be washing dishes. Fernie thanked me for having faith and believing in him. When I hung up the phone, I had tears in my eyes again. Just like the last time, he couldn't see them. I went to sleep, anticipating seeing my other starfish the next day.

~Natalia Lusinski

50

The Grocery Store in the Upper Room

Consider your own calling, my brothers.
Not many of you were wise by human standards,
not many were powerful, not many were of noble birth.
~1 Corinthians 1:26

The gray foggy mist in the air and the cold teamed together to chill to the bone the people shopping, out and about, on Tuesday before Thanksgiving. Jack Frost had kissed all the leaves and the wind swirled and tossed them into the air forming a kaleidoscope of color.

I viewed this beautiful scene from my office window on the stately nineteenth century campus of St. Peter Home for Children. A Dominican priest established it in 1858 and many children were raised there. Now we had sixty-eight girls, wards of the city, county, and state courts. They all knew the horrors of the world—to be hungry, homeless, abandoned, abused, persecuted, neglected. What they really wanted now was someone to care about them, love them properly, and give them a chance at life again and a new start with God.

As Spiritual Director to the girls, I learned they were all seeking God in an enormous, desperate way. Through the grace of God, the girls trusted me and looked forward to talking to me. To many of them, I was the mother figure they never had.

As the colorful leaves swirled, the ringing of the phone startled me back to my responsibilities. The repairman was telling me the cost of fixing my car would amount to the entire two week's salary I'd just received. My husband Harry had a stroke, grand mal seizures, cancer, Alzheimer's, and would never work again. We had five children, plus a son who died at seven months. I trusted in God, Our Mother, and Divine Providence... but had no money left for food.

Hunger is difficult to endure, and it was especially hard seeing my husband hungry when he now had the mind of a child. And I was hungry too, physically and spiritually. Harry's hunger, my inability to provide food, and my desire for God became greater in my desperation.

The mechanic delivered my car to me at work. I paid the bill and went to Mass at 5:00 P.M. before going home. I arrived early and I knelt in the church and poured my heart out to God, my head in my hands. I felt like a complete failure because there would be no money for food and Thanksgiving was only two days away. I knelt in silence before the tabernacle, tears running down my face, dripping to the floor. This was the only place I could cry. Everywhere else I had to be strong and positive. Here I could be the vulnerable person I really was. The silence in the church was deafening.

Then I realized someone was standing beside me. I looked up. Father Maury, the Franciscan pastor said, "Terry, I'm sorry for disturbing you in your prayer but today we received some food for the soup kitchen and there are quite a few items we cannot use in making soup for the homeless. I hope I don't offend you, but I think you may be in need of food."

I was so startled, for a moment I couldn't say anything. Father Maury knew nothing about the recent events in my life. The hardest words I'd ever had to say were, "Yes, Father, I do." I felt touched by God. His grace brought the words to my mouth.

As I stood up, Father Maury said, "Please come with me into the kitchen." Again, I was humbled to my soul. Father didn't ask any further questions but just said, "Help me sort these cans of food. You know what we use to make the soup and the rest of the cans we will put in the little room upstairs along with some grocery sacks. Every day when you come to Mass, you can just go upstairs to the room, take what you need, put it in a sack and your family will think you went to the grocery store."

Father and I sorted the cans, side by side; for a minute I didn't think I could do this. Each can felt ten times its weight. It was like a knife turning in my heart and stomach. I knew then what it was to depend on God for my daily bread, and Harry's. I thought I was self-sufficient. I knew the social service system and had helped many homeless and destitute people when I worked for Catholic Charities. I knew how to get help, but had been too proud to ask.

Father Maury and I carried many boxes of canned goods up the winding narrow stairs, which led up to an old library filled with spiritual books. This grocery store in the upper room now contained nourishment for our souls and bodies.

When Father and I carried the last of the boxes upstairs and descended the narrow winding staircase for the last time, he said, "Follow me to the kitchen." He opened the refrigerator. "Someone brought a turkey to us, for a person in need, and I want to give it to you and Harry and your family for Thanksgiving." In true humility, I could only say, "Thank you Father Maury for being an instrument of God's kindness." He hugged me and patted my back.

Every day at Mass, the Eucharist fed my soul, then St. Mary's Upper Room Grocery Store fed our bodies. But those cans of food also became food for my soul, because I was shown my pride and how I must use the grace God sends. Nothingness is a great class-room of spirituality.

My physical and spiritual being was filled to overflowing with God's mercy, love, and kindness. The rich pride-filled person I had been was "sent away empty." But God filled my emptiness and made me hunger to grow more and more in His love and to always do His Holy will.

After twelve years of suffering, Harry went to his eternal reward. Then I became a Consecrated Widow. I've taken a vow to devote myself to prayer and service of the Church. When my five children, thirteen grandchildren, and two great-granddaughters see me in my full habit they call out, "Sister Mammaw!" as do the children at the Catholic school of 1,600 students at St. Francis of Assisi Church where I am Director of Religious Studies.

From my abyss, God lifted me up in total loving union with Him.

~Sister Mammaw C.W.

51

Becoming Catholic

Thus, faith comes from what is heard,
and what is heard comes through the word of Christ.
~Romans 10:17

have avoided writing about this time of my life, because it was so painful. At the time, the aching hollow feelings often threatened to surface, screaming so loudly I wondered if other people could also hear them. Yet to others, I was sometimes envied as a popular university student. But instead of being happy, I was miserable. In fact, I was so depressed, death seemed attractive. No matter how much I accomplished, nothing seemed to fill my empty void or erase my self-hate. Friends, sorority sisters, family, even the school psychologist all tried their best, but to no avail

Finally, I decided only God could help. I longed to be filled with a strong healing faith. I had visited churches of various religions with girlfriends and relatives. Praying for an answer, I suddenly remembered my aunt, whom I had attended Mass with years ago. She was the first Catholic to join our extended family, and I marveled at her faith. Born with a crippled hip, she never complained. After she married my uncle, she suffered numerous miscarriages before my cousin was born. Yet her faith never wavered. Remembering her now, I recalled how I used to look forward to their Wisconsin dairy farm, so I could to go to Mass with her. As we knelt in prayer, I felt surrounded by a peace I hadn't known.

I began to study my Catholic friends, including my roommate, and realized how much I admired them. They had something I did not. Their faith had made better people of them. I noticed how confident they were, how caring for others. I especially appreciated their attentive support as I struggled.

When I started dating my future husband, Bob, we had long discussions about religion and faith. One sunny fall afternoon as we sat alone in my sorority's living room, Bob said, "I hope you don't mind? Last night, I kept thinking about you so I wrote this little poem." He smiled his warm smile. "Remember, I'm studying engineering, not English like you."

Looking at the small hand-written note, I read the refrain, "Carol is like a leaf floating down a stream..."

I sat very still, stunned.

"You're not mad or anything?"

"Oh Bob, you understand. And now I understand. I've been trying to please everyone, parents, teachers, and friends. I feel overwhelmed, guilty and frustrated. It's too much. I don't know which way to go!"

"I do understand," Bob said as he wrapped his arms around me.

During the next few weeks, I prayed and thought frequently about our talk. I listened and what I heard was, "The Catholic Church will help you find what is important, what God wants." For the first time, I felt embraced by safe boundaries and forgiveness. The Catholic Church was a theology on which I could depend to pardon my guilt. Harming oneself was a sin. I could close the door on those thoughts. I began to feel more alive, almost as if numb from frostbite and now tingling with a new faith. I could feel a presence, a love touching me, not for what I did, but who I was. I began taking lessons, and a year later, in front of family and friends, I was baptized Catholic. For the first time, I felt safe and secure, trusting in my new faith.

It has been more than forty years since I joined the Catholic Church. With counseling, prayer, study, and a loving family, I have found a miraculous life. It hasn't always been easy being Catholic. And it hasn't always been easy being me; I am not perfect. I have made mistakes and had my doubts, but the Catholic Church has always been there to welcome me home.

Now, as I celebrate Mass with Bob, my patient husband of forty-five years, I pray for our three beautiful daughters, their husbands and our three grandsons. During the summer months, Bob and I help at our small mountain Catholic mission church, Our Lady of the Lakes. We usher, lector, distribute Communion, publicize services, and even clean the church sometimes, so others may be filled with the healing faith, hope, and sense of direction that I found as a Catholic.

~Carol Strazer

That's Good Stuff

Instruct a wise man and he becomes still wiser;
teach a just man and he advances in learning.
~Proverbs 9:9

My wife attended church regularly, but I accompanied her only occasionally. After a few years of on-again, off-again, I started attending every week. One day I announced I would like to join the church. This meant a yearlong process of attending meetings once a week. I eagerly complied, as I found the classes very interesting.

There were several teachers, called team members, who conducted classes. One class had a very special guest named Dick Wellington. He was wheelchair-bound, had shoulder-length white hair and always began his presentations with, "Hello Saints." He was in his sixties, very thin and frail-looking. He had an oxygen tank alongside his chair with a nosepiece to help him breathe. But emphysema did nothing to sway his spirit. He told us how he and his wife Kay had raised forty-one foster children and that's why he looked the way he did. He said, "Would you believe I'm actually thirty-five-years old?" Everyone roared with laughter, and he had us right where he wanted us. Then he began to teach and every time he finished making a religious point he would add, "That's good stuff."

I continued to attend classes for the remainder of the year and was inducted formally into the church. I was so fired up, I decided to become a team member myself. I joined the group of teachers and started preparing for my own presentations. Our deacon brought Dick, and it was a pleasure to be around him. He was so upbeat all the time, even though he was in great physical distress.

One night the deacon said he couldn't pick Dick up to bring him to the meetings anymore and asked for a volunteer to help. Remembering what the Lord said about helping others, how could I not volunteer? So I drove to Dick's house, helped him get into the car with his oxygen tank, and placed the wheelchair in my trunk. Dick never missed coming to the meetings, even on cold Michigan winter nights. These nights were especially bad for him, because it aggravated his condition and made his breathing very difficult.

We talked about everything on the way to and from the meetings, but mostly we talked about religion. His knowledge was amazing. He had studied every religion before joining our church and was quite an authority on all of them.

"Now that's good stuff," he'd add with a smile. His sense of humor and conversation made the time spent in the car fly by.

I personally did not have a problem with Dick's long white hair since I was a child of the '60s. But my mother thought he was trying to look like a rebel or something and she didn't care for it. One day Dick came to church and his hair was cut short. I asked him what happened. He said he'd been growing it for the Locks of Love organization to be made into a wig for children without hair. "I can't do very much, but I can grow hair." My poor mother was very embarrassed, but I had yet another good laugh, thanks to Dick.

As time passed, I learned that Dick had been in the Air Force and was stationed in Japan. While he was there, he saw a need to help the Korean War orphans. So he grabbed the bull by the horns and with the help of a few other servicemen, set up an orphanage to help those poor children. Later, as a civilian, he worked for the church and became the religious education director.

His emphysema eventually caught up with him and he was nearing his final reward. I played the piano and I enjoyed the music in the church so much that I asked the choir director to order piano songbooks for me. The day after they arrived, I got a call to come to

Dick's home because he was going to pass soon. When I got there, Dick was still able to see people around him, but he was unable to talk. He noticed me right away when I went into the bedroom and he tried to lift his head. Kay was right there to comfort him, and I asked her if she thought Dick would like to hear me play their piano. Kay said Dick would like that very much. So I went into the living room and began playing from my books, just flipping through the pages, whatever caught my eye. I played "How Great Thou Art" and Kay sang to Dick while I played. The nurse said it was as though the Holy Spirit was guiding my hands, as if heaven was saying, "Dick you did such a good job, we are going to give you a musical send-off."

When we gathered at the cemetery to say our goodbye, there was a lone bagpipe player in full dress standing off from the crowd playing "Amazing Grace." My heart was broken.

While I lay in bed that night trying to sleep, all I could think about was losing my friend. I cried and then I started to get angry with God. I asked him why He did this to me. I did what He wanted; I did my best to help a fellow human being in need and this was my reward?

Then in the midst of my anger, a beautiful voice in my head said, "Be comforted in knowing that Dick is with us." I immediately stopped crying and became calm, with a great feeling of relief enfolding me.

And when heaven tells this story, I know Dick will say, "That's good stuff!"

~Donald Cracium

If I Could Just Phone Home

*There is an appointed time for everything
and a time for every affair under Heaven.*
~Ecclesiastes 3:1

While saying my prayers late one night, I was praying for comfort for the families of two relatively young men who had recently died. As I pondered their passing, I fervently wished that I could somehow comfort their families by giving them a glimpse of God's promise of "Eye has not seen, ear has not heard, what God has prepared for those who love Him" (1 Cor. 2:8).

Suddenly, I remembered the time when my oldest son, Jerome, went to Mexico for two weeks with one of our priests and several boys from our local Catholic high school. He was fifteen at the time, and I had never "let him out of my pocket," so to speak. I'd never been to another country, so my view of Mexico was skewed by television. I pictured banditos and drug busts and my son being unjustly arrested by the Mexican police. I know it sounds silly. But it was hard to let go.

It was a tearful day when he left. I repeatedly told God that I was sorry for crying over a two-week trip to Mexico, but I knew there was more to my tears than just worry. It was the whole "he's growing up" thing.

The first night after he left, the priest had all the boys phone home. I'll never forget that call. Jerome was so excited, he couldn't talk fast enough:

"Mom, you should see the ocean! It is so beautiful here! Mom, you should taste the food! We are living with this little Mexican woman who makes us fresh tortillas and real refried beans! Mom, you should see the all the flowers! You would love them! The weather is so perfect here! I am having so much fun!"

He went on and on and on. The joy in his voice alone was enough to put a stopper in my tear ducts. When I replaced the receiver I thought, how can I possibly be sad that he is gone when he is so happy? It was at that very moment that a thought came to me. It's too bad that our loved ones can't "phone home" from heaven. If they could just tell us how happy they are, then our pain would be greatly reduced.

As I lay in bed, I realized that maybe I could write a song about "phoning home." Though it was late, I jumped out of bed and went to the computer. I knew from past experience that when God calls me to write something, it comes out very quickly. It did. I knew it was from God and I cried. I always feel so humbled and in awe that He works through me.

I had just completed the long and costly process of recording my second CD, and needed to get it submitted for printing soon in time for Christmas deadlines. I questioned if I could swing payment for another song. I decided to leave it in God's hands by praying, "Okay, God. If this is really Your will that I add this song to my CD at this late date, then please help me write the music tomorrow, and let it flow quickly."

He did. The music came very easily, and so with joy, I added the song to the CD.

However, I never really got very much feedback from that particular song. It was strange. I couldn't imagine that something that was "so from God" hadn't had a bigger impact than it did.

Recently, a woman whose relatives live in my mother's apartment building lost her seventeen-year-old autistic son. I had met him several times and he was a sweetheart. Always smiling. Always a kind word.

My heart just ached for his family, and though I didn't know the mother well, I kept thinking that I would like to give her a copy of the song, "If I Could Just Phone Home." I kept putting it off, thinking it was too soon. Another time I would think about it and realize I didn't have her address. There were several times the idea popped up and I would say to myself, "I've got to get that song to that boy's mother!"

One morning after Mass, I stopped by the apartment complex to see my mother, and thought of taking the song with me. I dismissed the idea when I realized that there was probably very little chance of seeing the boy's mom that day, since I had only met her there a couple of times.

Sure enough, she walked into the apartment building. I excused myself from the group of residents sitting in the lobby having coffee and ran home to get the CD. I quickly printed off a copy of the words and headed back over to catch her before she left.

I wasn't even sure of her name, so I felt a little awkward. As I handed her the CD and the folded up words, I said, "I am so sorry to hear of your son's passing. What a good young man you raised." Tears filled her eyes as she thanked me and began talking about her pain.

Then she patted her shirt pocket that held her cell phone and sadly said, "My phone used to ring all the time. I used to get calls many times a day from my son. He would call me to tell me little things, like what he was eating, and... now... my phone... it never rings."

I could not believe my ears. I had not told her the name of the song. Through God's grace, this hurting mother was going to get her phone call after all.

~Elizabeth Schmeidler

If I Could Just Phone Home

I see your tears that fall down like rain.
And I know how hard it is to carry on,
But if I could do one thing to help you to get through,
I would ask the Lord for one more chance to talk again with you.

If I could just phone home,
I would tell you that today I soared with eagles!
And the peace that I'm feeling just cannot be explained;
And the love that fills my joyful soul just cannot be contained!

If I could just phone home,
You could hear it in my voice that I'm so happy.
Now I can sit within God's presence; rest in His secure embrace.
I can laugh and talk with Jesus while His light surrounds my face.

If I could just phone home...

Now, I know that it's easy for me to be brave,
Because it's you that's left behind so very broken.
But I promise you one thing, there's so much more than you know.
So try your very best to trust in God and let your grief go.

If I could just phone home,
I would tell you not to worry, please don't cry,
Because God's love can move mountains and take away your pain.
And what looked to you like loss and death has really all been gain.

And though I can't phone home,
When you need me I will meet you in your heart.
Talk to me like you used to and though you might not hear a word
You can find me in the starry night and in the sweet song of a bird.

Until we meet again, know I love you and forever always will.
Death can't separate our love,
Our hearts will always be as one.
Our love's not finished now, but only just begun.
My life has just begun!

Elizabeth J. Schmeidler ©2004

54

The Greater Faith

Now, faith is the substance of things hoped for,
the evidence of things not seen.
~Hebrews 11:1

"I love you, sweetheart." My husband, Bruce, leaned closer to me and reached to hug me. "You're a remarkable woman. Happy anniversary."

"Just be quiet!" I snapped through gritted teeth.

This certainly wasn't the way we had planned to spend our ninth anniversary, in the hospital laboring toward the birth of our fourth child. If I could just hold on for a few more hours, our baby would be born the day after our anniversary and we wouldn't have to share our special day forever.

Then the alarms went off. Nurses and doctors broadcast codes and hurried feverishly about the room. Every heartbeat pumped red onto the stark white around me as our baby slipped from my womb, blue and limp and lifeless.

Suddenly, we went from regretting that we would be sharing our anniversary with our baby's birthday, to fearing that our anniversary would forever mark the day she died.

I was barely aware of the transfusions and emergency measures so many were administering to me. My pain couldn't pierce the growing silence of waiting for my baby's first cry. I could see the backs of the medical team working frantically to revive her, each moment lasting longer than the next. When one of the nurses glanced over her shoulder at us, the probable outcome was written in the sympathy on her face.

"Please God, please," my husband's distressed voice cried out. "You allowed us to give our daughter physical life but only You can breathe life into her. Please, Father, give us this child!"

Our baby's cry was God's answer to his prayer. God delivered her into our arms, her breath warm and sweet against our cheeks.

We celebrated her and proclaimed God's great love to our families and friends and all who came to see our baby. They witnessed the powerful miracle of our peaches-and-cream little girl in her pink ruffles and bows.

On her first Sunday of life, we polished up her brothers and sister and went to Mass. As we settled into the pew, I glanced across the aisle and noticed the woman I had visited with a few times at the doctor's office. We were due on the same day and had a running joke about who would be most overdue.

I caught her attention with a little wave and then pulled back the pink blanket to give her a quick peak of our newborn. She gave a half smile and nodded.

When we stood to sing, I was surprised and pleased to see that she was no longer pregnant. She must have had her baby too, and I looked forward to sharing her good news after Mass.

It was during the intercessory prayers that I found out there would be no good news. I was shocked into disbelief when we were led in prayer for the soul of their baby. Their daughter had been born and died of a heart defect the same day our daughter was saved.

My heart crumpled and I looked over at her. She was leaning into her husband's shoulder; her face was streaked with tears and her husband's was taut with their shared pain.

While we had rejoiced with our baby's first breath, they had waited for their baby's last.

As we embraced the gift of our child, they had trusted God to embrace theirs.

While our baby went home in our arms, their baby went home to the arms of God.

As we went forward for Communion, she and I stepped into the aisle side by side.

We reached for the Body of Christ at the same time; her hands that had stroked her baby lovingly for the last time, and mine that had stroked my baby for the first of many times.

Her reverence, her trust, her willingness to see God through her anguish touched deep inside me.

My heart pondered and then asked, "Father, which one of these mothers stands here before You with the greater faith? Me, the mother whose faith was strengthened because my arms are filled with the life you saved? Or is it this mother whose arms are empty but stands here on the strength of her faith?"

At that moment, our eyes met and our hands reached for each other.

"God bless you," we both whispered, her rejoicing for me, and me sorrowing for her. God's love radiated between us, one to the other.

The years have passed and my baby girl is now a woman with a baby daughter of her own. The mother who lost her baby daughter danced at my daughter's wedding a few years ago.

The experience of God's hand reaching down and saving our child has not dimmed, nor has the memory of that day at the foot of the altar where I witnessed such a pure reliance and belief.

Which mother approached the altar with the greater faith? Only God can see into the heart of the answer.

~Cynthia Hamond

55

One Mother to Another

*The prayer that begins with trustfulness, and passes on to waiting will always
end in thankfulness, triumph, and praise.*
~Alexander Maclaren

My Catholic upbringing and education served me
well. To this day, I can recite parts of the Latin Mass
and many of the prayers from memory. The smell of
incense still brings me back to Benediction in our beautiful church,
with the girls on one side of the aisle and the boys on the other side.
My future husband was among them.

However as fond as the memories of growing up Catholic are to
me, they don't constitute my adult faith. I have been blessed abun-
dantly, and I have been tested to the limit. When my sister was near
death from a car accident, I turned to God. When my husband faced
cancer, I turned to God. I visited Him often to pray or touch base in
whatever Catholic Church I might have been passing. All my life, I
whispered to Him about my fears, worries, hopes and dreams.

Then the big challenge came... the one everyone fears the most...
the stuff of nightmares. My married daughter, mother of an infant
baby girl, contracted meningitis early one December, the day after we
all took her baby to her first Christmas tree lighting. I suffered with
her as I watched, helplessly, as she endured blinding headaches.

The hardest and longest night of my life was keeping vigil at
my daughter's bedside while she struggled to remain with us. I felt
God's presence when I asked for strength to sustain me through the

agonizing hours. I prayed for wisdom to know the right course of action despite the inertia of my daughter's physician. Eight hours later, our girl was moved to the intensive care unit where she lapsed into a coma and her bodily functions began to fail.

On December 23rd, she was visited by the same priest who married her. She was anointed. Together, my son-in-law, husband, some friends and I held hands and prayed. I never thought I'd see the day my child would receive the Sacrament of Healing. Referring to it by its previous name, the Last Rites, sent a chill through my body and made my knees go weak.

I had put up the manger right after Thanksgiving, a bit early for us. However, something prompted me to do it. Now I know it was a nudge from heaven. Each time I went home briefly, I'd stop to gaze at the mother of Jesus in that dimly lit stable. I connected with her in a way I did not think possible. She watched her son suffer and die. I was watching my daughter suffer. I prayed she wouldn't die

Later in the day, after she had been anointed, we saw barely perceptible movement in our daughter's fingers. When asked her if she could hear us, she fluttered her eyelids! Relief among the hospital staff was palpable; our joy was pure and deep. Our daughter was coming back to us!

After several weeks, she returned home to her infant daughter. It was months before she regained her strength, but she was alive and that's what mattered most.

A Christmas miracle took place in that hospital on December 23rd. Everyone said so. They talked about it on the elevators and in the cafeteria. The housekeeping staff spread the good news from room to room and floor to floor.

That year we didn't turn on the Christmas lights until the crisis was over. We had no tree but it was the best Christmas ever. I stood again before the manger and looked into the eyes of Mary. From one mother to another, my prayers were answered. Through the intercession of the Blessed Virgin, I was spared what she had endured.

~Eileen Knockenhauer

56

Christ Bearer

*Amen I say to you, whoever does not accept the kingdom of God like a child
will not enter it.*
~Mark 10:15

My husband and I elected to stay in our home city for Christmas since we were dealing with health problems. Traveling to visit one of our daughters would be too stressful, so we anticipated a quiet holiday season spent with friends.

We lived in the neighborhood and had belonged to our parish only three years. Although we didn't know many fellow parishioners, we found our faith community welcoming. I expected satisfying spiritual experiences while celebrating the coming of the Prince of Peace. I had no idea what a moving event awaited me.

I signed on to serve as Eucharistic minister at the 8:00 P.M. Mass on Christmas Eve and my husband volunteered to usher.

In the sacristy, we prepared for Mass and the coming of the Son of God by reciting the usual prayer together. Then our pastor, Father John, instructed us to prepare for a different kind of processional. He said, "We're going to assemble in the rear of the church. I'll have one of the children bring up Baby Jesus."

We headed to the back of the church where a couple with three children sat in the last pew. All were dark-haired except for the child next to the father. As we stood behind the rear pew, Father John leaned toward the mother and spoke to her. She motioned to her husband. The man exited his seat and came over to the priest. They talked briefly. Then the dad pantomimed to the youngster who had been sitting nearest him to take off the winter jacket and come to both parents.

The child looked thin and so pale; huge brown eyes dominated the face. Sparse, wispy light-colored hairs barely covered the child's scalp. The loose-fitting slacks and long sleeved shirt gave no hint of the child's gender.

Father John bent toward the child and handed over the plaster Baby Jesus. The child tenderly cradled the Baby and stood ready to walk down the aisle. The father stood close as if he meant to accompany us.

Then, Father John turned toward us and said, "Jeremiah just got out of Roswell Park Cancer Institute today."

I turned to the boy. "Jeremiah, you are going to be like an angel delivering the Baby Jesus."

He did not say a thing, but his smile could have served as a beacon. In fact, it did lead us.

We lined up to process to the altar behind Jeremiah and his precious cargo. His father seemed reluctant to watch his son walk away, but finally stepped aside.

While we processed, Jeremiah alternately looked tenderly down at the Baby and then up toward the simple manger scene at the foot of the altar. At the end of the aisle, we ministers stood in our usual location in front of the first pew.

Our young leader and Father John advanced toward the crèche. Jeremiah carefully placed the Baby in the manger. Then he and Father John knelt and adored the Child. Jeremiah's look of gratitude and joy made my eyes tear. The young boy represented all of us at that moment. He had brought Christ to a parish full of people burdened with fears of disease, financial ruin and all kinds of insecurities. He presented God among those of us suffering from despair, illnesses and loneliness. Like all of us baptized believers, Jeremiah brought Christ to others, those he knew and loved and those he had never met.

As he turned to step away from the manger, I noticed his father standing at the end of the aisle ready to guide his son back to their pew. The boy still wore that huge smile. Just looking at him filled me with joy too.

After Mass, I walked to the manger scene. Jeremiah's family approached, knelt and prayed. When they turned to leave, I commended the youngster. "You did a great job bringing Jesus to us."

His mother smiled and said, "You know he just got out of Roswell today."

In her eyes, I could see a kind of sadness. "I recognized the hairdo," I said. "I'm living proof that cancer can be beat."

"Oh, God bless you." She hugged me tightly.

Jeremiah brought Christ to our parish on Christmas Eve.

And when He comes, we feel great joy.

~Sandy McPherson Carrubba

57

A Mother's Guiding Hand

But those who hope in the Lord will renew their strength.
They will soar on wings like eagles; they will run and not grow weary,
they will walk and not be faint.
~Isaiah 40:31

ightning ricocheted in the sky like a Fourth of July fireworks display, while rain beat a steady rhythm on our roof. Although I was about five years old and accustomed to rainstorms, this one was different. Instead of rumbling thunder, the air reverberated with explosive thunderbolts that shook our house.

Frightened, I ran to my mother who was ironing in the kitchen. "Is our house going to fall down?"

Mother set aside her iron, led me into the living room and sat me on her lap. "You mustn't be afraid of rainstorms."

I shivered. "I'm not afraid of rain. I'm scared of the thunder."

"You want to know how to not be afraid?" she asked.

Relaxing in the warmth of her arms, I answered, "How?"

"Prayer," she stated simply. "When his disciples asked Jesus how to pray, he taught them the Lord's Prayer, the one you've been learning. You've learned it, but do you know what it means?"

Although I had memorized it by rote, I didn't understand several words so I shook my head.

Mother said, "Let's say it together and if you don't understand something, speak up."

"Our Father who art in heaven."

After the first sentence I paused and asked, "Does that mean everyone gets two fathers?"

Mother smiled. "Yes, we all have another father who lives in a heavenly kingdom we can't see. We call him God. He sent his son, Jesus, to teach us how important love is."

That seemed like a good idea to me, but the word "hallowed" followed right after that. "What does 'hallowed' mean?"

"'Hallowed' means to love and honor God, our Heavenly Father."

We moved on with the prayer until we got to "trespasses" where I paused again and asked, "What does 'trespass' mean?"

Mother patiently explained.

By the time we finished the prayer, the storm was over and sunshine blanketed the sky. I looked out the living room window to see ribbons of color forming an arc. I pointed at it and gasped at its beauty. Mother hugged me. "God made rainbows to remind us not to be afraid of rain. Anytime you're afraid, think about rainbows and The Lord's Prayer and you won't be afraid anymore."

That happened many years and thousands of Lord's Prayers ago. By saying this short prayer over the years, I've overcome fear and endured many stormy events in my life.

During the Great Depression, when I overheard the doctor tell my parents, "I don't expect her to survive."

"Our Father who art in heaven..."

A tumor...

"Hallowed be thy name..."

Two near-drownings.

"Thy kingdom come, thy will be done..."

An armed robbery assault.

"Forgive us our trespasses..."

Aborted flight after take-off.

"And deliver us from evil."

Mother has been gone many years, but during rain and other storms of life, I remember that rainy afternoon and her secret to overcoming fear.

A generation later, my daughter came to me during a storm. "I'm afraid."

I pulled her gently onto my lap. "You want to know how to not be afraid? Let me tell you."

~Sally Kelly-Engeman

*Living
Catholic
faith*

The Power of Prayer

*Ask and it will be given to you;
seek and you will find;
knock and the door will be opened to you.*

~Matthew 7:7

58

Sacred Heart of Jesus

If you ask anything of Me in My name, I will do it.
~John 14:14

As a child, I was devoted to the Sacred Heart of Jesus. Fascinated by the red heart crowned with thorns and beaming like the sun, I treasured His holy card, prayed His litany, and even attended Mass on the first Fridays of the months.

Between eighth grade and adulthood, I deemed this devotion old-fashioned and ignored it... until 1996, when my twelve-year-old daughter Kate became anorexic. Depression and the loss of forty pounds sent her to the hospital that winter. She gained weight and was released but then dropped another ten pounds after she came home. Her weakening heart, ashen complexion, and relentless fear of eating warranted our scheduling her return to the hospital.

Friends and family stormed the heavens for her, sent Mass cards, and offered compassionate presence. My friend Denise gave me a tape entitled, "Our Lady's Role in Healing," a product of the Sacred Heart Institute, a healing ministry headed by Father Gerald Ruane. Father and his teams traveled to parishes all over the northeastern United States celebrating Mass and laying hands on the sick.

"I thought you could use this," Denise said, handing me the tape. At her suggestion, I called the Institute and put my name on its mailing list. Every few weeks, I received the schedule, but usually the masses were too far away or the date had already passed.

On June 1st, the first day of the month devoted to the Sacred

Heart of Jesus, Kate was deep in despair, sobbing and praying to die. As I wept and massaged her bony shoulders, I prayed silently, "Oh, Jesus, save us. I do not want to lose my daughter."

I cradled Kate in my arms until she slept, then I checked the mail where, among the bills and magazines, lay the latest schedule of Father Ruane's visits to parishes in our area. I snapped the seal of the pamphlet to learn that there would be a healing Mass that week in a nearby parish.

Amazed, I looked skyward and gasped, "Jesus, You really are listening!" Later I told Kate, "We're going to that Mass. It's the night before you return to the hospital."

So on a hot, muggy evening, she and I rode with the air conditioner off and the windows rolled up. Summer was near, but Kate remained cold and bundled up in layers of fleece pants, shirts, and jackets, trying to withstand her own personal winter caused by severe weight loss.

Father Ruane celebrated the Mass and addressed the deep love and healing of Jesus' Sacred Heart in his sermon and prayers. Kate and I listened, prayed fervently, and received the Eucharist. When Mass ended, we joined a line of people in the center aisle, where we awaited the laying-on of hands. At one point, a breeze swept into the church when someone exited through the oak doors. Concerned that Kate would be chilled, I immediately turned to check on her.

"It's really warm in here," she said in an upbeat voice I had not heard in months. Unbelievably, she removed her outer jacket and set it on a pew across the center aisle.

My eyes widened. Her fragile body had shivered constantly and felt no warmth since the previous September. I thought, "Jesus, is this Your healing hand I'm seeing in action?" I breathed in, waiting and watching.

We reached the front of the line where Father Ruane asked how we needed healing. I whispered to him, "My daughter has anorexia."

Without hesitation, he passed me, cloaked her shoulders with his arms, and began to pray over her. Ten minutes later, he made the sign of the cross over her and bid us good night.

Kate rested as I drove away. I, like Mary heeding Simeon's prophecies in the temple, pondered all these events in my heart.

The next morning, my husband and I took Kate back to the hospital to begin her second stay. As we said our goodbyes, she looked into my eyes and assured me, "Mom, it's going to be all right."

Indeed Kate worked hard on the issues tormenting her. Even the staff noticed her new determination and grew optimistic about her recovery. I too was able to face this struggle with renewed hope, as I held fast to the promise that I sensed the night of the Mass.

A month later, Kate earned her discharge after gaining an acceptable amount of weight. Still, it was a long stony path to complete recovery, but she stopped starving herself and never required another hospital stay, ending that brutal winter. My daughter was back.

I also got my old friend, the Sacred Heart of Jesus, back, or maybe it was the other way around. After all, hadn't I stopped calling Him? Even though I let the friendship lapse, He did not forget His long lost friend and made good on His age-old promise to comfort me in affliction and to establish peace in my home. An icon of the Sacred Heart of Jesus now hangs in my kitchen to honor the love, mercy and faithfulness of my dear old Friend... not to mention His wit.

Several months later, Denise called me on a Sunday afternoon. "Dottie, did you enter me in a contest? The Sacred Heart Institute just called and said I won first prize in their raffle!"

I exclaimed, "Yes, I did write your name on a raffle for their fundraiser, because you set me up with them."

Laughing heartily, Denise exclaimed, "You know what's so funny? The prize is a five-hundred-dollar gift certificate for King's Supermarket. It's for food, Dottie! Does God have a sense of humor or what?"

~Dorothy LaMantia

Like Beads on a String

Now My eyes shall be open and My ears attentive to the prayer of this place.
~2 Chronicles 7:15

We were nine women with only two things in common: the military and some connection to Catholicism. None of us expected our lives would change significantly in less than nine months, but God knew we would be together for only a brief military assignment at Fort Leavenworth, Kansas, and He worked quickly. One by one He tied us together like beads on a string.

He started with Tracy. A convert to Catholicism, she was a true cheerleader who made everyone want to be a part of whatever she had planned. We were all still new to a Catholic women's Bible study at the post chapel when a speaker presented an explanation of the rosary. Tracy sat smiling through tears the entire time. At the end, she grabbed the hands of her next-door neighbor and shared how she'd been part of a rosary group before moving and wanted desperately to start another here. Would her neighbor Tami be willing to come?

Tami wasn't even sure how she had ended up in a Catholic Bible study. She'd been raised Lutheran but was only recently getting serious about her faith. This Catholic stuff seemed intimidating and she thought quickly for a good reason to avoid the rosary group. She had to admit, though, that God regularly put people and situations right in her path and she could not deny His hand in Tracy's invitation. Not owning rosary beads, having no idea how the prayer worked, Tami said yes anyway.

On Tami's other side was her long-time friend Tanya. She too was intimidated by the rosary presentation and thought such a prayer group was certainly not right for her. However, the move to Leavenworth had started in her a hunger to know God better and his Church deeper. She did not know where it was all going to end, but she was intrigued enough to join.

I agreed to go in spite of my own unease. I was an adult convert like Tracy and, though I was fascinated by the Church and the sacraments, I was still skittish about praying in any way other than the intimate conversation I'd been having with Christ since childhood. The rosary seemed to be a rote barely-Christ-centered prayer. But many of my beliefs from my upbringing had proven untrue, so I was willing to follow this one and see what the truth really was.

Stacey had been suffering with severe anxiety since the birth of her third child a year before. She had attended Catholic schools as a child and suspected some regular prayer would help.

Jenn was a cradle Catholic who had struggled over the years with raising her children in a faith that was real and important. Military moves made it harder to stay consistent when it came to church-going and she suspected her own deeper dedication would affect her family in a good way.

Nikki had walked with Jesus consistently throughout her life. Raised in a happy Catholic family, her faith was shaken when a drunk driver hit her and a high school friend. Her faith was ultimately strengthened since she escaped serious injury and her friend made a full recovery. With three small children, including a two-year-old with autism, she knew she needed the support and she burst into tears when Tracy invited her to join the group.

Lauren was still grieving deeply over her mother's death three years before. Raised a Catholic, Lauren believed it all but had not truly sought comfort from her faith until arriving in Kansas. When unpacking her heirloom rosary beads, Lauren broke down as she realized that these were the very beads given to her by her dying mom. It was as if her mom knew she would need them. Finally she was ready to use them to let God heal her.

Janet was also raised in a Catholic family, but she spent most of her adult life surrounded by Protestant friends who challenged her with questions she could not answer. Expecting gray-haired ladies, she was surprised to find other thirty-something moms in the Bible study. Joining the rosary group would prove to be just what she needed to cement her faith.

What we did was simple. We gathered on Tuesday nights at 9:00 in one of our living rooms. We shared our prayer intentions and then prayed the rosary together, changing mysteries each week.

Our prayer requests were both light-hearted and heart-wrenching. We prayed for couples expecting or wanting to conceive, and with great joy we reported positive test results and new babies. We had a list of cancer patients and cried together over hopeful diagnoses and tragic deaths. We knew of many ill children and we prayed the fervent prayer of every mother who knows it could easily be one of her own suffering.

And we saw answers.

Tracy's prayer for her nephew's eye problem brought a happy diagnosis of no cancer.

Tami's prayer for understanding brought her peace as she delved further into the teachings of the Catholic Church.

Tanya's prayer for her own journey led her to celebrate her first Reconciliation and Confirmation with us cheering her on.

My prayer for our family's future was answered with the assignment of our choice and a perfect new home big enough for five children.

Jenn's prayer for her brother was answered as he began turning to God for the help he needed with an addiction.

Stacey's prayer when faced with an immediate move and imminent deployment of her husband, was answered as she handled the transition with grace and humor.

Nikki's son was placed in excellent autism therapy and progressed in miraculous ways.

Lauren found a way to grieve through praying the rosary with her mother's beads and began the process of truly healing.

Janet's desire to know more about her faith found her in an apologetics course and looking forward to taking the job of Bible study facilitator the next year.

It didn't take long, but we were all changed. We consistently had new insights into the life of Jesus as we meditated on those mysteries. We found ourselves praying more in our daily lives. And though we often prayed together until after midnight, we busy moms found lost sleep an easy price to pay.

Saying goodbye at the end of the year together was painful, yet we knew that one day in heaven we would pray together again. And in the meantime the rosary would continue to link us.

God had hand-picked each of us, strung us together like rosary beads, and tied us together forever.

~Susanna Hickman Bartee

"I find that Post-it noting a relevant Scripture passage is helpful throughout the day."

60

Prayer Shawl

You created every part of me, knitting me in my mother's womb.
For such handiwork, I praise you. Awesome this great wonder.
~Psalm 139:13-14

When our sixteen-year-old son, Justin, died by suicide... unexpectedly, with no warning... I slumped into an intense period of grief.

One long, gloomy February day, in the depths of my inconsolable suffering and angst, I opened a gift from Mary Jo, a friend in Denver. Inside I found loosely knitted yarn the color of tangerines, tied with a long fringe. A prayer shawl. I stood in my kitchen and began to weep, amazed at how the Spirit of God consoles. I had no idea what a prayer shawl was, or that an entire growing ministry existed. Included in the gift bag was a card and "Prayer of Comfort" blessing written by Cathleen O'Meara Murtha, DW. I knew Cathleen! Wrapped by the embrace of orange knitted prayers from Mary Jo, I read a blessing prayer from Cathy, my friend from Connecticut. The knitted love from my Presbyterian friend and a Catholic religious sister who did not know each other wove an embrace of love wrapping me tight, offering me hope.

A few weeks later, a friend showed up on my doorstep unexpectedly, on a day when my grief seemed beyond measure. She gifted me with her presence... and a second prayer shawl. This one was pure white, and large enough to hide under or swathe me completely in a pure soft embrace. Completely different from the tangerine shawl, this was a baptismal prayer blanket to remind me that the waters of baptism bring new life and resurrection from death.

Not long after that, I sat in the Denver airport on my way to California. My traveling companion met me at the airport and presented me with a package. Inside the iridescent paper was a third shawl, knitted by a friend from Indiana. Its royal blue and triangular shape had shimmering strands of pink, white, silver and turquoise tied throughout the shawl and fringe. Ruth wrote in the card that it was the first prayer shawl she had ever knitted. Furthermore, within a few weeks, she would begin a prayer shawl knitting ministry in her church. Wrapped in the royal blue threads, I knew the broad deep mystery of God's mission for our lives.

In August, a large parcel arrived in the mailbox. I immediately recognized the distinctive handwriting of Sarah, a former student during my years of working in campus ministry. Curious, I stood at my kitchen island and unwrapped the paper to discover a large gold and white checkered box, tied shut with a white ribbon. Words peppered the box lid: share, hope, wish, enjoy.

Tentatively I untied the bow, and gasped with dawning comprehension. Midnight blue yarn greeted my hands as I lifted a six-foot-long prayer shawl from the box and encircled my shoulders. Medallions, pins, and buttons were tied within the fringe. My fingers traced crosses of all sizes and shapes, shells, a ceramic rose, worn holy medals, angel pins, and even a fishing lure.

Looking back into the box, I saw a colorful piece of paper adorned with butterflies. In handwritten blue ink was a list of twenty names from young adults I knew well. All were former students I had served, played, and prayed with who now lived in cities throughout the United States and as far away as the Philippines and New Zealand. Beside each person's name was a description of the charm and prayer that they had contributed to the prayer shawl, each an offering of healing, hope, and loving compassion.

These young adults had all known our son. In fact, many had watched him grow through his early years with us. Justin had loved them, calling them his "adopted" brothers and sisters from the church.

Now, twenty of them wrapped my grief and loneliness, bestowing on me one thousand-fold the love I had once given them. This prayer shawl spoke to me of boundless grace and a multitude of small acts of sacrifice and kindness that bind us together.

I know that in time I will learn to knit and pray my appreciation, love, and compassion into prayer shawls for others who suffer unexpected grief. Threads of belonging that weave us together will continue to knit themselves into homes and hearts, offering whatever each recipient most needs and longs for, bringing courage, consolation, healing, and a deep acknowledgment of the interwoven nature of God.

~Pegge Bernecker

61

Just Pray to Saint Anthony

Even now I know that whatever you ask of God, God will give you.
~John 11:22

Our home was busting at the seams with Mom, Dad, five sisters, my grandfather and me. Every time we ran to my mother upset or complaining about not being able to find something, she would remind us, "Just pray to Saint Anthony." More times than not the item would eventually surface, but as kids we blew it off as a coincidence, never remembering to give thanks or credit to Saint Anthony once our lost item reappeared.

As years went by, my five sisters and I grew up and left home. By this time I had acquired a respect for the saints, in particular Saint Anthony. One memorable day my mother told me that one of my sisters called earlier, upset about her husband losing his wallet. Not only did it contain his driver's license, important papers, and pictures, but also a significant amount of money, since he had just cashed his paycheck.

There was nothing much for Mom to do to comfort her, but she did ask my sister, "Did you remember to pray to Saint Anthony?" In my sister's own words, she pretty much asked Mom to "get serious." This was a lost wallet, and this was a crisis! Mom replied, "Well if you won't pray to Saint Anthony, I will pray for you," which Mom did as soon as she got off the phone. I added my request and prayers for Saint Anthony's assistance in finding the wallet.

My sister's whole family tore the house and the cars apart, mentally retracing their weekend, but no wallet was in sight. Most of the weekend had been spent in the yard after a long winter. Both my sister and her husband were very proud of their neatly groomed lawn and beautiful flower beds. Eleven large garbage bags full of weeds, leaves, clippings, and grass, all neatly lined the side of the house behind the gate. Garbage day was the next day.

Bright and early the next morning, my brother-in-law set the bags out at the curb. Like clockwork, the trash hauler arrived and picked up the weekly garbage, including all the large lawn bags.

Later that day, my sister and brother-in-law realized that just maybe the wallet got into one of those eleven large garbage bags already picked up. Sick at the thought that the wallet was gone for good, my sister called our mother again and told her there was a strong possibility the wallet had somehow dropped out of my brother-in-law's pocket while cleaning up the yard, and ultimately got scooped into one of the garbage bags. Once again Mom mentioned praying to Saint Anthony. "Your sister and I have been praying through him."

My sister's patience was wearing thin, hearing about Saint Anthony and that silly prayer. "There is no way possible now to find the wallet," she sighed, and she hung up.

In his grief, my brother-in-law walked outside and paced around in the yard, sick with the thought of his wallet mixed in with tons of garbage. He walked around to the side of the house where the eleven large bags had been lined up the night before. To his amazement, one lonely bag leaned against the wall of the house. He couldn't believe it! He knew he had taken out all eleven bags that morning. This couldn't be happening. No way. He nervously walked over to the bag, opened the drawstring, and on top of the yard waste lay his wallet!

~Connie Vagg

Extra-Strength Prayer Power

The Lord had heard my plea;
the Lord has accepted my prayer.
~Psalm 6:10

The tables were turned. I'd been an operating room nurse for many years when my doctor told me I had a quickly growing suspicious-looking cyst in my belly. It had to come out as soon as possible.

Why me? Why now? After working more than twenty-five years as a staff nurse, I had given up a full-time job and all my benefits, including paid sick leave, so I could complete my bachelor's degree and begin a teaching career. Abdominal surgery with a six-to-eight week recovery was not on my agenda. My salary now was based only on the hours I worked. I pushed frantic thoughts regarding money, job loss, and the possibility of postponing my degree away so I could focus on a professional analysis of the situation.

I begged the doctor to try to remove the cyst through a laparoscope so there would be no incision. The two-week recovery required for that procedure would be manageable. The doctor explained that I might have scar tissue from a previous surgery that would obstruct a safe laparoscopic procedure. I pleaded with him to try. He thought it over and recommended one of his partners, a man especially skilled in laparoscopy. This partner agreed to try, but offered no guarantees.

He would have to do a large abdominal incision if he was unsuccessful with the laparoscopy. I acknowledged that, and surgery was scheduled.

I spent the next two weeks in a state of turmoil, wondering what would happen if I needed to stay out of work and away from school for eight weeks. I prayed and meditated between bouts of worry, yet my imagination continued to run wild. I had twenty-five years of participating in all types of surgeries. I knew the risks better than anyone.

Two days before the operation, I approached my professor and explained why I might not be returning to class for awhile. He seemed quite concerned and wished me well. He reminded me that he was the chaplain for the college, and although we are committed to different religions, he asked permission to pray for me. Touched by and grateful for his offer, I accepted. He then requested permission to ask the class to pray for me. Assuming he would make a general announcement for class members to include me in their personal prayers, I agreed.

At the end of class, he announced my impending surgery. Most of my classmates seemed startled or upset. The chaplain went on to discuss the power of prayer, and asked if anyone would like to stay after class and join him.

Here? Now? Oh, how embarrassing. All eyes were on me and I could feel my face getting hotter and hotter. I looked down at my books so I wouldn't have to make eye contact with anyone. I wanted to run out of the room, but I couldn't move.

A self-described "hands-on" minister, he walked to my seat and placed his hands on my shoulders. Before he could begin, a classmate suggested that everyone hold hands to form a united circle of prayer. They did.

The chaplain closed his eyes, gripped my shoulders, and began with, "Heavenly Father..." He prayed passionately for at least five minutes... for skilled doctors, a good outcome, a speedy recovery, and family support.

At first, I kept my eyes closed to absorb his words. After a minute or so, I opened them to watch my classmates' reactions. Some were looking at me with great intensity, as if their concentration could make the prayer more powerful. Some were crying, and others had their eyes closed as they mouthed private prayers.

We'd barely said, "Amen" when the class moved forward, hugging me and wishing me well. Two classmates asked if they could light candles for me. I accepted gratefully. One woman lingered to ask when the surgery would take place. I told her it would begin at 8:00 A.M. on Friday morning. She worked as a Captain in the Salvation Army, and said all the Army officers gathered at 9:00 A.M. Fridays for a prayer session. Could she include my name at the session?

"Yes, please," I replied. I was overwhelmed by my classmates' efforts to reassure me. A sense of peace and calm, and the conviction that everything would be all right, flooded over me. Those feelings remained with me for the next nine days... up to the time the anesthesia was administered.

I half-woke in the recovery room grabbing at my belly, trying to determine the nature of the surgery by the size of the bandage. The recovery nurse was at my side saying, "It's all right, Susan, they were able to do it through the 'scope. There's no incision."

I couldn't even open my eyes yet, but I sure could smile! "What time is it?" I mumbled.

By then the surgeon was at my side. "It's after ten," he said. "You had so much scar tissue in your belly it was almost impossible to do the procedure through the 'scope. I was ready to give up after an hour or so, when all of a sudden, everything seemed to shift and I was able to see the cyst clearly. Somehow I was able to do it. You can go home tonight and be back to work in two weeks."

I was stunned. An hour into the "impossible" surgery would have been exactly when the prayer session at the Salvation Army headquarters was convening. Just when the doctor was about to give up, the group was praying for me, as were family, friends, and classmates.

The surgeon thought I had fallen back to sleep and began to walk away from my stretcher. "Thank you!" I blurted out.

"Oh, you're welcome," he tossed over his shoulder.

As I drifted back into a medicated haze, I murmured, "I wasn't just talking to you."

~Susan M. Goldberg

Short Prayers

I call out with all my heart. Answer me oh Lord.
~Psalm 119:145

hen I was a young girl, the Dominican nuns at St. Dominic's school taught us to say short prayers throughout the day, while walking down the street, riding a bus, or peddling a bike. They cautioned us that there might come a time in our lives when we faced a life-or-death situation. What would you do in that brief instant as you considered your fate? Say a short prayer such as, "Jesus, Mary and Joseph pray for us."

My family encountered that situation on a dark, cold, and icy January night.

That Saturday packed a full schedule for my husband, our three teenage sons and me. The boys had spent hours that morning building a large stadium with Legos to enter into a Lego contest at the local mall. Although they did not win a prize for their creation, they were happy to pack it into the back of the station wagon for the next event, our oldest son's high school basketball game some fifty miles away.

"Lord protect us."

After a thrilling game, everyone was tired as we loaded up the car and headed home. As we drove through the frozen, dark prairie night, our station wagon suddenly hit a patch of black ice. The car began to spin in circles, out of control on the highway, then careened to the side of the road. It crashed into a mileage marker and began to roll.

"Jesus, Mary and Joseph pray for us."

The car continued to roll four times until it landed back on its wheels with a thud at the bottom of the ditch.

"My Jesus, mercy."

The windows shattered; glass and Legos peppered the interior of the car. The boys were shaken and moaning, but we were all alive.

"Mother of Mercy, pray for us."

The first two people on the scene offered to take us to the hospital, since we were in a remote area and help was miles away. One son gripped his painful shoulder and ribs; the other two boys were remarkably unharmed.

"Our Lord and our Savior."

A van stopped to help. The Lutheran minister and his family would take the older boys to Denver while we went to the nearest hospital with our youngest son. We did not know these strangers who came into our lives on that night, but somehow we knew God had sent them and we could trust them with our children. The state patrol officer told us we were very lucky the accident happened in that location, where sandy soil slowed the car before it flipped; a short distance down the highway was a deep and dangerous culvert.

I gazed at the Lego stadium now scattered in hundreds of pieces in and out of the car, and wrapped my arms around my family, still together.

"Thank you, Jesus."

~Shirley Dino

64

The Perfect Cabin

In his heart a man plans his course,
but the Lord determines his steps.
~Proverbs 16:9

"Are you sure you want to consider buying this one?" my husband Mark asked with understandable doubt. The lonely, weathered and worn A-frame cabin stood orphaned among the pine trees. Part of the railing on the deck was missing and wind-blown forest debris littered beneath it.

"It could be perfect," I assured him.

We'd driven by this obvious "fixer-upper" several times when I finally asked our Realtor, Steve, to show it to me the week before. I'd been happily surprised to find that the couple who owned it the past three years had remodeled the interior.

"Wait till you see the river!" I said, trying to contain my excitement.

I'd dreamed of a cabin in the mountains since I was a little girl and had begun my serious search three years before. Though I had prayed God would find me my perfect cabin, locating one with all four of my strict criteria had not been easy. It had to be a simple cabin (not another home to maintain!), on a road with no traffic, within one hour of our home, and on water. I'd had three Realtors looking in five canyons for three years.

I began to question if it was God's plan for me to own a cabin. "If it is not Your will, Lord," I prayed, "please take this desire from me."

But my yearning... and searching... persisted.

Then I discovered the beautiful Crystal Lakes area, with cabins nestled quietly in 5,000 acres of mountain wilderness. I appreciated the remoteness, but also the amenities of being part of a community association. Steve showed me lots of cabins there, but some were too fancy, others had too much traffic, and still others, no water. One day I drove the fifty miles of gravel roads myself and decisively told Steve, "I want a cabin on Blackfoot Court. I'm going to put signs on the doors of the six cabins on that quiet road and tell the owners to let me know if they ever want to sell."

Steve smiled. "I know everyone on that road. No one is selling now."

"Then I'll wait."

The next week I said, "I know I told you Mark and I didn't want the headaches of building or rebuilding a cabin, but will you show me that fixer-upper on Blackfoot Court?"

Now rain spit from the sky as Mark and I walked up the rickety steps and into a surprisingly lovely small kitchen with new wood cabinets and floor. The log walls, cozy wood burning stove, small bedroom and bath were almost as impressive as the huge loft... a writer's loft, my friend had called it. Perfect! Most of the seven books I'd written and all of my keynote speeches were penned in borrowed or rented cabins... on the water. I could explain to no one how that setting inspired me. I knew other writers claimed that same muse. As a matter of fact, two women in my weekly writer's club had owned cabins, further proving and justifying my inspiration theory.

Although its "perfection" was less than apparent to Mark, he trusted my certainty and we began the process of arranging inspections by plumbers, electricians, and engineers to determine just how much "fixing up" this investment would need. When it was built thirty years before, the county didn't require so many safety regulations. The long lists of repairs needed to bring it to code had no doubt discouraged other potential buyers. But I was undaunted.

"Somehow I know," I sighed to Mark, "that God wants us to have this cabin."

We were as surprised as delighted when the sellers took our low offer, with a list attached of all the structural improvements required after many years of apparent little use.

One week before the closing, I returned to the cabin with Steve and a builder/repairman in tow. This time I made no attempt to stifle my joy. I bounded up the stairs, two at a time, to the loft, and envisioned a large picture window to be added so I could write while overlooking "my" river. Skipping down the hill to the water, I walked our 200 feet of shoreline. Under the swaying ponderosa pine, I inhaled the balsam scent and listened to the river ripple by. Squirrels chattered the end of winter... and I whispered a prayer of humble thanksgiving.

Too soon, yet three hours later, it was time to leave. The builder had his list full of repairs and supplies and I had a heart full of gratitude and joy. We pulled the cabin door shut and Steve placed the key in the lockbox. "LeAnn, you'll own this in a week, so if you need to come back in the meantime, I'll tell you the combination to the lockbox... it is J-A-V." Then he added offhandedly, "The first owners were Javernicks."

Stunned, I said, "Not Ellen Javernick."

"I don't know first names."

"Not my dear friend Ellen Javernick who invited me to her writers group twelve years ago?... who helped teach me to write?... who read us stories about her family of seven building a cabin in the mountains by hand?... not the Ellen Javernick who went to four years of biblical school with me?"

Now Steve looked stunned. "I... I don't know."

"What are the odds?" I shook the notion from my head. "Maybe that's a more common last name than we thought."

But as soon as I got home, I called my dear friend. "Where was your cabin, Ellen, the one you wrote about?"

"Crystal Lakes."

I could barely speak past the ache in my throat. "Ellen, I'm buying your cabin!"

Choking back tears, I shared the afternoon's Divine coincidence.

Her voice trembled as she shared how difficult it had been for her and her grown children to sell the family cabin after her husband's sudden death five years earlier. By now her children were doctors and pilots and nurses and teachers all over the country, and gathering at the cabin had become a rarity.

"My kids will be so happy to know it's yours!" she said gleefully.

"And now they can come and stay in it whenever they want. You can still gather there!" I declared.

Then I recalled and repeated the congratulatory e-mail she had sent me the week before. "LeAnn, I hope you and your family find the same joy and great memories in your cabin as my family did in ours."

Indeed, God did want us to have this perfect cabin.

~LeAnn Thieman

65

Blaise

Oh Lord, my God, by day I cry out;
at night I clamor in your presence.
Let my prayer come before you;
incline your ear to my call for help.
~Psalm 88:2

A typical pregnancy is supposed to last forty weeks. I was only in my twenty-fifth week. I had just had a prenatal checkup two days earlier and the doctor had pronounced that everything was going along smoothly. My stomach felt funny. Maybe I had eaten something odd.

I walked hunched over to the bathroom. With a sickening feeling I realized I was bleeding rich red blood.

My husband immediately called the nurse. I was in too much pain to talk to her. "You have to get to the hospital right now," she told us. "It sounds like you might be in labor."

The trip to the hospital only took five minutes, my husband looking over at me as I twisted in my seat with each fresh pain. "I can't do this, I can't do this, I can't do this," I said over and over again, aloud and in my head. I clung to the tiny hope that because my water had not broken yet everything was fine. This would be over soon. I was sure of it. Things like this don't happen to people like me. For sure God had made a mistake.

"Is she okay? She looks pale," a paramedic said as he brought out a wheelchair. My eyes closed, I concentrated on trying not to vomit. I was wheeled quickly to the maternity ward, put in a bed, and warm jelly was spread on my belly as they started an ultrasound. The nurses moved at lightning speed. Medicine dripped into my veins to stop the contractions. My husband, who had been holding my hand, had to sit in a chair in the corner and put his head between his knees. All the needles, he said. It was after he sat down that my water broke.

"We have to do an emergency caesarean," the doctor said all of a sudden. "Your baby is in distress. I need your consent."

"Yes, yes!" I said. It seemed like it only took seconds for the nurses to wheel me into surgery. The contractions were horrible and I started yelling for my husband. I didn't even have time to tell him I loved him. The mask of anesthesia jerked over my head. "In a little while, you won't feel a thing," they told me. I remember a blue cloth being lifted up, the clinking of surgical tools and then silence.

I woke up and turned my head to see my husband pacing back and forth by my bed.

"We had a baby boy," he said. "He is very small, but he'll make it. He can't breathe on his own yet. They had to put a tube in his throat. He's in intensive care."

We had already picked a name for a boy — Blaise. I was tired but happy. I couldn't wait to take him home.

Little did I know that our baby would be in the neonatal intensive care unit for six long months. He only weighed one pound, five ounces at birth. The diapers they had for him, even the tiniest ones, almost covered his whole body. His skin was paper thin and covered with fine downy hair from head to toe. His footprints were barely as long as my thumb. We were not allowed to hold him for the first month because he was so fragile. He was up and down so much for the first several months that many times we were unsure if he would make it. He had infection after infection, and several blood transfusions.

At three months, he had to be transferred by helicopter to another hospital for an emergency procedure. At four months he had a tracheotomy tube, a hole in his neck to breathe; his vocal cords were severally damaged.

Two years later we realize he is one of the luckier ones. His physical and mental delays are very slight. He still undergoes therapy three times weekly, but will no longer need it in several months. His scars are fading. We are still in and out of hospitals for checkups, but his doctors are surprised at his progress. His ability to cope is astounding. His constant smile will light up any room. He is social and loves making people laugh. Doctors are hoping that his tracheotomy tube can be removed so that some day he may be able to have a voice. We pray to be able to hear it someday. For now, we communicate using sign language.

Through all of this pain, God has shown us that He was with us since the beginning. I always had a profound interest in sign language, taking classes in both high school and college. I had been a special education teacher. All of these things prepared me for taking care of my own son.

The name Blaise we had picked out randomly. But now it has new meaning. St. Blaise is the patron saint of illnesses of the throat.

~Beatrice Catarello

My Mother's Novena

I have been driven many times to my knees
by the overwhelming conviction that I had nowhere else to go.
~Abraham Lincoln

My mother loved to recount the story of God's hand in her marriage. In 1941, when she was twenty-one years old, she fashioned her own novena. For six weeks, she visited St. Patrick's Cathedral in Manhattan every evening after work. There, she contemplated the stations of the cross and asked Jesus to bless her with a caring husband. On the night she completed her novena, she volunteered at a USO social, serving doughnuts and coffee to U.S. servicemen. A tall soldier, or "a long drink of water," as my mother described him, asked her to dance. During that first waltz, he jokingly proposed marriage to her. One year later, she accepted his more heartfelt proposal, and he remained devoted to her for more than fifty years.

Not long after their marriage, my father received orders to fight in WWII. My mother presented him with a Sacred Heart of Jesus medal and sterling silver rosary beads before he was deployed. Dad was sent to pilot a B-17 bomber, the Lady Lylian, over Germany.

As soon as he left, Mom rallied the prayer troops. She wrote to the families of the Lady Lylian's crew and requested that they pray for the safety of the entire flight crew. My mother taught the fourth grade in a Catholic grammar school, and each morning she had her students recite a special Our Father for my dad's men.

My mother added her private prayers to the others. She asked God to please protect her husband and his men from harm; in return, she promised to attend Mass and receive Communion daily for the rest of her life. Miraculously, after an extended tour of forty bombing missions, each man on the Lady Lylian came home safe and well. Mom faithfully kept her end of the bargain.

My parents settled into married life and hoped to begin a family. In high school, my mother had written an essay about how she hoped to use her God-given talents in the career that her heart most desired, motherhood.

Sadly, for sixteen years, she could not conceive a child. Obstetricians said that her chances of becoming pregnant were next to none. She continued her education and became a college professor, but her heart quietly ached every time one of her friends gave birth to an infant.

My mother held a strong belief in the Communion of Saints and in their abilities to intercede on behalf of the prayerful. She prayed to the Virgin Mary for a baby because she knew that Our Lady would sympathize with this particular hope. Mom also had a special admiration for St. Therese, the Little Flower, and petitioned her too.

In 1960, I was born, and to honor her intercessors, my mother named me Marie-Therese.

Throughout my childhood, my mother was a fine example of a faithful woman. Every morning, I watched her race from the house, still applying her lipstick, to make the 7:30 Mass. We attended church as a family on Sunday, and Mom would help guide my hand as I lit candles for friends and family members who needed God's blessing.

Just as important, she made God and prayer part of everyday life. I can still remember her dashing around the house with her bifocals on her head muttering, "St. Anthony, please help me find those darned glasses." Preparing large multiple course meals was a joy for my mother. Before we could partake, though, we thanked God for the gift of his bounty and for one another. At night, she had me kneel next to my bed and pray. "Talk to God just as you would to your most trusted friend," she told me.

I married a U.S. Army Lieutenant when I was twenty and moved across the country from my parents. They missed me terribly. When my husband's military commitment was finished, he received two civilian job offers. One was located in Oklahoma, and the other was in New York, a mere one-hour drive from my parent's home. Again, Mom hit her knees to share her heart's wish with God. Who would have imagined that God would consider Poughkeepsie, New York, such a heavenly place for us to put down roots?

In his late sixties, my father was diagnosed with a virulent form of lymphoma. The doctors gave him six months to live. He underwent chemotherapy and radiation treatments; he fought to live and spend more time with my mother. My parents held hands and recited prayers. Dad lived five more years, long enough to celebrate their fiftieth wedding anniversary at their church, Sacred Heart.

In 1996, my mother was visiting me when she suffered a stroke. She had a choice of two local hospitals, and, not surprisingly, she said, "Take me to St. Francis Hospital." During her CAT scan, she stopped breathing twice, so the neurosurgeon was forced to perform an emergency craniotomy. The doctor told me that she had suffered extensive brain damage and might not recover well.

I went home to rally the troops, just as my mother had taught me. I telephoned relatives and friends from all over the country and asked them to pray for her recovery. I contacted the pastor of Sacred Heart Church, and he had the parishioners remember my mother in their prayers. Then, I brought my children to church and had them light candles for her because Mom always said, "God especially loves the honest and pure prayers of children."

When my mother awoke from unconsciousness, her seemingly nonsensical conversation concerned me. "Do you know about St. Francis's stigmata?" she asked me.

"It's okay, Mom. I'm here," I told her.

Weeks later, I did a bit of research and discovered that her stroke and operation fell on the Feast Day of St. Francis's stigmata.

My mother's recovery was slow. She had to re-learn to walk, to swallow, and to communicate. The hospital's chaplain visited each day, and as soon as Mom could have food by mouth, he brought her Communion. After six months of rehabilitation, she was able to live independently again.

On my mother's first Sunday back at Sacred Heart, the pastor asked her to stand and say a few words. She said, "I am your miracle. My recovery... and life... are proof of the power of prayer."

~Marie-Therese Miller

67

The Healing Power of the Family Rosary

My dear children, I call you anew to pray, pray, pray and do not forget that I am with you. I intercede before God for each of you until your joy in Him is complete. Thank you for having responded to my call.
~The Blessed Mother to visionaries in Medjugorje

My five-year-old niece snuggles in closer to my daughter and another cousin. As she smiles up at the older girls, I can tell she feels safe and content. She concentrates on the moment. All three girls finger their rosaries.

"Holy Mary, mother of God...," the three recite.

Across the room, my dad sits with my sister and her daughter. Dad prays with eyes closed. My niece squirms. Next to me on the sofa, my son and a nephew, both nearly teens, sit quietly together. Two younger nephews cozy up to their parents, my brothers, in chairs flanking the crackling fire. One nephew sucks his thumb. My two sisters-in-law, husband, mother, and brother-in-law reverently add to the chorus.

"Pray for us sinners..."

As the busyness of my day is calmed by the meditative prayer of the rosary, I silently thank Jesus for this gift of time to share prayer with my family. Once a month, the eighteen of us, ranging from age three to seventy-two, join the Blessed Mother to pray for peace, for one another and for others we know in need of intercession.

Our communal prayer has bonded, grounded, guided and healed us for nearly a decade.

Hardly saints, and sometimes sinners, my family is like many others. We juggle commitments, struggle with setbacks and try to count our blessings as we work, raise our children, nurture relationships and journey in faith. Sometimes when the monthly prayer meeting rolls around, we get distracted by work, school and travel schedules. Sometimes a bad mood or illness interferes with our willingness to pray. Sometimes, when the weather is bad, we question whether we should drive across town to the host's house. Sometimes we're just plain tired, and would prefer to crawl into bed.

But we persevere because we know that regular prayer, including prayer with others, is essential to sustain our faith. Through prayer, our faith comes alive.

Glancing at my dad, I thank Jesus again, this time because Dad feels and looks great. Diagnosed with kidney cancer almost three years ago, his stage IV disease has been stable for months despite predictions to the contrary from his doctors at the Mayo Clinic. My family prays daily for a miraculous healing... and also for acceptance of whatever God wills.

Seated close to my dad, my sister-in-law is peaceful as she journeys through chemotherapy. Her battle with major surgery and treatment is nearly over, and she has great hope for her future. Nearby, my younger brother looks rested and strong as he leads our prayers. I'm grateful that he no longer wrestles with chronic fatigue syndrome, a debilitating illness that kept him from a full life for nearly four years.

It is through family prayer, joined with Mary's powerful intercession, my family believes, that we have experienced these physical healings. Just as powerfully, our prayers have led to spiritual and emotional healing too.

The gospel tells us that prayer can change anything. It provides spiritual protection, discernment, comfort and grace. It can convert hearts and produce peace. It can heal sinners and lead souls from purgatory. On occasion, prayer can even result in miracles.

My family continues to face challenges and crosses, as does

every family. But when we bring our petitions to Jesus through family prayer, even the youngest members feel his presence. When, as parents, we model our faith for the next generation, we grow in grace.

"Hail holy queen..."

My family finishes five decades of the rosary, offers special intentions and concludes with a Memorare. Now my little niece squeals. It's treat time. Tonight she helps serve rich gooey chocolate brownies, her favorite. As the kids chatter and play and the adults mingle as friends, I offer a final silent prayer: "Thank you, Jesus, for the divine blessings and hope you offer.

"Thank you for the gift of this family praying together... and staying together... in You."

~Cathy Kruse

68

The Connection

Have no anxiety at all, but in everything, by prayer and petition, with thanksgiving, make your requests known to God.
~Philippians 4:6

I was born into a Catholic faith and attended a Catholic elementary school. I went to church every Sunday and I could recite Mass in Latin, even though I didn't understand a word of it. Timing was everything. I knelt and stood at the appropriate times. I made the sign of the cross in record speed and even wore that silly doily on the top of my head. Concerning the confessional, I was a repeat offender. "I hit my brother and sister and took the Lord's name in vain."

As a young adult, I was still reciting the same old sins. Too embarrassed to upgrade to more serious offenses, I stopped going to church. God didn't really exist for me outside of church. The only time I thought about God was when I said bedtime prayers and asked for favors. The requests started out simple and advanced into the more complex. I want a: puppy, boyfriend, car, career, marriage, house, child, etc.

I shouldn't complain; I got all the things I had asked for. It might have taken longer than I wanted, but eventually I got what I wanted. Somehow, I never really felt the connection that God was at the bottom of all of this. I just attributed it to a lot of hard work and perseverance on my part.

Still, something was missing in my life. Physically and mentally I

244 The Power of Prayer: *The Connection*

was in good shape, but my soul needed nourishment. At age fifty, one ponders more philosophical questions. I wanted to know if there was a good reason why I existed in this universe, that I made a difference, and that I was on a path to salvation. I came to the realization that I needed God on a more personal level. When I spoke to God, I wanted to feel as if He was in the same room listening to me. "Ask and you shall receive." I always wanted to believe in this simple phrase.

One day when I was out walking on an early January morning, the brisk air had quickened my pace and I felt invigorated to repeat out loud *The Prayer of Jabez*, which I'd recently read. It was helping me reconnect with God. I came to the passage which says, "And Jabez called upon God of Israel saying, 'Oh that You would bless me indeed.'" The author's interpretation of this particular section was that God was waiting to shower us with blessings, big ones; all we need is the courage to ask, as Jabez did.

Well, I substituted the name of Jabez for mine and added a few twenty-first century verses of my own. I said, "And Karen called upon God of Israel saying, 'Oh that You would bless me indeed.' Pile it on, God — give it to me — heap it on — sock it to me — sock it to me — sock it to me!"

Okay God, if you are listening, show me a sock!

I knew it was silly, but I needed something, anything, to know He was listening.

I walked a few feet ahead and glanced to my left at a snow bank. There lying in the snow, next to the curb, was a wet dirty sock. Not a comb, not a glove, but one sock.

Now, I have the proof that God does listen, that He can be spontaneous and humorous.

That day, not only did I take home one slightly used sock, but a renewed faith in God.

~Karen Adragna Walsh

69

Listening for Bells

*For the eyes of the Lord are on the righteous
and His ears turned to their prayer.*
~1Peter 3:12

Thirty-two years old, ten years of marriage and no baby. I'd pretty much given up hope.

My husband Mickey and I were stationed with the Canadian Armed Forces in Lahr, Germany in 1984. At a conference held on a mountaintop, at a healing service, I prayed to become pregnant. But that year it was not to be.

The following year, I attended again. The same priest who had conducted the healing service the year before recognized me, blessed me, prayed for me to have a baby, then anointed me.

Five days later I was home, full of peace and joy after the faith-filled inspiring conference. Tired from my travels, I took a letter I'd received while I was away to bed with me. It was from my sister, Angie, in Saskatchewan. Eighteen months younger, but married three years longer, she was feeling depressed that she and her husband Boris had not been blessed with children either. With stationery propped on my pillow, I replied to her letter immediately, saying perhaps we had not prayed with enough conviction.

I told her about a story I'd heard once about a man who had a dream that he was on a tour of heaven with St. Peter and upon seeing a room full of beautifully wrapped presents, asked what that room was. St. Peter replied that it was the room where God had stored all the prayers that people had given up praying for. God was still waiting for more prayer, but they had given up too soon. I wrote Angie that I wasn't finished praying yet. With that, I got out of bed and knelt down. "Father, you know I want children and perhaps I haven't been praying hard enough. Whenever I hear a bell ring, I will remember to pray for a baby, for me and Angie."

In Germany the church bells rang every fifteen minutes. And I prayed. I also used the telephone's ring and any other ring or ding I heard to remember to pause for prayer.

Ten months later, I gave birth to a beautiful baby boy, Christopher John.

A year later, Angie and Boris's name rose to the top of the adoption list in time to be blessed with twin baby girls.

Now when I hear a bell, I pray in thanksgiving.

~Terri Scott

70

St. Ann, St. Ann

Prayer is not overcoming God's reluctance;
it is laying hold of His highest willingness.
~Richard Trench

My friend, Patty Duffy, had all the beauty of an Irish colleen, with silky chestnut hair, a heart-shaped face and laughing eyes. She was tall and athletic, friendly and funny, yet since she had left college and begun her internship at the local newspaper, there were no men on the horizon. Zero.

One Saturday night on her way to Mass, she stopped at her grandmother's house to share her misery, one single gal to another. Patty was happily surprised to find her grandma alone and anxious for a chat. When she began to bemoan her dateless status, her grandmother had asked, "Do you ever pray to St. Ann?"

"St. Ann? Why?"

"Well, she was the mother of Mary, the Blessed Mother, and she is considered one of the patron saints of single women. What you have to do is say 'St. Ann, St. Ann, send me a man as fast as you can.'"

Patty burst into peals of laughter. "That's like little kids saying 'Rain, rain, go away!'"

"Well, you go ahead and laugh, Miss Smarty Pants... Miss Single Smarty Pants, but don't knock it till you've tried it."

Still smiling, Patty finished her coffee, kissed her grandmother goodbye and headed off to church.

She silently lamented, "Here it is Saturday night, and I'm sitting in church... alone."

She glanced around at the plaster statues and located one of the Virgin Mary as a child next to her seated mother, St. Ann. She looked kind, and she certainly looked as though she was keeping a close eye on her own daughter.

"I have no idea if Grandma is even right about this... but what could it hurt?" Feeling unbelievably silly, she began the little prayer. "St. Ann, St. Ann, send me a man as fast as you can."

For the next two days, any time Patty thought of it, she repeated the little prayer.

On the third day, an old friend from college called and asked her out for a drink.

Then a guy from work, whom she had never even spoken to, asked her to an opening of an art gallery.

By the end of the next week, she had three dates.

Eagerly, she told her grandmother how the plan had worked. Grandma wasn't surprised. "Oh, honey, how do you think I ended up with your grandfather? He was the sweetest man, and he really fit all my specifications."

"You had specifications?" She crumbled another cookie into her tea and studied her grandmother. "What exactly were you looking for?"

"Oh, I was very specific. I wanted a man who didn't drink, because that would mean that he could manage his money carefully and he wouldn't be drinking it up at a bar while his wife and kids did without. He also had to wear his seatbelt. A man who wears his seatbelt is aware of his own mortality, and he wouldn't risk his life in any stupid daredevil sort of way. Finally, he had to be a Catholic. If we were Catholics together, then there would be so much for us to share and enjoy every day in our beliefs and our future together as a family."

At first glance, Grandma's list seemed a little superficial, but the more Patty thought about it, the more it showed how carefully considered it was. Each of those requirements represented something important in the character of a prospective mate.

"What the heck," thought Patty. "St. Ann, St. Ann, send me a man who wears his seatbelt, doesn't drink, and is a Catholic!"

On Tuesday of the following week, a colleague of Patty's invited her out after work to meet a friend of her fiancé.

Patty said her revised prayer.

The friend was stereotypically tall, dark and handsome. He had chiseled features, an easy smile and friendly eyes. His faint German accent made him not only mysterious but exotic, in a romantic sort of way.

"Hi, I'm Joe," he said extending his hand to Patty. She felt a little shock as she took his hand in hers. They laughed and talked easily. He asked her out for dinner and she happily accepted.

When he picked her up, he helped her into her side of the car, went around to the driver's side, slid into his seat and latched his seatbelt.

"That's one," she thought to herself. After they settled themselves in a booth at a local restaurant, Patty ordered a beer and Joe ordered a diet soda. "I never drink when I'm driving," he said, unwrapping the straw.

"That's two, St. Ann!" Patty tried to keep herself from smiling. Joe was telling a serious story about attending a camp in his native Germany.

"What kind of camp was that?" she asked trying to refocus her thoughts on the conversation.

"Actually, it was a church camp, a Catholic church camp where I worked with the boys teaching them soccer."

Patty almost choked on her drink.

"Joseph," she began, "you are really something else."

"My name isn't Joseph."

Patty thought to herself, "Here we go. I knew he sounded too good to be true. He's probably got an alias or several ex-wives. He probably..."

"Patty, are you listening to me? I said my name isn't Joseph; it's Joachim."

"Joachim? Where have I heard that name before?"

"In the Bible. St. Joachim was St. Ann's husband."

It was a few moments before Patty could speak. "Thank you!"

"For what?" asked Joe.

Patty looked at the man who was literally a gift from heaven and said, "I wasn't speaking to you."

~Rosemary McLaughlin

Living Catholic Faith

A Matter of Perspective

*We ourselves feel that what we are doing is just a drop in the ocean.
But the ocean would be less because of that missing drop.*

~Mother Teresa

71

Tuesdays with Sister Mary Patrick

Character building begins in our infancy and continues until death.
~Mrs. Franklin D. Roosevelt

I grew up in the '60s. It was a time of constant change and rebellion, yet as the daughter of devout Catholic parents, part of my weekly activities included attending catechism class on Tuesday afternoons. I hated it. I wanted to be at the local family-owned corner store smoking Parliaments and planning the next revolution, but I was forced to focus my attention on a nun with a reputation as a drill sergeant.

Being a cheerleader was a large part of my high school ritual. Unfortunately, one of the weekly practices was held on Tuesday afternoons, the same time as catechism class with Sister Mary Patrick. My parents wrote a letter to my principal excusing me from the first forty-five minutes of cheerleading practice. Following my reluctant attendance at catechism at St. Cecilia's, I would run the two blocks back to the high school to attend practice for the last hour.

Even as a teenager, I was extremely strong-willed and, following my sometimes weak attempts at humor, I tried to match wits with Sister Mary Patrick. I rarely won.

One memorable Tuesday afternoon, the entire class received new rosary beads from Father as a reward for a job well done at the food pantry drive. He announced that the white beads were for the girls and the black beads for the boys. Sister asked me to distribute the rosary beads to my classmates. I proceeded to ask each and every student what color beads he or she preferred, ignoring Father's instruction regarding color distribution. Who the heck cared about the color? I, for example, much preferred black, and black beads were what I took.

Sister stood in front of the class and asked us to hold up our rosary beads. She took a quick look around the room and walked to my desk. Without so much as a blink, she slapped the "I'll do whatever the heck I want to" grin off my sixteen-year-old face. I sat there ashamed and embarrassed with my cheek red and stinging.

"Fix it," she said quietly.

I did as I was told, but in my mind, a battle had begun. I was out to get Sister Mary Patrick. This was war.

Week after week, I challenged Sister's every word and move. I disrupted the class and made inappropriate jokes. I talked out of turn, questioned each and every one of her orders and mocked her at every opportunity. One cold Tuesday afternoon in November, just before Thanksgiving, I decided that cheerleading practice was more important than aggravating Sister. I blew off religion and cheered my heart off till 4:30. I walked home with a bunch of the other heathens and arrived just in time for dinner, as usual.

My parents questioned me about religion class. What did we learn today? How was Sister? Did I see my friend Mark? I answered almost robotically. I hardly raised my head to look up... but I sure felt my father lift me from my chair and stand me in front of him.

"Sister Mary Patrick called me at work today. It seems you never showed up for class, and she was worried about you. Are you going to keep lying to me?"

My father was beyond angry, and I was beyond dead!

I saw no reason to lie anymore, so I proceeded to tell my dad all about the evil ways of Sister. I poured my little heart out about how mean and nasty she was and finally confessed to him that she had actually slapped me several weeks ago. "Now she was in for some real trouble," I thought.

Dad looked at me and said, "Sit down." He then gave me a forty-five minute lecture on the importance of religion and the evils of telling untruths. He also informed me that if Sister had indeed slapped me, it was because I deserved it, and that if she ever hit me again, he would make sure that he would be the one I would answer to.

Now I hated her more than ever.

I was forbidden to attend cheerleading for one month, and missed the all-important pep-rally. I was so angry with Sister, I plotted and schemed of ways to torture her. I sat at my desk and waited for her to arrive. A few minutes past 3:00, Father entered the room and said, "Sister will no longer be teaching your class. She is ill and will spend her remaining days in the infirmary in the convent next door to the church." He explained that he would be our new instructor.

She had won.

Only upon the direction of my father, I visited Sister Mary Patrick in the infirmary. I entered her room to see a tiny woman who reminded me of my grandmother. She looked thin and pale, but quite lovely. I had never before seen her like this. She held out her hand to me. I took it and she smiled.

"I have always admired your spirit," she said softly. She went on to say that as a young girl she, too, was a rebellious soul. I listened to her tell tales of her youth and of her decision to enter the convent. Her stories intrigued me.

I visited her again. And again.

One visit, she held a package. In it was a strand of black rosary beads. She smiled. "You were right, color doesn't matter. Remember that lesson in all aspects of life." She kissed the beads and handed them to me.

It was the last time I saw her.

I think of her often when I pray with those special black beads, I remember that few things in life are black and white.

~Marianne LaValle-Vincent

72

Uninitiated Child

Childhood and genius have the same master organ in common — inquisitiveness.
~Edward George Bulwer-Lytton

As a Jewish child, all of my friends were Christians, mostly Roman Catholics, but some Lutherans. Two of my friends... Irish Annie with the smiling green eyes and pretty Barbara with her long, thick, blond braids... lived on my block. They attended St. Patrick's Church and school at 95th Street and 4th Avenue in Brooklyn.

One afternoon, on an impulse, they decided to take me to church with them. At seven years old, this would be a new adventure for me, because I had never been inside a church before. Walking the few blocks to St. Patrick's Church, or Saint Pat's as everyone referred to it, we talked and laughed as we ambled along.

The beige brick church took up most of the block. Three long stained-glass windows glimmered on the sides and above the front doors.

We ran up the stone steps in front of the church and opened the beautiful carved wooden doors. When we entered, we were in a small room facing huge ornate brass doors with inlaid figures. These majestic doors would lead inside to the main chapel where Mass was being held.

Before we went in, I looked around and saw small fountains of water. After checking them out, I asked Barbara and Annie, "Why are the fountains broken?"

They looked at me strangely. Perhaps, they were beginning to realize that bringing a "heathen" to church wasn't their best idea. They panicked, no doubt worrying that I might ask the nuns and priests questions, too. Apparently they decided the better part of valor was to quickly run inside the sanctuary and get away from me.

Undaunted, I raced after them. As I entered the dimly lit church, I saw both girls walk toward the front, then stop to kneel at the end of a row of pews. Thinking that they dropped something I said, "What are you looking for?"

Instead of answering, they disappeared into the pew and vanished from sight.

I started slowly walking and peering into each pew to find them. There weren't many other people there and three rows down I spied them, crouched down at the end of the row. I slipped into the pew.

"Go away. You're going to get us in trouble with Sister Alice Marie," Annie whispered.

Barb's eyes were wide, and she looked scared. Looking around to see if anyone was watching us, she said, "We never should have brought you here. Leave... please... now. My mom's gonna give it to me if she finds out what we did."

"Why? Why can't I be here? What are you afraid of? What's the matter? Who are you looking for?"

Barb and Annie popped their heads above the pew, looked around quickly, and crawled out the end.

"Don't follow us... you can't come with us," hissed Annie.

They skedaddled away.

By the time I reached the end of the row, they had disappeared completely.

When my eyes became accustomed to the soft lighting, I began to walk around the sanctuary. Tilting my head wa-a-a-y back, I looked up to the ceiling and saw all the decorations and glass that made up the dome. Wow!

Gawking at the other sights, I strolled by rows and rows of

candles, some lit, some not. I watched a woman put some money in a small wooden box next to the candles. She then took a long stick to light two of them.

I walked along the right side of the church, my footsteps echoing, and I came to three green-curtained booths. Curious, I stepped inside the first booth, which had a small wooden bench. Where I expected to see a telephone, there was a screened window with a metal grate. How odd.

Going back out and meandering further down the aisle, I came to a railing.

Behind it, a tall man in a fancy white and gold robe and a tall, pointed white hat with white flaps stood talking. I couldn't understand a word he said.

Behind him, I saw beautiful statues, rows and rows of candles glowing brightly, and a pretty tapestry hanging on one side. A huge cross hung in the center of the back wall. Beneath it, on a pedestal, was a miniature house shaped like a church. I was fascinated and continued to stare at all this.

By now, another man in a long fancy robe noticed me standing at the railing. He came up to me and whispered, "Can I help you?"

I whispered back, "What's that little house for?"

"My child, that is God's house," he said.

"It seems a little small for Him to fit in there, don't you think?"

Smiling, he leaned down to my level and said softly, "I'm Father Lynch, one of the priests." He was tall with a kind face and friendly eyes. "And what's your name, little lassie?"

"Marissa."

"Well, Marissa, how about walking with me?"

Together, we walked up the aisle toward the door.

"Who's that man in the long white robe and pointy hat, the one who's talking gobbledygook?"

Father Lynch explained that he was a Monsignor conducting the Mass in Latin.

When we reached the front doors, I said, "This is a nice church, but you have a lot of repairs to make."

"Repairs?"

"Yes, so many things are broken."

"What's broken?"

"Look at these water fountains. There's no way to get a drink. And all your phone booths are missing their phones!" I explained.

Looking slightly perplexed, he asked, "Have you never been to church?"

"This is my first time. I came with Annie and Barbara, but they disappeared. They said they had to leave me. Barb said Sister Alice Marie and her mom were going to be angry they took me here. But, I don't know why."

"Ah. And where do you go to school?"

"I go to P.S. 104, two blocks over."

"Well, since your friends have left you, why don't I walk you home?"

Walking the three blocks to my apartment building, Father Lynch asked about my family. "Where do you go to pray?"

"The 81st Street Temple. We're Jewish."

A few minutes later, we were ringing my doorbell.

Mom opened the door to see Father Lynch with me in tow. Recovering from her initial surprise, she nodded when he introduced himself.

"Please, please, come in," she said, still a little flustered, looking at me with a question on her face. "Please sit down," she motioned to the priest. "I have a fresh pot of coffee on the stove and a lemon meringue pie."

"Thank you. Sounds great," he said.

While she served the food, he began relating the afternoon's events of our meeting at church.

My mom was still getting over the shock of seeing me with a priest. Upon hearing my comments about the state of disrepair in the church, she was mortified.

"Please forgive my daughter's rude comments and behavior," she said as she poured more coffee.

Laughing, he said, "No apology is necessary. After all, she was just seeing the church through the eyes of an uninitiated child. I assure you, I don't believe for a minute she was being rude. She was honestly reporting the facts as she saw them."

With a twinkle in his eye and a grin, Father Lynch finished his pie and said it was time to leave. "I have a holy water fountain to repair."

~Margo Berk-Levine

"May I have a word?..."

Sacraments Make Me Hungry

Jesus Christ, the condescension of divinity and the exaltation of humanity.
~Phillips Brooks

t was an evening wedding during the Christmas season, elegant with poinsettias, hurricane lamps, red velvet dresses and boutonnieres. The string quartet played Purcell's stirring *Trumpet Voluntary* for the entrance procession. As the bride and groom, shaking with joy and fear, said their vows to one another, so full of gratitude for this wondrous love, I turned to my husband, Ben, and said, "I'm hungry."

He rolled his eyes. "You're always hungry at weddings."

I had to admit he was right.

The truth is, give me a bride and groom, a room full of love and hearts full of hope and I start hungering for champagne and wedding cake.

A wet and squirmy baby, newly baptized and held up to the adoring congregation, makes me think of cookies and punch and bowls of salty cashews.

I remember everything I had to eat at all the sacraments of my childhood. My baby brother's baptism party, held in our garage, had platters of Sloppy Joes and corned beef sandwiches, icy bottles of beer and pop, chips and dips and... oh, blessed of childhood memories... homemade ice cream and chocolate cake. Now that's a baptism!

Confirmation was spaghetti and meatballs, garlic bread and salad, brownies and ice cream and special Shirley Temples for the new soldiers in Christ.

But the most indelible memory is the reception our parents gave us after our First Communions. At Mass, the girls all had crisp, crinkly white dresses and the boys wore white or black suits. We carried our white missals or our tiny colored rosaries up to the altar where we knelt on soft leather as the priest placed the host on our tongues. We returned to our pews and placed our heads in our hands, doing our best to imitate the piety of our parents. And then afterward, Sister Vivian led us into the school cafeteria, now transformed with balloons and beautiful tablecloths. There were little paper cups of mints and nuts at each place, and plates of pancakes and scrambled eggs, tiny glasses of orange juice, and even cups of hot chocolate.

Ben nudged me from my caloric reverie and I watched as the bride and groom received Communion.

Suddenly I knew.

"I know why I am always hungry at weddings," I whispered to Ben. "Because the Eucharist, the mother of all sacraments, relies on food to bring us God. Food. Real bread. Real wine. Real Jesus." *For my flesh is true food and my blood is true drink* (John 6:55).

I knew it that day I walked into the transformed cafeteria, with beaming parents and sweet pancakes. I've known it after every sacramental celebration, with its punch and cookies and buffet tables and sit-down dinners.

It's all about food... real food that sustains real people, hungry for a relationship with the Real Jesus.

No wonder sacraments make me hungry. They're supposed to.

~Kathy McGovern

74

He Didn't Ask Me

And you yourself a sword will pierce so that the thoughts of many hearts
may be revealed.
~Luke 2:35

The priest moves to a position in front of us. He wants to be sure Grandma can hear. I take my mother-in-law's hand. This second memorial service was planned for her because the trip to our hometown would have been too taxing.

Determined to be strong, I focus on the statue of the Virgin Mary. She looks so serene.

The priest begins the words he hopes will bring comfort. He speaks loudly so Grandma will hear. "It's God's will that his faithful servant join him in heaven today."

"Well," I think angrily, "God hadn't asked me." My husband was far too young to die. I think of the happy times we'd never share, the graduations he would never attend, the grandchildren he'd never bounce on his knee.

My mother-in-law's shoulders shake silently.

God hadn't asked her either.

She'd often expressed her readiness to die. Why, she wondered, hadn't God taken her instead? Losing a child, I'd read, was harder than losing a husband.

For Grandma's pain, the tears I'd been holding back fill my eyes. The statue of Mary blurs. I think of Mary. God hadn't asked her if she wanted to be the mother of His son. She probably would have declined politely. After all, having a child outside of marriage then was not politically correct, and imagine how she must have felt explaining her condition to Joseph.

Had God asked, Mary would probably not have given permission for her son to die on the cross, even if His death was for the salvation of the world.

God did not ask, but Mary did not complain either. In fact, when the angel told Mary of God's plan, she said, "Be it unto me according to Thy word."

My eyes clear. I look closely at the statue of the woman who models the true faith I'll need in the weeks and months to come. The congregation is saying the Our Father. I join in... "Thy will be done."

"Please Lord," I add, "give me the strength to accept God's will."

~Ellen Javernick

75

My Son's New Job

No joy in nature is so sublimely affecting as the
joy of a mother at the good fortune of her child.
~Jean Paul Richter

Most little boys want to be firemen or cowboys when they grow up. From the time my son was eight and watched Neil Armstrong walk on the moon, he wanted to be part of NASA's space program. Twenty-five years later, I was asleep when he called to tell me his new plan.

"Mother, I've been trying to reach you for four days."

The hand that wasn't gripping the phone fumbled for the light switch. "Been gone." My voice sounded mushy. "Busy visiting people with bathrooms in surrounding towns." Des Moines was in the middle of the Flood of '93 and didn't have running water for two weeks. "Good thing your sister moved to Bondurant. I take my own towel." My mind began to clear and I plunged on with details. "A lot of businesses are closed. Restaurants in West Des Moines are open, but they serve steaks on paper plates with plastic utensils."

I continued along this life-is-tough vein until I noticed the clock and realized his call pertained to something bigger than a water shortage. For one thing, it was past ten o'clock and my son knew a late-night phone call meant a death in the family. Even worse, he called me Mother. For everyday good news, he said Mom: "Mom, I got a raise." Mother, on the other hand, preceded more serious remarks such as, "Mother, what have you done?" the time I voted for a Democrat.

So now I tensed at this call from my son, the rocket scientist. Yes, he really was one. No one at his ten-year high school class reunion believed him, especially when his friend claimed to be a brain surgeon.

"Enough about me," I said. "What's up with you?"

"Not much. Just wanted to see how you were. Oh, and I have some good news."

I sat straight up in bed, ideas bouncing around my brain. Suddenly, with a streak of motherly insight, I knew what he was going to tell me. He had a different job... the research and development one he'd had his eye on... and it was in Iowa... plus, he had a fiancée! Although his thirties were oozing away, so far he had not shared my interest in locating feminine companionship for him. While romantic details were scarce, he had promised to invite me to the wedding should one occur. So far, the closest I'd come to meeting a woman friend was the time he'd asked whether he could bring someone home for Christmas and showed up with two cats... both male. His college friends had long since married and provided their parents with grandchildren. The new graduates he befriended at work referred to him as the old guy.

"What's going on?" I asked.

"The Rockies won last night." Definitely news, but not what I had in mind. He recapped the activities of Denver's baseball team, although he knew I really didn't care unless he was telling me he'd made the squad.

I endured what seemed like hours, and was at least several minutes, before interrupting with, "Quit teasing. Anything else? Something more personal?" I thought I sounded casual.

"Let's see. Oh, I'm thinking of trading my pickup. It's either that or put in a new transmission." As he discussed the pros and cons of purchase versus repair, I got out of bed and started pacing around the room. One does not hurry an engineer.

Then while I was trying to think of a way to move the conversation past finances, he segued to the headline topic: "And I'm going to become a priest."

I stopped dead. What? Priest? Priests don't marry, and they have to work every Christmas.

"Wait a minute, honey. There's static on the line." I shook the receiver hopefully. "Now, what did you say?"

"I'm going to become a priest."

"That's what I thought you said." Glimpses of him treating lepers in South Whatever, some place with no phone system, flashed through my mind. I struggled to control my breathing. "Are you serious? I thought we discussed this before and you said religious life wasn't for you."

He sighed. "That was in the fourth grade. I've changed my mind."

"You realize you'll be forty by the time you're out of the seminary. Look, I know you don't like to decide what to wear every day and the black suit must seem appealing, but you have all those blue shirts."

"I can wear them on my day off."

I tried another tack. "You'd leave the Broncos and the Rockies?"

"I've already broken up with a girl who had season tickets behind home plate."

Girl? So close.

"Oh, honey, are you sure you're doing the right thing?"

"Yes."

"I see. Well, when you're a priest, will you move to Iowa?"

"Probably not."

"And I guess you're not getting married."

He coughed. "Hardly. What made you think I was?"

"Just an idea. Never mind."

Okay, new job but no Iowa, no engagement. One out of three...

I was being selfish. The Denver Archdiocese would assign him to a parish in Colorado, which was twelve hours away and you had to cross Nebraska to get there. I pictured myself breaking the news to his father. "You know our only son, the one we were expecting to carry on the family name? Well, guess what." And his response would be, "But he's a heck of an engineer." Perhaps I needed to reconsider the wording.

In developing a more positive spin, I found my attitude changing. Let's face it; our son's chances of finding work in Iowa had always been remote, rocket launches being in short supply here. As for a wife, why would I want to share him with someone who'd expect to spend every other holiday with her family? All any mother really wants is for her child to be happy. If he preferred sending people upward by prayer rather than rocket, then that was what I wanted too.

The clincher came when he said, "Mom, I used to pray that God didn't want me to be a priest. Now I pray that He does."

Six years later, he was ordained a Catholic priest.

By that time, I knew what a chasuble was and how to spell it. But it was at the reception following his ordination that my role became clear. As I stood in the buffet line patiently listening to one of the church ladies chastise me for being late, another volunteer asked, "Does Father liked mustard on his ham sandwich?"

"Yes," I said.

The first woman, now much friendlier, exclaimed, "You're Father's mother!"

I thought about it. "Yes, I am. It is the best thing I can be."

~Sally Jo O'Brien

"Are you gonna make your sermon on
the evils of technology available on
your podcast?"

Baptized Conditionally

Go therefore and make disciples of all nations,
baptizing them in the name of the Father, and of the Son,
and of the Holy Spirit.
~Matthew 28:19

Niki, my oldest grandchild, was baptized in the Lutheran tradition. When her brother Robert was born four years later, his family belonged to St. Joseph's Catholic Church, where he was baptized.

After many more cousins were baptized Catholic, Niki asked her pastor if she could be baptized Catholic, too. Father Joe assured Niki that the Catholic Church recognized her baptism. "One baptism for all," he quoted. "But if you really want to be baptized again, I can do it conditionally."

At her mother Kim's prompting, Niki decided we'd all think about it. My mother and I were visiting them at the time, so four generations of first-born girls gathered to address the issue.

Mom and I were raised in the pre-Vatican II church and were taught that unbaptized babies went to Limbo, so we had our babies baptized within weeks of their birth. Although that theology had changed, old beliefs die hard. Although many of the babies I saw baptized at Mass were old enough to crawl, I wanted to claim my kin for Jesus as soon as possible. Therefore, I baptized most of my sixteen grandchildren when I held them for the first time. I no longer believe it was necessary, but it was tradition.

So during our discussion of Niki's "conditional" baptism, I confessed, "You had some breathing problems when you were born, Niki. I baptized you in your mother's hospital room bathroom."

My daughter Kim looked at me in surprise. "So did I," she said. "I was afraid she wouldn't make it."

My mother said, "So did I."

"And then I was baptized in Dad's church?" Niki asked.

We nodded.

Niki looked pensive, as though pondering the fact that she is the most baptized person in our entire family. She smiled and said. "That's enough."

~Diane C. Perrone

77

And for the Others... You Sing

Look at the birds of the air, they neither sow nor reap nor gather into barns,
yet your heavenly Father feeds them.
~Matthew 6:26

One of the great works of charity of the Knights of Columbus, the largest Catholic fraternal organization in the world, is something called the "Vicarius Christi Fund," which is a $20 million endowment earmarked for the Holy Father. The interest from this fund each year is given to the Pope for his private charities.

Because of this unique relationship between the church and the Knights of Columbus, some representatives have the honor of a private audience with the Pope from time to time. Heck, $20 million will get you dinner at the Vatican.

I've sold life insurance to Knights and their families for more than thirty years and in the mid-1990s, our family had a private audience in the Vatican. Christine and I, along with my twin sons, Cory and Jason, got to meet and shake hands with the Pope in his chambers. It was a high point in my life, to say the least.

While in Rome, it coincidentally happened that a conclave of sorts was going on during our visit. Many of the American bishops, archbishops and cardinals were in Rome at the same time.

We were delighted to meet many of them at a lovely banquet hosted on one of the Seven Hills of Rome in a setting unlike any

I have ever attended. To my surprise, I met one of my old Sunday school teachers who had been a priest at St. Peter's Catholic Church in Columbia, South Carolina, where my family went to Mass every Sunday. That young priest, Father Joseph Bernardin, was now Cardinal Joseph Bernardin. He had taught many of my ten brothers and sisters while at St. Peter's, and my late parents knew his parents quite well. Still, I was surprised that he remembered the Aun name.

We were enjoying cocktails together outside the banquet chamber, under glorious trees, as the sun was setting. We shared a lovely conversation with the cardinal recalling his days at the University of South Carolina.

While talking with him, the birds came home to roost in the huge tree under which we were chatting. In the course of our conversation, one of the birds, which obviously enjoyed a bountiful day of scavenging, did what birds do when they eat their fill—it voided itself. Unfortunately, the good cardinal was right in his path.

Let the record reflect that I am a pretty quick wit and always have a comment in my hip pocket. However, you just don't tease a cardinal when a bird poops on his hat. Cardinal Bernardin felt the bird droppings hit his beanie. He reached up to see what it was and realized that he then had poop on his hand.

I didn't know where to go with this, but I knew that no confession I would ever make again would excuse me for making one of my typical off-the-cuff "poop comments." So, for once in my life, I kept my mouth shut. I did not say a word, mainly because I wanted to hear how the good cardinal was going to deal with this.

Realizing that he had been nailed by a wayward bird from above, he looked up at the tree, looked down at his hand, and then looked back up at the tree and said, "... and... for the others... you sing!"

~Michael A. Aun

78

Coloring the Road to Calvary

All history is incomprehensible without Christ.
~Ernest Renan

I hated Lent when I was a kid. Lent meant that I had to give up fudge and chocolate bars. Lent meant I had to try harder to be good so that I could color the rocky road to Calvary that the teacher handed out. Each stone stood for a good deed, a prayer or a sacrifice offered. A few kids whizzed through forty Hail Marys and colored in inches at a time. My conscience wouldn't allow me that luxury.

Lent meant that we were lined up in school by the nuns and marched over to the church for the stations of the cross, confession, or choir practice. Lent meant that it was possible when I called on a friend, her family would be on their knees saying the rosary. I would be expected to join them even though my family had just finished ours.

If we called on more friends, we could run into three, four or five rosaries a day. I considered these sacrifices, as well as prayers, and colored two stones for each... perhaps a shortcut to the Cross, but the road to Calvary was a long one.

Near the end of the season of prayer and sacrifice was a shopping trip in preparation for Easter Sunday. My sister and I would withdraw all of our money from the Credit Union, about fifteen dollars each.

We bought new dresses... Ann's pink, mine blue... shiny white shoes, new ankle socks, new white straw hats with ribbons and flowers on them, small plastic purses and white gloves. We weren't allowed to wear these things before Easter but we modeled them for anyone who came to visit.

My mother was forever reminding me that this was a holy time, and that I should be thinking about the suffering of Christ, but my mind was on my new Easter bonnet and how I'd wear my hair that day.

I went on like this for several years until our parish received a new parish priest. This priest was a Monsignor. He told us the name meant he was a special friend of the Pope. We were impressed. He was a large man with a deep voice and a talent for the dramatic. My first Way of the Cross with the Monsignor changed Lent for me. He prayed quietly at the first station and the congregation made the appropriate responses. He paused and stared at the scene.

The stations in our small chapel were plain beige plaster images of Christ's journey. I stared at them for years and saw nothing. Now the Monsignor spoke as if he were an eyewitness. As he moved from station to station, Christ became real. I saw Him fall. I felt his mother's tears. I was not alone. People wiped their eyes as this man described our Savior in words that hurt. His voice rose and fell from tragedy to tragedy.

We stared past the plaster, past the present, back in time to a tired, weakened, battered man who struggled for us.

When it was over, people left, a bit embarrassed by this show of emotion, disturbed by this man's vision, yet determined to return. So it went all that Lent. We got to know Jesus as a flesh and blood being who was afraid, betrayed, alone in his agony. We prayed with new vigor and actively looked for ways to be more Christ-like. When Monsignor read the Passion, I grieved as I would for a family member wracked by pain I could not relieve.

On Easter Sunday I went to church with my family. I felt a boundless joy. The sun shone with a new brilliance, the Easter lilies looked whiter than last year, the leaves greener. I can't remember what I wore or if I managed to get a new hat in time for the big day. I do know that for the first time the road to Calvary had been colored for me and I was truly prepared to rejoice.

~Donna D'Amour

So Far Away

The Lord will watch over your coming and going both now and forevermore...
~Psalm 121:8

The Lord seems far away at times, though I can't reason why
He was right here, just yesterday, as I was passing by
I told Him in the morning that my time was really tight
But promised I would talk with Him, sometime, perhaps that night
Yet as the shadows cast their gloom 'round evening colors deep
I barely whispered thanks to Him as I fell off to sleep

The Lord seems far away at times, the reasons: hard to say
He tried to reach me in my thoughts, but work pushed Him away
I promised Him at lunchtime I would read His Word and pray
Instead I worked right past my meal and through the rest of day
At dinnertime I bowed my head, to Him I gave a nod—
And wondered, as I watched TV, where's time to spend with God?

If God seems far away at times, the reasons are all mine
He's always there to hear my prayers, yet He must wait in line
There's time each day to talk with Him, to read His word and pray
When it seems God's not reachable, it's 'cause I walked away
He's never changed His whereabouts, His steadfastness He's proved
If God seems far away from me... it wasn't God who moved.

~Michele Dellapenta

Living Catholic faith

Lessons

Hold fast to instruction.
Never let her go; keep her,
for she is your life.

~Proverbs 4:13

80

A Cord of Three Strands

Where a lone man may be overcome,
two together can resist.
A three-ply cord is not easily broken.
~Ecclesiastes 4:12

When my husband and I were married, there were several things we didn't see eye to eye on. The fact that he was of one political party, and I another, was challenging. We both wanted to sleep on the left side of the bed. I liked modern furnishings and he liked Chippendale. But the single most difficult challenge facing us was finding a balance spiritually.

Ryan had grown up attending church every Sunday, rain or shine. My family, while spiritual in their own way, had not been active churchgoers.

"I think it's important for us to go to church as a family," he often told me. "When we have kids I want that to be a part of their life, too."

"Why do we have to go to church to be religious?" I argued. "Can't we be spiritual at home?"

"It's not the same," he'd say. "When you go to church you are a part of a larger community. It's important to me."

I thought long and hard about the dilemma. I knew how important it was to my new husband and I wanted him to feel fulfilled and happy. I grudgingly agreed to give church a try. But after several weeks of attending his childhood church I felt unsatisfied.

"Look," I told him bluntly one Sunday after service had ended. "I want to do this with you. I want to make this a priority, but can we look for a church together? Can we try something different? I know this is the church you grew up in, but are you willing to go out on a limb for me and try a different denomination?"

In a testament to his commitment to me, he readily agreed to go church shopping.

Over the next couple of years we were sheep without a flock. We attended services of every shape and size. Lutheran, Methodist, Baptist, non-denominational, Congregational, Presbyterian... you name it, we tried it. Along the way we met many wonderful people, and yet we still hadn't found a church family to call our own.

One day, while running errands in the city we had recently moved to, I saw a sign in front of a church.

"Interested In Becoming Catholic? RCIA Classes Forming Now!"

Hmm, we hadn't tried a Catholic church. I'd never thought about it. In fact I was pretty sure that you had to be born Catholic. Who ever heard of anyone converting to Catholicism?

"What about the Catholic Church?" I asked Ryan at dinner that evening. "Maybe we should try it out."

"Don't you have to be born Catholic?" he asked. "And don't they have really complicated services? Kneeling and standing and saying things in other languages? I want to be able to understand what I'm hearing."

"I don't know for sure," I admitted. "But I could at least call and find out about these RCIA classes they're advertising. What have we got to lose?"

The next day, I called the church and spoke to the priest. He was a very gentle soul, easy to talk to and not intimidating as I'd imagined priests could be. He encouraged us to attend Mass the coming weekend and see what we thought.

On Sunday, Ryan and I snuck into the church just as Mass began, and hid in the very last pew. At first it seemed a little confusing. We tried to watch the parishioners around us and take their cues as to when to kneel, stand, etc. We were pleased to hear that the entire service was in English and found the priest's homily to be very enlightening.

Soon after that Sunday morning, we jumped headfirst into the RCIA program. The people we met during those weekly classes were amazing and one couple became our closest friends. It was like a new chapter in our lives had begun. The discussions and insights at RCIA classes on Wednesday night were the highlight of our weeks. We felt like we'd found a home away from home. And suddenly I began to understand why this had been so important to my husband.

On the night of the Easter Vigil, we sat in the front row of the packed church and awaited our turns to be blessed by the priest and become full members of the Roman Catholic Church.

Right before my husband's name was called, I leaned into him and whispered into his ear, "I feel closer to you now than I ever have before. Thank you for pushing me out of my comfort zone and allowing me to see how important it is to make a place for God in my heart."

He could've said "I told you so," or something equally snide. But instead he kissed me gently and smiled at me. And in that instant I knew that the author of Ecclesiastes was so right; "A chord of three strands is not quickly broken."

The fabric of our marriage became so much stronger that holy night before Easter. And though the journey was long and sometimes frustrating, I am so glad my husband insisted we travel it together, to find the third cord that bound our marriage in faith.

~Emily Weaver

81

Father McKeever's Lesson

Beware, so as long as you live,
of judging men by their outward appearance.
~Jean de LaFontaine

I remember Nancy. We were both in second grade. I was the "smart" one; she was the "dumb" one, or so I thought. I made life a living hell for that poor girl, and she just took it. Gentle and shy, Nancy was about eleven years old, and it had taken her years to reach second grade. She had difficulty reading and writing. All the kids made fun of her, especially me. Nancy would just stand there, avoiding my eyes, tears rolling down her cheeks. Cruel and clever, I manipulated the crowd so that the taunts of the audience would increase Nancy's misery and shame.

We called her "Stupid." "Ugly!" "Smelly!" "Dirty!" Nancy never fought back, which was a riot to her tormentors.

Then one day, everything changed. I went to a Bible class and Nancy was there sitting by herself in the back of the room. The Bible story was about the trial of Jesus, who had been sent to King Herod. The story went on and Father McKeever, who taught the class, became quite animated, in his wonderful Irish fashion.

He told us how the Son of God was spat on, beaten, and kicked. Father McKeever made us wince as he described the crown of thorns being pushed and pounded into the flesh and bone of our Lord's skull. I could feel the nails piercing His wrists and feet. Then Father repeated the mocking words that had been hurled at the "Holy Innocent."

Father paused for a moment, his eyes filled with tears, and he looked at Nancy in the back of the room, all alone, her head bowed. A look of intense sorrow passed over his features; and then his eyes were on me. Steel blue points pierced mine. I felt as if I were the only one in the room, and this decent kind man of God was speaking only to me.

"How would it feel to be all alone and innocent, I wonder?" he asked, softly, in his rich Irish brogue. "How would it feel to be hauled in front of your enemies, dirty and unloved, with no one to protect you?" Tears sprung to my eyes, because at seven years old, I loved Jesus only a little more than I loved Father McKeever.

I understood the message immediately. I was overwhelmed. I looked back at Nancy in her tattered clothes, covered with dirt that I had helped to smear on her face. I felt shame.

It seemed as though everyone else missed the point that pierced my heart that day. I suddenly saw myself in Herod's courtyard, mocking and striking... Jesus! In my mind's eye, I saw Him lift His head and look at me. My seven-year-old heart broke. I sat there stunned for a moment, and then I gathered my things. I stood up and walked to the back of the room. I pulled a chair up next to Nancy and sat down. With hands shaking and the most incredible sorrow in my heart, I reached over and took Nancy's hand. She looked at me, her eyes round and her mouth in the shape of an "O."

"Nancy," I began, my voice breaking, "I want you to be my friend... my best friend."

Nancy looked at me for a long time. The room was silent. I noticed that her eyes were an incredible shade of blue, framed with lovely, dark lashes. She smiled, her lips framing perfect white teeth. Why, Nancy was pretty!

After that day, I tripped over myself to become Nancy's friend and protector. I spent the rest of that year with skinned knees, bruises and a few bloody noses. We moved away at the end of the following summer. I never saw Nancy or Father McKeever again, but they have lived in my heart, ever since.

Nancy taught me forgiveness, and Father McKeever taught me redemption.

~Jaye Lewis

82

Mother Superior

Blessed is the influence of one true loving human soul on another.
~George Eliot

The black-clad figure with the wide white wimple ruled the classroom with unquestioned authority. As she spoke, her first-grade charges sat up straight behind the well-worn wooden desks in neat rows of ten. In their pressed navy jumpers and starched white shirts with Peter Pan collars, the girls were quiet and well behaved as they waited for the school bell to signal the end of the day.

Since the desks were assigned according to carefully calibrated height measurements, the diminutive little girl in the first seat in the first row was the shortest by far. Nervously twirling her strawberry blond hair, she was worried about the homework that Mother Superior was about to distribute. The diligent student was already spending hours each night on the worksheets designed to drill the lessons of the day into the first-graders' tiny heads.

Mother Superior gave the littlest girl ten papers and moved on to the next row, and the next, and the next, until all the papers were distributed. As the school bell rang, the young pupils filled their book bags and lined up to say goodbye to their teacher. Filing out of the classroom, the smallest girl ran into her mother's arms and walked home to their apartment.

After school, children of all ages spilled out onto the concrete streets and played spirited games of Double Dutch, Hopscotch, and

Ace-King-Queen. As dusk set in, moms up and down the block leaned out apartment windows and chanted familiar refrains summoning their youngsters home for dinner. The little girl joined the groups of exhausted kids and reluctantly headed inside. After washing her hands, she dragged a kitchen chair over to her mother's side at the big, white enamel oven to help her prepare the family meal.

With dinner over all too soon, it was time for the dreaded homework to begin. The first-grader's mother was becoming increasingly concerned about the ten pages of homework that her little angel was getting each night. Since she didn't have older children, she couldn't determine if this was normal for this grade, but she was worried that it was excessive for such young children.

Despite her daughter's pleas not to speak with Mother Superior and get her in trouble, the concerned mother marched into the first-grade classroom the next morning and asked for a quiet word with the teacher. Observing her mother with the nun, the little girl was puzzled to see them smiling as they concluded their chat. Waving a cheery goodbye, the mom promised to pick up her daughter promptly at 3:00.

Throughout the day, the young girl paid close attention to the reading, writing and arithmetic lessons. As the big hand on the clock slowly made its way to the number twelve and the little hand inched towards the three, Mother Superior approached the first desk in the first row with the usual ten homework sheets. The nun handed the worksheets to her smallest student, who respectfully bent her head and obediently accepted the pile. Before moving on to the next row, Mother Mary leaned in and whispered, "Take only one, dear. You're supposed to pass the other nine to the girls behind you."

~Pamela Hackett Hobson

Halloween, 1958

What gift has Providence bestowed on man that is so dear to him
as his children?
~Cicero

The September my parents enrolled me at Saint John Kanty School marked my entrance into a spiritual world inhabited by Jesus and Mary, downy-winged angels, and haloed women and men called saints. I was enthralled, like Lucy stumbling through that wardrobe in *The Chronicles of Narnia*. Best of all was the new stuff to collect: rosary beads of every color, medals, prayer books, and holy pictures of all the saints. My assortment of holy pictures rivaled the size of my brother's collection of baseball cards.

Early that October, Sister handed out a white memo, still damp and fragrant from the mimeograph machine, outlining plans for a Halloween party. Calling it a "Come as a Saint" party would be more accurate, as the Sisters put the accent on the All Hallows rather than the unholy ghosts.

I returned home breathless that day. "Mom, we're having a Halloween party and I have to dress like a saint!" I pranced around the kitchen excitedly. "Who can I be, Mom? Where will we get a costume?"

"You decide who you want to be, and I'll make the costume,"

replied Mom. "It'll be easy. All you will need is a long dress with wide open sleeves."

"And a veil!" I interjected, draping a tea towel over my head. "Like the Blessed Mother! Ooh! That's who I'll be!"

That Saturday, Dad drove us to Kresge's Five and Ten, where we bought two pieces of cotton broadcloth, one in the traditional Blessed Mother blue and the other in white. While I was in school, Mom and her Singer sewing machine tackled the project. I checked her progress daily and grew more excited as Halloween drew closer.

October 31st dawned gold and crisp. The party was scheduled for after lunch; the fact that we got any schoolwork done that morning should be declared a miracle. At noon we went home to gobble down lunch and assume our saintly identities.

Mom had a cream cheese sandwich and the costume ready. The veil lay flat on the bed, and the blue dress hung safely in the closet where her ironing job would not be spoiled.

"Wash and dry your hands well," Mom cautioned. "You don't want to mess the costume before we even get to the party."

When my hands and face were clean and dry, I took off my uniform. Mom slid the blue dress over me and tied a white sash around my waist. She combed my brown hair, set the veil on my head, and secured it with bobby pins at my temples. Two side curls spit out on either side of my face. From the mirror, a Blessed Mother with a pixie haircut stared back at me.

"Am I ready? Can we go?" I asked.

"In a minute," answered Mom. "We have a finishing touch. We can't forget the Baby Jesus," she said, as my arms received my Betsy Wetsy baby doll swaddled in cloth left over from the veil. I held the bundle close to my heart, just the way the Blessed Mother did in one of my holy pictures.

Mom and I smiled confidently at each other and then walked the two blocks to the church auditorium, which was decorated with orange and black crepe paper, pumpkins, black cats, and, most importantly, tables laden with cider, cupcakes, and enough candy to sate or sicken every one of us.

The children wowed and oohed at each other, while the moms sized up the competition for the costume judging. We quieted when the PTA president stepped up to the microphone. "Attention! Children, form a circle. When the music starts, march around the room. If a judge taps your shoulder, go to the middle of the circle. Everyone keep marching until the music stops."

The stylus of the record player sizzled for a second before Mitch Miller and company belted out, "Oh, When the Saints Go Marching In." Sister signaled, and a seven-year-old Saint Joseph sporting brown burlap and a burnt cork beard took the first steps. A cardboard-mitered Saint Patrick followed, with a staff fashioned from a broom handle. Saint Cecilia, patron of musicians, plinked a xylophone, while Jesus, in white toga and red cloak, displayed red marks in the middle of his palms. "Think those are mercurochrome?" one of the angels asked as three feathers defected from her wings. Michael the Archangel unsheathed his sword. A number of Blessed Mothers marched that day, but the moms spaced them out so they all could receive their due. A fireman and three cowboys brought up the rear.

A PTA mom tapped my shoulder and nudged me to the circle of semifinalists.

The music stopped, replaced by murmurs and tense glances of those awaiting judgment. Cheers rose when the emcee declared Saint Patrick as third place winner and Jesus as second. She interrupted the din with "First prize goes to..." A few seconds later, I recognized my name. Pats on the back propelled me to the stage amid acclaim and applause. We winners basked in our glory and accepted the prizes, pictures of our guardian angels for our bedroom walls.

In the middle of the crowd, Mom clapped her hands widely, her eyes sparkling. She never looked as happy as at that moment when she stood savoring our shared victory. Struggling to hold the prize and Baby Jesus, I ran to her, and her arms simultaneously hugged me and rescued Him from an imminent fall to the floor.

Heading towards us was my teacher, Sister Azaria, looking pleased with the parade of saints. Only a teacher could find a lesson in those events, but it is an invaluable one for someone taking the first step... or the hundredth... towards the kingdom of God.

"Dorothy," said she, "other girls dressed like the Blessed Mother, but only you brought the Baby Jesus. Always remember that."

~Dorothy LaMantia

84

Confession Anxiety

In praising or loving a child, we love and praise not that which is, but that which we hope for.
~Goethe

The mysticism associated with Catholic rituals awed me to no end during my youth in the late 1950s. The stern demeanor of the priests and nuns during that period, accompanied by the solemn nature of the holy sacraments, were close to overpowering for a young boy. This was especially the case for a young orphan with an overzealous outlook on life Monday through Saturday, who was then expected to be pious enough to receive the sacrament of Holy Communion on Sunday. But, in order to receive Communion, one had to cleanse himself by confessing his sins prior to Mass.

To this young Irish Catholic lad of eight, the thought of entering a small dark closet and pouring my guts out to an unseen, but all-powerful, priest on the other side of a thin wall was daunting.

In the weeks leading up to my First Communion, the nuns at my Saturday morning catechism class prepared us in the proper way to confess our sins, a prerequisite for our First Communion. As with most Catholic procedures, protocol was very important. In fact, the senior nun arranged a series of "dry runs" just to make sure each of us understood the sequence of things to say while inside the confessional. The only point of the entire experience that seemed "ad-libbed" was when you actually stated your sins. During the mock rehearsals, with the nuns playing the role of priests in a makeshift classroom confessional, one can imagine how creative these "unofficial" sins could be.

At last, the big day the nuns had drilled us for finally arrived... the real confession in a real confessional with a real priest!

I arrived at the church early that Sunday morning for my first confession before Mass. There were about a dozen parishioners already standing in a line along the inside wall of the church, waiting for their turn. Since my town was home to only 853 people, I recognized several of the folks in line. There was Mr. Cox, the local television repair man, and Ray, the barber. I was amazed to see the town's librarian, Mrs. Dillard, in line. What possible sins did she have to confess?

I took my place in the queue behind the town cop, Chief O'Callan. I barely recognized him in a brown suit and tie, compared to his blue lint-laden uniform. All those in line stood in solemn silence, with their heads bowed and hands clasped in front of their waists. Each person shuffled about three steps forward as the one at the front took his or her two minutes in the confessional.

As the line of sinners progressed, so did my anxiety. I kept going over the procedures and my rehearsed lines. "Bless me father, for I have sinned..." I also kept silently repeating the words of the Act of Contrition prayer, as I always stumbled on it in catechism class, to the dismay of the nuns. "Oh, my God, I am heartily sorry for..." For what? What came next? Anxiety mounted. Would I remember what I had to say? Would I remember what sins I needed to report? Would I reach my turn in the confessional before I hit puberty?

When there were only a couple of people in front of me, I saw something for the first time that wasn't part of our rehearsals. Each time a person entered the sinner side of the confessional, a small yellowish exposed light bulb came on over the heavy dark velvet curtain. I noticed the bulb stayed illuminated until just before the person exited the confessional. I quickly surmised this was in fact, an indicator to the rest of the parishioners that the confessional was occupied. The nuns hadn't said a word about this, but I made a mental note to remember to find the light switch as soon as I got inside that small cubicle. I wouldn't want anyone entering by mistake when I was in the middle of my confession. More anxiety, in addition to everything else that morning. Would I find the switch? Where was it? How would I turn it on?

Just then, red-faced and looking repentant, Chief O'Callan emerged from the confessional. I realized his confession had lasted about three times longer than anyone else. His bowed posture made me think his penance must be to say 400 rosaries and make a couple of trips to Lourdes.

It was my turn!

I couldn't even feel my feet as I advanced to the confessional and pulled the heavy curtain back. Blackness was everywhere except for a small purple glow about the size of a book cover emitting from what I guessed was the wall separating the priest from the sinner.

Gathering my wits within the strange dominion of the confessional, I remembered the exterior light bulb. I had to get that illuminated before I got down to the confession procedures.

I began running my hand up and down—first to the left inside the darkened wall, and then to the right, searching in vain for the light switch. With no results, I started waving my hands madly overhead in an attempt to find a pull-string for the light. Just as I was panicking with the thought I might be too short to reach a string from the ceiling, a rather frustrated sounding, deep male voice slowly asked, "What are you doing, my son?"

"I'm looking for the light switch, Father," I answered nervously.

There was a long minute of silence followed by an audible sigh coming from the other side of the purple opening. "Please kneel in front of the screen, my son. The light outside will come on automatically!"

What a relief.

Now, if I could just get through that Act of Contrition.

~Thomas L. Reilly

85

Catholics Don't Drink...

As are families, so is society.
~William Makepeace Thayer

Growing up in the Washington, D.C. suburbs in the 1950s, there were two things we knew for sure about our family: we were Catholic and we were Union.

My dad, Jimmy Noonan, was an Irishman with beautiful burnt sienna-colored hair and a ready twinkle in his eye. He was very committed to our Catholic parish and to their grammar school that my brothers and I attended. Dad was a member of the Holy Name Society, the men's prayer and service group. He also did a huge amount of electrical work for the church and school without taking any pay for it. While my mom, Juanita, a spirited, dark-haired stay-at-home mom, took great care of us three kids and the house, Dad worked hard as a union electrician and as an active member of the International Brotherhood of Electrical Workers' Local #26. On many an evening, Dad came home, greasy and tired from a hard day's work that had begun at 5:00 A.M. Yet he would jump in the shower, down a quick dinner, and head out for an important meeting at the local union hall. Dad always said, "We all have to do our part."

Since Jimmy Noonan was such a committed union man, he insisted that whenever any union, no matter what kind, was on strike against a company or organization, our family would not buy the product or service made by that company until the strike was resolved. It was our whole family's way of "doing our part."

When I was about seven and my brother, Billy, was five, there was an extended union strike against Coca Cola, so we became a Pepsi-only family during that long period.

One crisp autumn Sunday, some family friends called to say they would like to stop by our house for a visit later in the day. In the '50s, people often went "a visitin'" on Sunday afternoons for a nice family outing to stay connected with family and friends. Mom and I had gone to an earlier Mass, so Mother asked Dad to stop by a small local delicatessen and pick up some sodas for our guests on his way home from church.

When Dad and Billy arrived, all of the parking spaces were taken. My father pulled up close to the door, handed five-year-old Billy some money and told him to go in and get the sodas. Dad said he would be right in, as soon as a parking spot opened up. When Dad finally got into the store, the owner had the most puzzled look on his face. He told my father, "I am so glad you came in; your son has me confused. He told me he needed some colas and so I brought these up." The merchant pointed to the container of Cokes. "When I showed these to your son and started to take his money, he quickly pulled the money back and said, 'Oh no, sir. We can't drink Coke. We're Catholic.'"

~Nancy Noonan

" I CAN'T EAT QUAKER OATS. I'M A CATHOLIC."

86

David's Gift

The heart of the giver makes the gift dear and precious.
~Martin Luther

I grew up in the neighborhood by the railroad tracks in Fort Dodge, Iowa. In this particular area, there was a long stretch of property overgrown with scrub trees, ragweed and discarded sidewalk slabs left by a local contractor. The drainage ditches on both sides of the tracks usually had a small amount of flowing water, a great place for catching tadpoles and crawdads. This area, stretching a couple of hundred yards and up to the wooden bridge over the railroad tracks was known to all neighborhood kids as the Jungle.

It was a great place for kids to play and let their imaginations roam pretty much unfettered or bothered by adults. We dug tunnels, built forts, rigged booby-traps against real and imagined intruders. We learned how to catch crayfish, pollywogs, frogs and lightning bugs, and an occasional snake or two.

We cut down the small saplings to make homemade bows and arrows. It was a perfect place to play cowboys and Indians or Jungle Jim, another movie hero.

By the time I was in third grade, my friend David and I would walk and talk and daydream like all young kids do. We wanted to graduate from cap guns to Daisy BB rifles, but our parents wouldn't let us. We both coveted the Hopalong Cassidy bike because it came with the best stuff: battery-powered headlights, a deluxe seat that resembled a saddle, handle grips with multi-colored plastic tassels, a big Hopalong Cassidy name plate, a Daisy BB Gun in a big sheath holster, and then the crowning touch... dual matching saddle bags with pictures of Hopalong Cassidy on the side.

We spent a lot of time discussing these and other weighty problems of the day, like who was the better hero, the Lone Ranger and his silver bullets, or Straight Arrow and his fabulous Cave of Gold. Straight Arrow won pretty much because he was an honest-to-goodness Native American, and it was widely believed in our circle that all Indians were pure of heart. We all knew pure of heart was better. Sister St. Zita, at Sacred Heart Elementary School, had told us this, and we would never doubt her. Everyone knew that you only doubted Sister St. Zita at your own peril. If she said it, it must be so, case closed, end of discussion.

Now Sister St. Zita was reputed to be a really tough nun, and most kids in the first and second grades dreaded moving up to her third-grade class. Many of us had spent the entire second-grade year praying that she would be transferred, to no avail of course.

Fortunately, for us, Sister St. Zita's bark or reputation was worse than her bite. Almost none of us ever got our knuckles rapped with the metal edge of her ever-present ruler, and we only occasionally had our ear lobes tugged to keep us in line.

One day, while on our way home from school, David had exciting news. His dad was getting him the Hopalong Cassidy bike, full-sized saddlebags and all! Wow, I was stunned! The only one anyone could remember seeing was the display model at Sears Roebuck. Excitement reigned supreme; all of us kids were almost as excited as David. When was he going to get it? We couldn't wait.

Sears said it should be delivered in three to four weeks.

After two weeks of agonizing waiting, David announced that the bike had arrived at Sears and would be picked up when his family returned from their weekend trip.

The night before their return, I had a life-like dream with David in it. In the dream, David had the Hopalong Cassidy bike and we were examining it and testing it out on the wooden bridge. It was a magnificent bike, and we spent a long time with it. But it was getting late, and David had to go home. He took off over the top of the bridge and out of sight. I started to take the short cut through the Jungle, when I noticed that David had left the bike behind. I grabbed the bike and raced up to the top of the bridge, all the while yelling for David to come back. As I reached the top, my progress was halted because the middle section of the bridge was missing. David reappeared from the other side and asked, "Why'd you call me back?"

"Your bike," I shouted. "You left it behind, but now part of the bridge is missing, and I can't get it over to you."

"I have to go now," David replied. "I'm really late!"

"But I could run it down the path at the side of the bridge and up the other side. I'll meet you at the corner," I called.

I started to move swiftly to complete the task but David stopped me. "I have to go now. I'm late, can't wait. My father will be mad, gotta go."

"But your bike?" I said. "What about your bike?"

"You keep it Rich, you keep it. My father will get me another one." With that he waved goodbye and ran off home.

I never saw David alive again. It turned out that the weekend trip was because David needed a heart operation. He died during that surgery.

In class the next morning, Sister St. Zita told us she had an announcement. She had a melancholy smile on her usually stern-looking face. "David won't be with us anymore. He has gone to live with God in heaven." She led us in prayer for David, and the rest of the day seemed like a big blur.

Later in the day, the class was marched in line to the funeral home. We were greeted by David's father, a solemn man, who led us in prayer for David. How that man could look at all of our inquiring eyes without breaking down, I'll never know.

Some days after the funeral, I started to go over to David's house. I felt that there was a certain bond between his dad and me, and I wanted him to know how much David meant to me, and how much I missed him.

Then there was the matter of the bike... hadn't David given it to me? I was only a third-grader, for goodness sakes. What did I know?

As I approached David's house, it occurred to me that these people most assuredly had no idea he had given me the bike from "beyond." So I rode my bike on by and went on home. I wouldn't miss the Hopalong Cassidy bike... I missed my friend.

~Richard J. Mueller

87

Never Walk a Road That Doesn't Lead to Your Heart

Humor is anger taking one step back.
~John R. Powers

ister Lee was the most vicious, violent, intimidating human being I had ever known. On the day I started eighth grade, she was about a billion years old. At that time, the Catholic schools had a rather unique retirement system. It was called "Death."

Sister Lee was three feet tall and getting shorter every day.

We children feared Sister Lee more than we feared God. We believed in God.

We had met Sister Lee.

She was a legend among us kids. To this day, you can go into my old neighborhood, walk into a tavern, step up to the bar, and announce, "Sister Lee taught me eighth grade," and people will begin buying you drinks.

When I first walked into my eighth grade classroom, I expected to see autumn leaves on the bulletin board or cutouts of children playing on swings. Not Sister Lee. She believed in the power of words. On the bulletin board, the very first day, were the words, "Discipline is remembering what I wanted." Every week, there would be a new proverb. I don't remember all of them but a couple of the others were,

"Idiocy is doing the same thing over and over and expecting different results," and "The Lord's coming. Look busy."

During the school day, Sister Lee might point to the proverb on the bulletin board and ask you how those words were enriching your life. If you could not give a good answer, your life might come to a sudden and abrupt end.

You did not want to annoy Sister Lee. No one ever did it twice.

Each proverb spent a week on the bulletin board except for the last one, which went up there in mid-April and stayed until the end of the school year. "Never walk a road that doesn't lead to your heart."

The last day of eighth grade; the books had been collected and the papers turned in. We were sitting in our desks just running out the clock. A student asked Sister Lee, "Sister, why do we have to go to school?" That was a very bold question to present to a nun, particularly this one. We held our breaths fearing a final explosion.

Sister Lee thought about it a moment and then replied. "I don't know the purpose of school. But I do know the purpose of education. It's to set you free..." she pointed to the phrase on the bulletin board, "...so you can walk the road that leads to your heart."

As a kid, Sister Lee was the kind of teacher who you would go blocks out of your way to avoid when you saw her walking down the street. But when you grew up and came back, she was the very first person you looked for.

After I'd written four bestselling novels and the Broadway musical, *Do Patent Leather Shoes Really Reflect Up?*, I drove back to the old neighborhood and parked across the street from the school. At three o'clock, the kids came out. A little while later, all the teachers but Sister Lee came out. As the neighborhood was growing dark, the door creaked opened and out hobbled Sister Lee.

She must have been five billion years old by now and an inch and a half tall.

I walked up to her. "Sister Lee, do you remember me?"

She stared up.

"I'm John Powers. You taught me eighth grade."

Finally, she smiled. "Oh, yes... John Powers. I'm sorry. All grades are final."

~John R. Powers

88

Treasure Beyond First Prize

Correction does much, but encouragement does more.
~Goethe

Squeezing his six-foot, one-hundred-seventy-pound frame into a desk designed for an eighth-grader looked uncomfortable, but Paul never complained. Or maybe he did. The bits of broken English he offered as conversation were often impossible to understand. The solution, of course, for his fellow classmates, was to shout at him s-l-o-w-l-y, and c-l-e-a-r-l-y. We discovered none too quickly that volume and clarity, even in slow motion, had no bearing on Paul's level of understanding. The prominent furrow in his forehead and his bewildered look gave testament to the fact that most of the time, he didn't have a clue.

Paul D'Orazio arrived in America from a small town in northern Italy. His sparkling dark eyes and friendly smile, under a crop of thick shiny black hair, drew us to him immediately. He was thirteen then, and assigned to the fifth grade by some mysterious process the principal at Holy Cross School did not share with the rest of the class. If he felt out of place, he didn't show it. He was warm, genuine, and very good-natured when someone occasionally poked fun at him.

Though Paul didn't understand much about our language, our classwork, our games, or our music, when Sister Frances Patrice started and ended the day by making the Sign of the Cross, he never failed to reverently bow his head and fold his hands in prayer. As hard as he tried, Paul never really caught on or caught up with the rest of us.

Then one day in eighth grade, Sister Frances Patrice announced an art contest for which we were expected to create a model of a musical instrument. When she tacked up the poster on the corkboard and explained the details, I noticed Paul perk up in his seat.

After school, as I finished my turn at erasing the blackboard, I noticed Paul studying the poster. Sister walked over to him and traced around the musical instruments with her finger. "Can you make one of these Paul?" she asked.

His eyes flipped from Sister to the poster and back. Immediately Paul began to nod his head with the speed of a bobblehead doll. "Does he really understand?" I wondered. With one final nod Paul said clearly, "Okay! Can do." He had eight weeks to make good on his promise.

On the day of the contest, Sister set up a folding table and asked each of us to explain our individual items as we placed them on display. One by one the expected collection of *papier maché* and construction paper *objets d'art* made their way out of paper sacks and cardboard boxes to a spot on the display table.

Paul was last. Slowly he walked to the front of the class carrying a large, flat, cardboard box, which he set down on the crowded display table. Without fanfare, he opened the box and gingerly lifted out his project for the class to see. Then he said in perfect English, "Guitar." And a guitar it was, only not one fashioned from poster board and school paste. This guitar, every inch of it, was hand crafted. Its smooth wooden body was the product of incredible creativity and skill. The room fell silent and a worried look replaced the smile on Paul's face. Timidly he presented it to us saying, almost in a whisper, "You like?"

Oh, how the thunder of applause, stomping feet and cheering voices broke the silence that had settled over the class upon our first glimpse of Paul's amazing guitar. Sister Frances Patrice swished up the aisle toward him, her rosary beads and leather-soled shoes clicking and tapping in synchronized rhythm.

She wrapped her arms around Paul and hugged him, the exact way Annie Sullivan hugged Helen Keller in *The Miracle Worker*. Paul's triumphant smile spoke volumes, as now he held aloft his work of art with pride. All barriers had been broken.

Many years have passed since that day in the eighth grade when, hands down, Paul had won first prize for his beautiful handmade guitar.

Just the other day I looked out my office window and watched as a white van with bright red lettering rolled down the street. The letters on the side of the van shouted s-l-o-w-l-y and c-l-e-a-r-l-y, "Paul D'Orazio—Carpenter and Cabinet Maker."

~Annmarie B. Tait

A Eucharistic Experience

Come to me all you who labor and are burdened and I will give you rest.
~Matthew 11:28

It was December 24, 1961, midnight Mass, one of the most joyous celebrations in the liturgical calendar. Why was I trying to convince myself that I should remain in the choir loft at Communion and deprive myself of the precious Body and Blood of Jesus Christ? My misery and pain were standing in the way of my wanting to go to Communion.

Following a routine bone graft, there had been months of frequent surgeries and long hospital stays, leaving me with uncontrollable infections in the wound. The end of treatment came on the day my doctor said the words no one wants to hear, "I cannot do anything else to help you. You'll just have to live with it."

"It" was a swollen, angry red foot that had a three-inch round hole eroded in the side and a frozen ankle that did not bend at all. This created a deep limp resembling a pumping motion when I walked. I could not stand to wear a regular shoe so I wore a canvas tennis shoe split all the way down to the rubber toe to allow room for the swelling. The worst of it all was being in pain all day, every day, and sometimes throughout the night.

The hospital and doctor bills had financially devastated us, and there was no money to buy more than one pair of canvas shoes, so the pair I wore was slightly soiled. Definitely, there was no money to buy festive holiday clothing to wear to the midnight Mass.

My return to our church choir, following my extended illness, had been an effort as I tried to rekindle my connection with God and with my church. My faith had become shaky due to pain, disappointment, worry, and having my whole life turned upside down. I felt God had all but abandoned me. I had gone to confession to prepare for the holiday season and was determined to participate, as I always had in the past. I had attended all the choir rehearsals and I was ready, or so I thought.

Christmas Eve arrived and, as always, the church was filled to capacity, and then some. As I entered the church, the smell of incense filled the air, combined with perfumes belonging to the many ladies wearing their beautiful furs, hats, and holiday best.

Although the stairs were a struggle, I welcomed the chance to disappear to the choir loft where I couldn't be seen by the congregation. I wore my gray and blue plaid wool skirt and a light blue sweater. These were the best I had and, of course, my feet were clad in my slightly-soiled, slit to the toe, canvas tennis shoes. But, it really didn't matter, no one would see me.

We sang the half-hour Christmas program we had been rehearsing for the past few weeks and the lovely joyous music penetrated my very being. I was caught up in the celebration and feeling very good when the Mass began. As we progressed toward the Communion part of the Mass, my stomach began to feel queasy and my heart was beating faster. Panic was setting in and clouding my concentration. I could not bear the thought of limping pitifully all the way down the center aisle to the Communion rail wearing my plain clothes and split tennis shoe. I quickly decided I would just stay in the choir loft and let everyone else go without me. I would be safe. I started to feel a little less nauseated.

Suddenly, another feeling surged over me—a longing so great I could not ignore it. I desperately wanted to receive the Eucharist. I needed to receive the Eucharist. The internal struggle was overwhelming; my fear of being stared at and pitied, battling with my desire to receive the Body and Blood of Jesus Christ. I was singing, but my mind was whirling out of control. Then, I heard myself saying the words aloud, "Lord, I am not worthy to receive you, but only say the word and I shall be healed."

It was time to go to Communion.

I sat frozen for an instant. All at once, I stood, started toward the stairs, down the center aisle, and toward the Communion rail. I walked, looking down at the floor and wishing I could vanish upward like the smoke from the incense. I fought back tears. I could feel heads turn and stares falling on me, like arrows from an archer's bow, as I limped down the aisle to where Father was distributing the Host. I looked up as he said, "Body of Christ." My response, "Amen," was loud and clear. Suddenly, I felt a warm feeling spreading over my whole being as I turned to go back to the choir loft. I suddenly felt different. I felt wonderful. I felt joy.

My journey back up the center aisle was not the same as it was coming down. I was still dressed the same, my gait was the same pumping motion, but this time my head was held high and I looked into the eyes of the people kneeling along the aisle as I walked. I felt great inside and out. The pain was lessened by this new feeling of peace and joy deep inside.

My life changed dramatically that night. I was no longer plagued by worry about what I wore or how I walked, nor did I let the relentless pain keep my mind from seeing what was really important in my life. God made me realize that my suffering wasn't from being poor or physically afflicted, but from my foolish pride and my own self-pity. God took away my feelings of sorrow and misery and gave me a renewed spirit to bear up under my hardships and go on living my life in a more spiritual way.

The Blessed Infant truly gave me a wonderful and lasting gift. The joy and true meaning of Christmas had settled in my soul and, from that night on, it was there to stay.

–Joyce Sudbeck

Faith

But let him ask in faith,
with no doubting, for he who doubts
is like a wave of the sea driven and tossed by the wind.

~James 1:6

The Boy

And the prayer of the faith will save the sick person,
and the Lord will raise him up.
~James 5:15

young boy lay in the critical care ward of Children's Hospital in Denver. He was thin and weak from years of struggling with uncontrolled asthma and chronic bronchitis. Even though he had been wasting away for years, he had never quit fighting for every breath. Now a severe case of pneumonia was taking away what little strength he had left. He lay in his oxygen tent listening to the muffled voices of those who came to visit him. He'd joke with his parents and tell them the worst part of being in the plastic enclosure was that it made the toast soggy, but he could see even through the foggy plastic that it was taking its toll on them, too. As he got sicker, he joked less, sat up less, and heard less of what was going on around him.

One morning, as his parents sat by his bedside, the boy's doctor came in and whispered something to them. What the young boy couldn't hear was that the hospital staff had done everything they could, but the pneumonia was winning. The doctor suggested they call a priest. Soon a man in clerical dress was standing next to the boy's bed. He pulled up the side flap of the tent and, praying, he anointed the child with oil.

The rest of the day passed in a flurry of activity that seemed to happen in silence. Things in the hospital changed. The staff rotated and new patients came, while the well patients were released. The one constant seemed to be the boy in the tent, and his mother sitting by his side, waiting.

His mother was a woman of faith. As she waited for the inevitable, she prayed, silently, so she didn't disturb her son. She prayed late into the night until she had said to God all she could say. And then, she waited some more, with only the sound of the machinery to keep her company.

The boy was waiting too. He waited to catch his breath. He waited for the pressure in his chest to go away. He waited for the struggle to end. He waited in silence. He was waiting and listening to the silence when he heard her voice. She said, "Don't worry. Everything's going to be alright."

He opened his eyes. The flap of the oxygen tent was still down. Funny, she had sounded so clear, like she was right next to his ear. He turned toward his mother and said, "Mom, you sounded just like an angel when you said that."

His mother looked up. "Said what?"

I think of this story whenever I feel alone. In today's world, sometimes it feels like the more people we have around us, the more electronic gadgets we have to help us communicate with each other, the more isolated we feel.

As Catholics we've got to remember that grace from our Father fills us, that intercession from the saints and our Holy Mother is only a prayer away, and that we are under the constant watch of the angels.

I know that for a fact. You see, I was the little boy.

~Jeffrey Brooks Smith

The Cabbage Patch Doll

When Jesus heard this he was amazed and said to them,
"Amen I say to you, in no one in Israel have I found such faith."
~Matthew 8:10

My daughter, Maria, was five years old, a bright bouncy little girl with solemn brown eyes and a smile that could melt a glacier. Maria was often referred to as my "surprise child" since there was an eight-year gap between her and her closest sibling.

This timespan also accounted for the fact that Maria usually managed to get whatever she asked for, if not from her father or me, from her big sister, one of her older brothers, or her Aunt Marilyn. Luckily, Maria was a sweet-natured child who remained unspoiled despite her privileged position in the family.

On this particular day, my nephew, Donnie, was visiting from Chicago, and the Arizona sunshine had suddenly dissolved into torrential rains. I was looking for an indoor activity for that evening. A man I worked with came to the rescue with four tickets to a benefit being held at a local dinner theater. It sounded like fun, and since my husband was working that evening, Aunt Marilyn and I took Maria and Donnie to the benefit.

While dinner was being served, a few people moved from table to table selling raffle tickets for a drawing to be held during the theater intermission. Set up on a table across the room were a number of prizes donated by local businesses for the raffle. It didn't take Maria long to fix her eyes on a Cabbage Patch doll, which at that time were hard to come by, and very much in demand.

"I want that doll," she announced. "Please can I have it?" she implored, looking from me to her aunt.

"We can't buy you the doll," I explained to Maria. "We have to win it, and with all these other people buying tickets, we don't have a very good chance of getting the doll."

Marilyn waved at one of the raffle ticket sellers and purchased five tickets for a dollar.

"When you win the doll, can I have it?" Maria asked her.

"Yes, but your mother's right. There's not much chance of us winning, so don't get your hopes up."

Maria quickly lowered her curly head, and looked down at her plate. She ate her dinner in silence and I assumed it was her way of showing her disappointment.

After dinner, we went into the theater to see the show. Our table was right down front, directly in front of the stage. The show was a rollicking farce with lots of laughs, but it was a little too adult for Maria. I thought she might get bored and fidgety, but she sat quietly while the rest of us enjoyed the show.

At intermission, the lights went on in the theater and the drum, containing all the raffle tickets of the three hundred people there, was wheeled on stage.

"I want that Cabbage Patch doll," Maria told us again.

"I know you do, honey," I replied. "But you're probably not going to get it."

"Yes, I am," Maria declared. "Ever since I saw it, I've been asking Jesus to let me win it."

Now I understood why my little bundle of energy had been so quiet all during dinner and the show.

Marilyn and I exchanged a look, and shook our heads at each other. Donnie just shrugged. He was the closest one to the stage, so Marilyn handed him the raffle tickets to monitor.

The drawing began and one by one the minor prizes were distributed. Donnie still held our five tickets, which so far had gotten us nothing.

The final two prizes were a clock radio and the Cabbage Patch doll. The winning number for the radio was read, and Donnie let out a cry of surprise. One of our tickets had won!

There was a brief smattering of applause as Donnie claimed the prize. Marilyn and I exchanged looks. Drawing one of our tickets from the hundreds in that barrel had been a real stroke of luck. The chances of another of ours winning the most coveted prize, the Cabbage Patch doll, were next to impossible.

"And now for the final prize," the announcer held up the doll and I dared to look over at Maria. She was sitting with her eyes tightly closed and her tiny hands clasped in prayer. Once again, I gazed around at the theater filled with people, feeling helpless. It didn't even occur to me to utter a prayer of my own. I was too busy trying to think of words that would soothe Maria's devastation when someone else walked off the stage with that doll.

Donnie was so startled to hear another one of our numbers that he jumped, causing his chair to topple over backwards.

Marilyn and I were too stunned to move.

Maria opened her eyes and stared at her cousin who was regaining his balance. "Who won?" she asked innocently.

"You did!" Marilyn and I shouted in unison.

Donnie handed Maria the winning ticket and lifted her onto the stage to collect her prize. She hugged the doll and twirled around in delight, while the audience gave her a thunderous ovation.

"Oh, ye of little faith," I whispered to Marilyn.

Today, Maria is a high school English teacher. The Cabbage Patch doll is faded and worn, packed away with other childhood treasures, but in my mind that doll is as bright and clean as my memory of a delighted child claiming a wonderful prize.

That image still fills me with hope and reminds me that when the odds seem hopelessly stacked against us, a little faith and a simple prayer can make us winners.

~Carol Costa

Ten Dollars in Faith

The steps of faith fall on the seeming-void, but find the rock beneath.
~John Greenleaf Whittier

When my husband and I first met, he was not Catholic. In fact, when we began dating, he admitted that I was the first Catholic he had ever met. I was very devout in my faith, and although I never pushed my beliefs on him, I tried to lead by example. He had been raised in a lot of different churches, but the common theme in all was that the Catholic Church was just wrong.

One windy date-night we were going to the store to get a late-night snack. When we got there, he realized he had lost his last ten dollars. In college, this is equivalent to a small fortune, so we dejectedly returned to campus to search for the money. After looking in all the places we had been, I suggested he pray to St. Anthony.

He angrily shouted, "Fine! St. Anthony, if you are real, help me find my ten dollars." We got out of the car and walked across the street back to his dorm. Leaves were blowing across the road. I crossed the road first, and turned when I heard an audible gasp. My husband found his ten dollars, in the middle of a busy road, on a windy fall night.

Needless to say, when he joined the Catholic Church three years later, St. Anthony was his patron saint. He helped us find a lot more than ten dollars that night, and I will be forever grateful.

~Christina Robertson

Beads

*Prayer is as much the instinct of my nature as a Christian
as it is a duty enjoined by the command of God.*
~Tyron Edwards

It was not the usual party talk.

"I know it sounds weird," confided my friend, Josie, between bites of brie. "But I've started saying the rosary again."

Josie is a thoroughly modern woman. She has a career, a husband, and three sons. She works hard to keep everything balanced, including the family's meals and her own checkbook.

When she told me about reconnecting with this ancient Catholic ritual, she lowered her voice and looked around to make sure no one would overhear. I think Josie considered her statement shockingly retrograde for a Southern California woman at the start of the millennium.

Her admission brought back my own Catholic girlhood. Through that tangle of early memories, winds a long string of rosaries... fancy First Communion rosaries with mother-of-pearl crucifixes and clattering cut-glass beads... light-weight glow-in-the-dark rosaries, tinged creamy yellow by day, shining ghostly green on my dresser in the dark of night. There were rosaries I made myself in youthful bursts of Catholic craftsmanship.

In summers, before the Sixties' heyday of macramé, my grade-school friends and I spent many August afternoons knotting thin waxy cord into misshapen beads. Not that we were particularly religious.

Making rosaries was a time-passing crafts project, something we did when it was too hot to roller skate. We'd lounge on collapsible lawn chairs near our mothers' rose bushes, talking about the boys in our class we liked and the girls we didn't. And when we weren't reaching for the Kool-Aid, we twisted twine. We had a certain-sized knot for Hail Marys. A larger one for Our Fathers and Glory Bes. And the most complicated of all for the Apostles' Creed, the lengthy prayer that got the whole thing rolling. Sometimes we'd save these creations to give to our grandmothers. More often, we'd drop them at afternoon's end into the kitchen's catch-all drawer, the one with all the ballpoint pens that didn't work.

Every funeral I ever went to when I was young featured a rosary resting in the deceased's eternal grasp. These were serious, grown-up rosaries. Usually black, with smooth, oblong beads linked by shiny bits of silver chain.

I remember rosaries as a kind of fashion accessory for the nuns who taught us, their woolen habits loosely cinched by a weighty strand of wooden beads. And a rosary was as much a part of my grandmother's hands as the age spots.

Rosaries were part of everyday life, like tuna sandwiches on Fridays and Ed Sullivan on Sundays. And saying the rosary was as natural to me then as outgrowing last year's saddle shoes.

Those days are gone. Not just for me, but for many Catholics everywhere. In less than one generation, a centuries-old tradition all but vanished, disappearing like a puff of incense in a cavernous cathedral. Choirs began singing "Kumbaya" instead of intoning Gregorian chants. In place of an old religion's incalculable mysteries, came something called "relevance." And fingering beads, while muttering more than fifty Hail Marys, seemed about as relevant as Sunday services in the language of Julius Caesar.

Many of the changes brought a much-needed breath of fresh air to an institution in danger of terminal mustiness. But the winds of change that coursed through those opened stained-glass windows blew a lot of people's rosary beads into a forgotten corner, mine included, along with Josie's.

And there they stayed. Through decades of anti-war protests and rising divorce rates, assassinations and a growing drug culture. Through the Cold War and free love, terrorists attacks and an AIDS epidemic. Into an era of race riots, drive-by shootings, and white-collar fraud. In a society that makes Madonna rich, and too often leaves its homeless hungry. In a country where a gruesome double murder trial was televised daily on the Entertainment Channel.

A faithless time, when you think about it. And Josie did, as she shook the dust from her rosary beads. She says she now finds praying the rosary meditative, almost mantra-like, and infinitely soothing to her soul. Peggy Noonan, a former speechwriter for the first President Bush, says the same thing in her book, *Life, Liberty, and the Pursuit of Happiness*. She admits that lunch hours today sometimes find her at church, kneeling with the old ones who through the years never put down their beads.

I know that two examples do not make a movement. But something seems to be going on here. Maybe we're slowly realizing that a custom hundreds of years old offers a permanence that we lost in the Age of Information. Could be that our grandmothers... and their grandmothers before them... were onto something. I'm beginning to see again that there's something to be said for a simple faith, a faith that embraces mysteries, a faith unafraid to offer awe instead of answers.

In a world spinning into the first decades of the twenty-first century, it's comforting to know there are still a few rosaries around to hold onto.

~Sue Diaz

Coming Home

Faith makes the discords of the present, the harmonies of the future.
~Robert Collyer

As a young child, I can honestly say I did not want for anything. My life really was perfect. And, as was typical for Catholic families in Southern California, God was a big part of my life.

My mother, and the nuns who came to our village every summer, taught us that God was everywhere. Though we may not have voiced it as we ran wild along the lake shores and through the forests learning about our world, we were aware of who was responsible for all of our blessings.

Oftentimes, Mom stopped quarrels among my eight siblings and me with the words, "Count your blessings." I grew up thinking God loved us better than most. After all, He'd given us a lot of blessings to count.

My life was perfect, until I turned four. Then everything changed. I watched in sadness as my oldest sibling abruptly changed into a teenager, followed closely by the next eldest. Slam! Bam! They pieced together a totally new existence.

With tear-filled eyes, my younger siblings and I waved goodbye as one by one the older kids deserted us and what they termed our childish ways. One by one they disappeared from the front pew and vanished to places unknown.

I promised myself if that was the way of it, I'd never grow up.

I had no way of knowing there was nothing I could do to stop my bones from lengthening and my mind from absorbing the outside world. Nor was there any way to stop the big hole that had begun expanding in the middle of my chest. Something was missing. A part of me was ready to move on, but a bigger part of me couldn't figure out the right direction. When my feet finally did move, I couldn't stop them.

As bits and pieces of the strange and complicated land my older sisters lived in filtered into my consciousness, the hole seemed to disappear. By the time I was fifteen, I knew everything. Seemingly overnight, my younger siblings became a constant source of bother and more and more I came to the realization that my parents were not as smart as I had once thought.

As soon as I was old enough to date, time existed solely for me. I'd seen this happen to my sisters and hadn't understood it, but it made perfect sense now. Oh, I saw the looks my parents and younger siblings gave me. What did they know? I hung near the back door of the church with the other teenagers and skipped out of Mass early. We had better things to do.

Then suddenly, just when I felt like one of the adults, my older sisters changed again. They wanted jobs, marriage and, heaven forbid, children!

I watched from a distance as they grew greedy with the money they'd made, and distant and remote as they spent more time with their coworkers and husbands. Hurt and baffled by their behavior, I tried to ignore them. But a funny new development caught my eye. They were starting to attend Mass regularly again, and this time with a new exuberance. They delighted in teaching their children about God.

Then one day I woke up and the desire to find a job was a constant itch just under my skin. It wouldn't go away. I begged everyone I knew for a job. Finally, a summer job at a small factory took me from poor teenager to rich teenager. I hoarded my money, spent time with my coworkers, and felt happy again.

By the time I was twenty, I had another hole growing. This time, the only thing that could fill it was marriage. I argued that my wedding should take place in an apple orchard. My mother was appalled. Her words were, "Inside God's house or I'm not coming!"

I argued that she'd taught me God's house was everywhere. She said His garden was everywhere, His house was the church, and it was a matter of respect. I finally gave in and got married, in the same Catholic Church I'd attended since birth. The Sacrament of Marriage was a bright and peaceful addition to my life.

I didn't want to admit it, but God had a lot to do with that feeling and Mass was now something I attended regularly on my husband's arm. A permanent grin on my face, I settled down to the perfect life... or so I thought. But, before I knew it, that hole had begun expanding again.

Why wasn't I happy? Why didn't I feel complete? I couldn't quite put my finger on it, but something made me cry myself to sleep. Then I realized what it was. Six of my siblings were married and pregnant. I was the only one married and not pregnant. Night after night, I knelt at my bedside, and prayed to God for the child I so desperately wanted. Next came rosaries, and before long, God answered my prayers.

For me, the moment my firstborn child was laid in my arms all things fell into place. Everything simple and delicious had been restored... running barefoot along the lakes and through the forests, skipping stones on calm waters, walking in the cool garden soil, and smiling proudly as chubby fingers explored the pages of a prayer book in the front pew.

That was twenty-two years ago. Since then my world has been complete. As I watch my three children grow, I see the same aloof teenagers as those I'd grown up with and I, myself, had been. I watch as my eldest two work on Sunday, sleep in and miss Mass, or simply forget there is such a thing as church. I frown. I purchase rosaries and nudge them in the right direction. I pray for them to return to the flock, as I'm sure my mother prayed for me.

The same bewildered look my younger siblings wore is now reflected in my youngest child's eyes as his sisters desert him for the realm of important things he's not invited to join. I feel his loss, but know it's only momentary. Soon, he, too, will stumble up through the ranks from childhood to adulthood, and by the time he arrives at the stage they're in right now, they'll be on their return trip.

Occasionally, on Sunday mornings I feel a presence at my side and move to make room for our eldest, who's found a need to be in God's house again. I smile, push my limits and offer her a rosary. She politely declines. I nod and return it to my pocket, but my smile doesn't fade. I pray for patience, and look forward to the not-so-distant future. I hold fast to my faith. I know the light will reach through and all of my children will find their way home just as their mother did.

~Norma Jean

Are You Catholic?

He that does good to another, does good also to himself.
~Lucius Annaeus Seneca

Ever since I can remember I have loved books. Having come from a family of educators and avid readers, I grew up believing that books can change the world and put us in touch with the most significant questions and most enduring answers.

Following graduation from the University of Notre Dame with a degree in English and philosophy, I worked in a bookstore for minimum wage and sent out resumes to publishers hoping to land a job as an editor. I finally got a call from the director of the Chicago-based Catholic publishing house, Loyola Press, asking me to interview for an editorial position. The pay was low and I was not sure I wanted to edit religious books, but I had grown up a Cubs fan and loved the idea of living near Wrigley Field, catching ball games, and getting paid to read. So I did the interview, they made an offer, and I accepted right on the spot.

After my first few months, my boss walked into my office and said, "Langford, I've got an important project for you. It's a book called *The Catholic Tradition Before and After Vatican II: 1878-1993*, and I think you're ready for it." At that point I had only taken an editing class at the University of Chicago, assisted other editors with their work, and handled only one project on my own. My only fear now was that my boss would figure out that I did not know much about the Catholic tradition and had no right to edit this book!

Throughout that fall and winter, I devoted most of my time and energy to that project. I was determined to learn about the Catholic tradition while making the book letter-perfect.

The day before the project was due to the printer, I took the galley pages home for one last review. I ended up pulling an all-nighter.

The next morning, overly tired and grumpy, I waited in freezing snow for the 152 Addison bus to pick me up for work. As the dime-sized flakes fell with increasing intensity, I retreated deeper inside myself. Eventually the groan of an approaching bus startled me back to the moment at hand, and I squinted to make out the number "152" against the blurry backdrop of the Chicago skyline. Soon I'd be on my way to work, and soon after that I'd be mailing the manuscript to the printer.

When the bus finally pulled up to my corner, I saw a middle-aged man coming forward with an elderly woman clutching his arm. I thought about shoving my way past them, but decided my kind act for the day would be getting out of the way so this other man could perform his kind act for the day. Within a minute, the man had deposited his delicate cargo on the corner and reboarded the bus. I started to follow in his path when I heard the elderly woman plead, "Oh my, it is so icy today, I don't know if I'll be able to make it to the hospital just down the street."

It was one of those moments when you want to pretend that you did not hear a plea for help so that you can just go about your business.

But I had heard it.

With one foot on the first step of the bus and the other on the curb, I looked at the half-smiling driver, then my watch, and finally the gray-haired woman.

In my bag sat the typeset pages to *The Catholic Tradition*. Chapters on peace and justice seemed to be whispering to me, "What are you going to do?"

In a great John Wayne-style moment, I looked at the bus driver and said, "Go on without me." He smiled, shut the door, and zoomed off. I turned back and offered the woman my arm as the exhaust fumes engulfed us.

"Thank you so much, young man," the elderly woman said in a half-fake tone of surprise. "Normally I make this walk by myself, but today it's too dangerous."

"No problem," I said, stifling a grumble.

Saint Joseph's Hospital was just down the street from my apartment. I'd passed it many times. But that day it seemed miles away as measured by our cautiously teeny steps on the snow-hidden glaze of ice. Gradually, I gave up trying to sneak peeks at my watch and fantasizing about throwing this woman over my shoulder and running her to her destination. I simply resolved to enjoy my time with this seemingly fragile soul. "My name is Frances," she offered.

Salutations out of the way, Frances and I chatted a little about the weather, my job as an editor, and our mutual love of Chicago. About halfway to the hospital, Frances asked, "Can we stop here a minute so I can catch my breath?" Though I wanted to say sarcastically, "Gosh, I'm glad you said it first because we've been sprinting like marathon runners!" I thought it better to hold onto her arm and tell her to take her time.

Without warning, she looked at me and asked, "Are you Catholic?"

The question caught me off guard. I'd been privately asking myself the same question for such a long time that it sounded foreign coming from somebody else's mouth. I felt my canned answer making its way to my lips. "Yes, I am...," I finally responded.

"I can tell," replied Frances with an assuring tone.

From the back of my mind sprang a haunting question I once heard at an Easter Mass: "If you were on trial for being a Christian, would there be enough evidence to convict you?" The answer had continually eluded me. Maybe Frances's "I can tell" was pointing to some truth about myself I didn't ordinarily acknowledge.

We continued on our journey, but my mind sat cold and numb as I pondered what I mean when I say I am Catholic.

We finally reached the hospital doors, and I wished my new friend well. "I hope it's nothing serious and that you're going to be okay."

"Oh," she said, delighted. "I'm fine; I just come down here once a week to volunteer, you know, cheer the patients up."

I stood awkwardly in awe of her as she read the surprise on my face.

I couldn't help but to ask Frances, "Are you Catholic?" to which she happily answered, "Yes, I am."

Somehow her answer sounded different from mine... stronger, more confident.

After leaning down to hug Frances goodbye, I headed back to my bus stop. It hadn't been terribly long since I was last there, but everything about my morning had changed.

As I caught the next bus, I replayed Frances's question hundreds of times: "Are you Catholic?" It was no longer a theoretical matter. Through her words and actions, she challenged me to examine how my being Catholic meshes with the all-too-often sloppy details of my daily life.

On that cold winter day I felt a powerful warmth that had been stoked by the humanity and Catholic conviction embodied in my unexpected companion, Frances. And as I mailed *The Catholic Tradition* typeset pages in enough time to meet the printer's deadline, I smiled to think that I'd come a few steps closer to understanding the message contained in its pages.

I haven't seen Frances since that day, but her challenge continues to take on deeper meaning each time I confidently respond, "Yes, I'm Catholic."

~Jeremy Langford

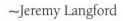

In Touch with Faith

The deepest wishes of the heart find expression in secret prayer.
~George E. Rees

"She's my grandmother. You can't..." I started to say. "You can't stop me." But we both knew he could. "Please, Daddy, I want to see her. I..."

"We all love her, Sissy, but this stroke has destroyed the person we know. She won't recover. All we can do is ease the pain of her final passage." His eyes got drippy, and he dabbed at them with a folded, linen hanky.

I'd seen my father cry once before, when I was thirteen and they were going to amputate my sister's leg. I came on him in the kitchen sobbing into a dishtowel. Those tears were wasted. The pathologist called a halt to the surgery. My father, a surgeon specializing in cancer before the age of specialties, was in the operating room as an observer during the initial biopsy. When the lab results came in, Daddy said that he had touched the tumor, and it didn't feel like a malignancy. The pathologist sent off the slides for another opinion. My sister's tumor turned out to be a benign look-alike mimicking a deadly malignancy. There was no cancer. She got to keep her leg.

Back then, my father was weeping; now, his eyes were damp and spilling over with sadness. He finally gave in to my persistent pleas. "Take Mommy's car," he said. "I have to make rounds." He took my shoulders in his hands. "She probably won't know you, Sis. She doesn't know me, and I've been her son longer than you've been her granddaughter. Will you be okay?"

I nodded and gave him a quick hug and a brush-by kiss before leaving. I was prepared for whatever awaited me, or so I thought.

Of my half dozen siblings, I was the closest to my grandparents. I often stayed with them in the small town where my father had been raised. Far from Baltimore and the perils of a city, I was free to roam, and it was fun to be an only child for a little while. Wrapped in my grandmother's ample arms, I felt loved. The memory of that feeling drove me to visit her at the nursing home, even if she had no memory of me.

Three months before the stroke, my grandmother had created her usual Christmas feast, spreading her love among her grandchildren like soft butter on warm biscuits and convincing each of us that we were the special one.

I felt special as I followed Sister Ignatius down the nursing home hall. At Ma's room, my heart froze; I didn't even recognize my own grandmother in that chair. The flesh had melted from her body, and her hair had gone from soft brown to wiry gray. A bed sheet was draped across her chest, wrapped under each arm, and tied behind her back. She dangled like the odd conjoining of a wooden marionette and a rag doll. Her left side was twisted and stiff, but her right side hung limp, as if someone had stripped the muscles out of her.

"Why did you tie her in the chair?" I asked, my eyes hot with accusation.

Sister drew a deep breath. "Your grandmother needs to spend time upright so her lungs don't fill with fluid. The sheets are gentle on her flesh."

Sister must not have held my hostile tone against me, because she asked if I wanted her to stay. I shook my head, and she gave me a hug. "I'll be right down the hall if you need me. Just give a shout."

I gazed at my grandmother through misty eyes and saw that she held her rosary in her right hand. On summer evenings, we'd sit on her big screened porch after supper and say the rosary. The olive wood beads had darkened with age and were worn smooth from years of passing through her supple fingers.

"It's Sissy," I said, touching her shoulder. "Come to visit."

She spoke, but not to me. She seemed to think I was my Aunt Fran, whom I had always resembled. I'd never heard most of the names she called me. She sounded as if she were talking to childhood pals. She asked me if I'd brought my "skip rope." Her words were gibberish, but she was calm and we chatted contentedly.

"Halo," she said, her good eye drifting above my head.

"Hello?" I asked.

She began humming a Christmas tune about angels. With her right hand, she touched the gold velvet ribbon in my hair.

"Halo!" she repeated.

There was no mistaking the word this time.

Suddenly she grew agitated... twitching, moaning, and straining against the straps. I shouted for Sister Ignatius, who hurried to find a doctor to prescribe a sedative for her comfort.

When Sister left, I tried to calm my grandmother, but nothing worked. As I leaned in to touch her, the silver sheen on the cross of her rosary caught my eye. I reached into the crumpled sheets and retrieved it from where it had dropped when she touched the ribbon in my hair.

The instant I placed the rosary in my grandmother's right hand, she turned as calm as an inland pond on a windless day. She didn't remember me. She didn't remember my father. She didn't even seem to know if she was in heaven or on earth. Her mind was gone, but her fingertips recalled the feel of that rosary and what it represented.

When I told Sister what happened, she canceled the sedative. During the next week, which was the last week of my grandmother's life, that rosary never left her hand. Sister tied it to her wrist with a white satin ribbon.

Touching those beads might have been all that my grandmother remembered of her long, full life, but it was enough. It brought peace to her passing.

~Carol Kenny

Irish Wake

Rejoice and be glad, for your reward will be great in heaven.
~Matthew 5:12

My dad possessed a special Irish sense of humor, filled with wisdom, love, and great trust in God and His care for us all. As my father's cancer advanced beyond all hope, in the winter of 1984, Dad set about putting his life affairs in order.

After his last surgery, when the doctor told him he could do nothing more to stop the cancer, Dad pondered this for a moment, looked the doctor in the eye and said, "Well now, it's January and Saint Patty's day would be a perfect time for an Irish wake, don't you think? I have always thought it is such a sad thing that the poor bloke who dies never gets to enjoy his last party."

With this somewhat unusual statement, the doctor just agreed, but told the rest our family that Dad probably would not last another week, two at most.

Obviously, the doctor did not know my father.

Dad made a list of final things he needed to get done. On the top of his list was a plan to throw his own Irish wake on Saint Patrick's Day, more than two months away. Even more startling to those who did not know him was a list of things Dad wrote on his personal calendar covering the whole year of 1984 up to Valentine's Day of 1985. The doctors humored Dad, while they planned hospice care for the end of his life, which, they were certain would be a week or two away.

Dad said he'd had enough of doctors and hospitals and decided he wanted to go home to die. The doctors agreed, so we took Dad home. He was so frail and weak, the end looked imminent.

My father set out to surprise us one and all. One day, a few days after he returned home, he disappeared when mom was shopping. Now that was no easy feat, since he was bedridden and on oxygen. But Dad had gotten up, dressed, and walked over to the funeral home to plan his own Irish wake. He expected his good friend Randy, the undertaker, to help him pull it off. My dad never let the moss grow under his feet in good times or in bad, and this situation was to be no different.

As the weeks passed, Dad seemed to grow stronger as he anticipated his goal of spending one last Saint Patrick's Day with his friends. Never mind it was to be his own wake... that thought didn't faze him at all. It seemed to give him strength and joy to check off on his calendar each task he felt the Good Lord wanted him to get done before heading home. Dad called it... "Home to heaven after finishing my mission, which only me and God seem to know the ending of."

To everyone's amazement, Dad made it to Saint Patrick's Day, and his own wake, just as he had planned it. He had picked out his casket, and with the Irish humor borne through the ages, he placed it in the living room. "After all," Dad said, "an Irish wake without the coffin and the dearly departed wouldn't be an Irish wake at all." With good humor, Dad lay in the coffin as any good Irish stiff would do. There was joy, and storytelling and remembering all the good times of our lives together. Our family and best friends from childhood all played up the Irish wake to the hilt, with Irish toasts and general foolishness born of the spirit of love.

Bernie, one of Dad's childhood buddies, reached over and stuck his hand in Dad's pocket. It was an old joke among friends, that whether they were rich or poor, they would trust in God's love and mercy and leave this world with empty pockets, except for their rosary.

My dad laughed and handed Bernie the rosary in his pocket, and said, "Now don't be forgetting to say the beads for me."

All in all, it was an Irish sendoff, better than any Saint Patrick's Day we had ever celebrated.

From that day on, my father remained optimistic and happy. Of course, his doctors were a bit stymied to say the least when Dad lived right up until the day he marked off the last "to do" item on his calendar.

The only item not crossed off was Valentine's Day, 1985. The day he died.

He must have even planned that. His grave marker, which he had picked out on the day he planned his own Irish Wake, was heart-shaped.

~Christine M. Trollinger

98

Welcome Home

The love of heaven makes one heavenly.
~William Shakespeare

Mrs. Phillips was one of my favorite residents at the assisted living facility where I worked. She was in the early stages of Alzheimer's, and spent much of the day asking me the same questions over and over. But it was her sarcastic sense of humor and complete honesty that endeared her to everyone.

When she'd get her hair done at the beauty salon, she'd look like royalty, and I'd go out of my way to let her know how beautiful she looked. Her face would glow with pleasure at the compliment, but her response would be most sarcastic. "Yeah, right!" she'd exclaim. That was her answer for any compliment given, and the entire staff smiled whenever we'd overhear those familiar two words.

Mrs. Phillips must have been an excellent secretary in her day, because she was always concerned about my getting the mail out on time and answering the phone right away. She often asked me how she could help.

"Hi Babe!" she'd greet me in the morning. "Need any help?" I'd reassure her that I was getting along okay. "Oh! You're a lefty!" (She'd say this every time she saw me using a pen.) "You know, left-handed people are very intelligent! My son is a lefty, you know." I'd smile to myself, because she'd only shared this fact with me a dozen times a day.

When she realized I was busy, she'd wink and say, "See ya

'round... if you don't turn square." I grew to love those old sayings, obviously handed down from generation to generation.

Afternoons seemed to be the hardest on the residents suffering with dementia.

One particularly busy afternoon, Mrs. Phillips came to my desk upset. "Where is Ed?" she asked. Ed was her deceased husband, and we often tried to explain this to her, but she would forget our ever mentioning it. Finally, after noticing that each time his death was mentioned, she reacted as if it were the first time she'd received the news, we decided it would be best to just let her believe Ed was still alive. She truly couldn't remember from one minute to the next at this point, and it was pitiful to have to put her through unnecessary trauma. I heard her approaching my desk some time later. "Have you seen Ed yet?"

"Well, no, Mrs. Phillips, not this afternoon I haven't."

"Well, I'll be! Where in tarnation has that scoundrel taken himself off to now?" This would go on and on, until she grew weary, retiring to her room, at last, for a nap.

Mrs. Phillips also was a devout Catholic. She asked for the priest to come and give her Communion often, and if I shared a concern with her, she would let me know which saint to pray to for help. When she became a bit upset over forgetting things, or felt insecure, I could always calm her down by mentioning our mutual faith in God.

As time wore on, Mrs. Phillips grew weaker. She had a hard time walking, and fell asleep sitting up a lot. Her sarcastic sense of humor seemed to lessen as well.

One evening, she came to me a little more excited than I'd noticed in weeks.

"My sister is coming to take me on a trip," she confided.

I was aware that her sister had also been deceased for quite some time, but it was the end of the day, and I was growing weary. "That will be nice," I murmured. "Maybe you should get your hair done for such a special occasion." I smiled, hoping to finish the menus for the next day before I punched out for the evening.

"Oh, do you think so? That's a good idea!" she said, shuffling off to the beauty parlor. Sometime later, she approached my desk, looking lovely once again.

"You look beautiful!" I exclaimed.

"Yeah, right!" she said. Then her eyebrows wrinkled up in a worried expression. "Listen, how will my sister know where to find me tonight?"

I was a little surprised that she was still dwelling on the idea that her sister was coming for her. "Help me with this Lord," I whispered to myself. "Well," I began, "why don't you put a flower in the window for her? That way, she'll know it's your room."

"I don't know where in the world I'll find a flower, but that's a good idea." She smiled. "See, I told you lefties were smart!"

I wished her goodnight, and returned to the task at hand, eager to get off work and out into the fresh air.

The next morning, as I approached my desk for report, a ringing phone greeted me. Answering it, I was surprised to hear the distraught voice of Mrs. Phillips' son on the other end. Suddenly, my heart raced uncontrollably.

"Mary, I'm calling to let you know that Mother passed away last night. One of the nurses on the midnight shift let us know."

Time stood still, as he explained the details. I hung the phone up, fighting tears, as I made my way in to console the director of the facility.

All morning, I thought of Mrs. Phillips and how much I had grown to love her. When it was time to deliver the morning papers, I made my way upstairs, placing the papers one by one outside each resident's door. When I reached Mrs. Phillips' room, I paused, noticing the door of her room was open halfway. I peered inside, my eyes glancing around the cozy surroundings she had called home. Suddenly, my eyes reached the windowsill, and I cried out, as my hands clutched the doorknob tightly.

I'll never know how she had managed it, but Mrs. Phillips had found the most beautiful potted pink rose and placed it where her sister, Rose, would find it.

"Oh, Mrs. Phillips," I whispered, clapping my hands together. "Bravo!"

And I could almost hear her answer me from the gates of heaven.

"Yeah, right!"

~Mary Z. Smith

99

Chicken Soup
for the *Soul*

Special Delivery

Whatever you ask for in prayer with faith, you shall receive.
~Matthew 21:22

One day my five-year-old son Jimmy came home from his summer day camp program and told us, "Peter's mother is going to have a baby any day now." The delight in his voice surprised us as much as his follow-up announcement. "I think we should get a baby, too. I'd like another brother."

A noble thought indeed, but I wasn't thinking about an "addition" to the family at the time. This wonderful, yet impractical, idea just didn't fit into my family planning timetable.

Yet the excitement, enthusiasm, and urgency in his voice showed me he expected an immediate and probably positive response.

Not knowing exactly how to explain the intricacies involved, I turned to one of my parenting techniques: encourage the use of prayer as an aid to achieving success.

"When you say your prayers tonight, why not tell God what you have in mind," I said. "Remember how we talked about the scripture, 'Ask and you shall receive'?"

Jimmy thought for a minute, and nodded.

"Why not give it a try," I encouraged.

"Good idea," said Jimmy. "God's always listening."

And listen He did!

The following May, my third son arrived to the surprised delight of all.

When Jimmy saw his brother, he made two proclamations.

"I guess this is my baby. I prayed every night for him." Then he added, "God really does hear our prayers."

Jimmy frequently reminded us of his miracle from God, and told anyone who would listen about how he "got to have a baby." For many years, my son believed he was responsible for the blessed event.

To this day, there's a special connection between the oldest and youngest brother. Not only are they bonded by blood, but by a belief in the power of God and prayer.

~Helen Colella

New Life

Jesus said to her, "I am the resurrection and the life."
~John 11:25

There I sat, reveling in my solitude, observing the hushed preparations for Easter Vigil Mass in the dim quiet. Street lights cast deep shadows through the stained glass, and the lessons in the windows seemed distant from the stories colored there when the sunshine danced through. I could smell the sweet mix of perfume, incense, and lilies. The stillness held me softly. Ah, alone at last.

Rather than rouse our energetic toddler from his sleep, his dad had offered to stay home so I could attend the Vigil. I did not hesitate, more from a harried mother's need for some time alone than anything else.

Actually, when I was growing up, Easter Triduum's traditions had always held deep significance for me. Christmas could never come close to the drama of Easter's agony turned to joy, the very crux of our faith. I loved how through Holy Week we experience the humility and forgiveness of Holy Thursday's foot washing, and as children of God we are invited to the banquet table of Eucharist. Good Friday's Passion, with the extinguishing of candles, and stripping of the altar, always tore at my heart, sending me home pensive and introspective. Of all the once-a-year ceremonies and rituals packed into Lent, from Ash Wednesday through Easter Sunday, the Easter Vigil had always been the most special.

This year, however, was not the same. Good Friday's fasting and abstinence had left me feeling tired, questioning if it was all still relevant to me. In the midst of feverish spring cleaning and preparations for Easter company, I'd boxed up the components for Sunday's feast anyway and participated in the Blessing of the Food Saturday afternoon. I'd even managed to squeeze in another trip to church for confession. Add a busy two-year-old to the mix and I was just plain exhausted, tempted to skip the whole Vigil thing.

Frankly, I came because I welcomed the opportunity for some downtime for me.

I was enjoying being by myself without the need to talk to or take care of anyone. Then Father said softly, "*Be* in the tomb. *Feel* its darkness in your soul. Participate mindfully. When we turn out the lights, listen to the silence with your whole self. When we bless the fire, know the reality of Resurrection."

At that very second, the church went black.

Even knowing it was coming, I was surprised at the pitch darkness. The red letters of the Exit sign did little to relieve the disconsolate weight of my human failings now pressing me. I realized there were no such exits in a tomb. Childhood fears of inky spaces niggled at the back of my mind.

Amazed such a large crowd could be so deathly silent, I felt alone. Not a hot-bath-in-fragrant-suds alone. More like forsaken-without-water-in-the-desert alone.

Then somewhere inside me came the crushing realization of what it all meant. From far away, I heard Father's unpretentious voice. He prayed the Blessing of the Fire. I could not have anticipated how my heart leapt with the eruption of flame in the container at the back of the church. From it, Father lit a single candle. He walked over to the last person in the last pew and lit her candle. She lit her neighbor's. He lit the person's next to him.

Flame to flame, candle to candle. The tiny flickering light moved row by row, slowly reclaiming the darkness. A golden glow grew to envelop us. In a pregnant silence, the first person in the front pew stood. He walked to the pure beeswax Paschal Candle on the altar and reached his candle aloft. His flame touched the wick.

Simultaneously, the "Hallelujah Chorus" soared to the vaulted ceiling as the lights blazed back on. Now we could see the altar, resplendent in crisp linens embroidered with gleaming threads, sumptuous in a sea of creamy fragrant lilies. Their very blossoms seemed to trumpet the instantaneous transformation from death to life.

We oohed. We aahed. Tears streamed down our faces.

The Liturgy of the Word sparkled that night as each scripture fell fresh on my heart. Eucharist fed my hungry body and nourished my receptive soul. The Baptism of the Catechumens flew by. I was astonished when we were already singing the recessional. The Easter Vigil was over. The plunge into darkness had opened my eyes to the Light.

My fatigued limbs hummed with energy. I surged with gratitude for all I had been given.

This was Resurrection. Yes, there was New Life, even for me.

~Maryjo Faith Morgan

Fallen Away

For the Son of Man has come to seek and to save that which was lost.
~Luke 19:10

"I'm not going to church any more," I announced, right before ten o'clock services.

My little brother, Bill, only twelve at the time and about to be confirmed, stared in open-mouthed amazement, as if suspecting I'd become possessed. Mom, Catholic through and through, immediately geared up for a showdown. She fired back, "You most certainly are going with us to Mass!"

But Dad defused everything. "No," he said. "He's eighteen. Old enough to make his own choices."

That was how I officially fell away.

We never talked about it, but I imagined Dad would have fallen away too, if he'd been Catholic. He had to be equally sick of all the ceremony and ritual. Maybe, like me, he wondered whether or not there was even a God. After all, he'd been raised in a non-religious family. He stoically attended Mass every week, but it was for Mom, not him.

The difference between us was that I didn't have to do it for Mom any more.

Being fallen away was liberating for a young guy trying to figure out the world. Exciting, even. I was finally free on Sundays!

It took a while to notice that I wasn't nearly as happy as I thought I should be. I felt off-balance, somehow. I rationalized that you don't do something every week... even something pointless, like Catholic Mass... and not feel its absence when you stop.

So, in my twenties, I began the long process of casting around for an answer by "trying out" services in various Protestant faiths.

I knew there had to be something better.

Episcopal, Evangelical, Presbyterian, Methodist, I went to them all. Each had their hearts in the right places, but in the end, none seemed right. The formats didn't have the substance I wanted, and the ritualized backbone of the services seemed "lightweight" and frivolous. They either didn't have Communion, or had it only inter-mittently... or when they did have a weekly Communion, it clearly didn't have the meaning I'd been raised to understand.

Not one church truly satisfied.

It was irritating that my Catholic-raised sensibilities seemed to have ruined me for other churches. But by that time, I hadn't been to a Mass in many years. I was determined not to let weakness lure me back.

I thought a lot about Dad. About how he sat by Mom every week, wasting all that time in a place he didn't want to be. I admired his sacrifice and love, but I wasn't going to make the same mistake. Anyway, I had a family of my own now, and I wanted it to be better for them.

By the time I was in my thirties, we were thinking outside of the Christianity box, and settled at a Unitarian Universalist church. This is a "religion" where you can believe in everything... or nothing... if you want. It seemed a good fit for a lapsed Catholic.

But being UU means being politically correct to a self-conscious extreme. It got to me after a while. It slowly dawned on me that you can't accept and applaud every point of view and value if you want to retain any of your own.

Our attendance gradually dwindled, then stopped.

During my forties, I went nowhere on Sundays. It was a sad time for me. Humans have an innate desire for spirituality, and I'd all but given up on finding an outlet for mine. The term "fallen away" was beginning to seem very descriptive. The sensation of being without a place to find balance and guidance and foundation really was like falling.

Then a couple of interesting things happened.

The first was that my brother and his family started attending a fledgling Catholic community. First Bill got my parents going, then they all worked on me to try it out.

After a while, I agreed. Only once, I told myself. Just to keep them company.

I was surprised by how different everything seemed. The music was modern, the congregation energized. And no wonder. At the center of Corpus Christi Church was Father Fred, a terrific priest who gave vibrant, intellectual, and often very funny sermons that challenged the mind and the conscience.

I began drifting in and out of attendance. Resisting. Going only on special occasions, like Christmas and Easter. I refused to take Communion, not wanting to give in and say I was back, not even to myself. Not wanting to admit that this might be what I needed and had been seeking.

But Father Fred got me thinking.

Then the second interesting thing happened: Dad decided to become Catholic. I was stunned. Was it possible Dad had been going to church because he chose to go, all along?

Bill sponsored him through his preparations, and the day soon came when the entire family, including me and my wife and kids, attended a special Mass in which Dad was welcomed into the church. I have a mental snapshot of him, his hair wet with baptismal oil, receiving Communion from Father Fred for the first time.

It was the last little push I needed.

Returning to the church in my fifties has been like coming home. The world is hard and confusing and divided, and it is a comfort, knowing I have a place to go for renewal. I take Communion, and am uplifted by the ritual of a Mass, the same ritual that used to turn me off. I grow closer to this nascent religious community all the time, bonded by the presence of my family, under the care of a truly inspiring priest.

Now, I call my parents each weekend. Like the fallen away declaration I made over three decades prior, the conviction behind the call is not for Mom and it's not even for Dad, no matter that I owe him for the example he provided.

It's for me.

"I'm going to church," I say. "Want to ride there together?"

~Craig A. Strickland

Meet Our Contributors!
About the Authors
Acknowledgments

Chicken Soup for the Soul

Meet Our Contributors!

Michael A. Aun of Kissimmee, FL., is the only living speaker in the world to be awarded the CPAE Speaker Hall of Fame from the National Speakers Association, the Certified Speaking Professional designation and to have won the World Championship of Public Speaking for Toastmasters International. Contact Michael at http://www.aunline.com.

Aaron Bacall's work has been used for advertising, greeting cards, wall and desk calendars and several corporate promotional books. Three of his cartoons are featured in the permanent collection at the Harvard Business School's Baker Library. He can be reached at ABACALL@msn.com.

Susanna Hickman Bartee is a military wife and mother of five. Her works were previously published in *Chicken Soup for the Military Wife's Soul* and *Chicken Soup for the New Mom's Soul*. She and her family converted to Catholicism in 2001. She can be reached at Bartees7@embarqmail.com.

Margo Berk-Levine always envisioned having three careers. Actress/model, gave way to founder/owner of a successful staffing service company, gave way to writing. She is currently creating a memoir and a series of short stories. She is a contributor and board member of the Scribblers' Society Journal. Contact her at mberklevin@aol.com.

Marla Bernard received her Master of Arts with honors from Baker University. She is an executive for a major teaching hospital in Kansas City. As a former police officer, Marla is a victims' rights advocate and is currently writing a true crime book. Please e-mail her at mbernard@kc.rr.com.

Pegge Bernecker is a spiritual director, retreat leader, and author of *Your Spiritual Garden: Tending to the Presence of God*, and *God: Any Time, Any Place*. The death of her son magnifies her desire for deep meaning and service. She lives in Kasilof, Alaska, with her husband and dogs. Pegge can be reached through her website at www.PeggeBernecker.com.

Jeffrey Brooks Smith is a comedian/writer/speaker who is proud to be Catholic. He works to spread that pride to everyone he meets. He performs his humor based apologetics programs to Catholic groups around the country. He can be reached via e-mail at Jeffrey.smoth@kofc.org.

Tom Calabrese is an Associate Professor at JWU, with degrees from New York University (Bachelor's 1981), Villanova University (Master's 1997), and University of Connecticut (Doctorate 2009). He authored a textbook and numerous educational articles. Tom is an accomplished guitarist. He enjoys family time and sports. E-mail him at tcalabrese@jwu.edu.

Martha Campbell is a graduate of Washington University, St. Louis School of Fine Arts and a former writer/designer for Hallmark cards. She has been a freelance cartoonist and illustrator since leaving Hallmark. She lives in Harrison, Arkansas.

Sandra McPherson Carrubba became a first grade teacher after graduation from the State University of New York, Oswego. She later taught at Villa Maria Academy, a private high school. The mother of two enjoys gardening, reading and interacting with people from other cultures. She cares for her husband and cat.

Beatrice Catarello is a stay-at-home mom of three boys. She enjoys painting and cooking with her children and playing the viola with the community orchestra.

Hugh Chapman is a business teacher at Izard County Consolidated High School in Brockwell Arkansas. You may contact him at Julchapman@yahoo.com.

Helen Colella is a freelance writer from Colorado. Her work includes educational materials, articles/stories for adults and children, contributions to *Chicken Soup for the Soul* books and parenting magazines across the country. She also operates a home-based business offering writing services to independent publishers. Contact: helencolella@comcast.net.

Carol Costa is an award-winning playwright and the published author of ten books including financial titles, mystery novels, romance novels, short story collections, and a book on video poker. Her short stories and feature articles have been published in newspapers, anthologies, and magazines. Contact her at ccstarlit@aol.com.

Don Cracium teaches middle school in Troy, Michigan. He and his wife, Mary have two daughters, Christina and Kathryn. He has a Masters Degree of Music. He also writes sacred music songs and hopes to publish them one day. You can e-mail him at donjames@ameritech.net.

John Crudele has been inspiring church, business and education audiences for over twenty-five years. His passion for the struggles of young people today, combined with his faith, led him to found Partnership for Youth, a nonprofit organization committed to providing dynamic Catholic programs for teens. Please e-mail him at john@johncrudele.com.

Donna D'Amour has been freelance writing for more than twenty years for newspapers and magazines. She also offers writing courses from her website, www.damourwriting.ca. Her writing career began when she submitted essays on everyday life to her daily newspaper. She lives in Halifax, Nova Scotia.

Lauren Aileen Davenport is a stay-at-home mom to five young children. Her daughter, Mary, is named in honor of VoVo, the inspiration of her story. Lauren earned her B.A. in Journalism from Taylor University in Fort Wayne, IN. Please e-mail her at laurenadavenport@gmail.com.

Lola DeJulio DeMaci is a contributor to several *Chicken Soup for the Soul* books, the *Los Angeles Times* and *My Friend — A Catholic Magazine for Kids*. She has a Master of Arts in education and English and continues writing in her sunny loft overlooking the San Bernardino Mountains. E-mail her at LDeMaci@aol.com.

Michele Dellapenta has been writing poetry since the age of nine and has had several minor publications through the years. She lives with her husband Lou, in Miamisburg, Ohio. She credits her sister, Jodi Severson, a current *Chicken Soup for the Soul* contributor, as her mentor and cheerleader. Please e-mail Michele at mdellapenta@earthlink.net.

Sue Diaz is an author, writing teacher, and essayist whose work has appeared in numerous regional and national publications, including *Newsweek, Family Circle, Woman's Day, Christian Science Monitor*, and *Reader's Digest*. Her website — www.suediaz.com — tells all. You can contact her at sue@suediaz.com.

Shirley Dino lives in Denver, Colorado, with her husband, Sandy. She is a lector at her parish and enjoys tennis, biking and gardening. In addition to her three sons and two wonderful daughter-in-laws, she has three grandchildren.

Carol J. Douglas is a freelance writer and has been published in *Woman's World* and *Petwarmers*. She also enjoys writing for children and has had poetry and nonfiction published in this genre. Carol lives in Dublin, Ohio, with her husband, Jeff, and children Justin and Emelia. Contact her at carol_jean_douglas@yahoo.com.

Sally Edwards is a clean corporate comedian and motivational humorist of twenty-five years who performs her one-woman show "Family Lunacy!" at parishes across the country. www.ComedyBySally.com. Sally Edwards is also the author of three illustrated humor books. Recently, Sally started her own clean comedy agency entitled "The Humorous Speakers Bureau." www.HumorousSpeakersBureau.com.

Judy Ann Eichstedt is the mother of six children and one granddaughter. A freelance writer and homeless activist, Judy is the coauthor of a book of poems titled, *Weary Souls, Shattered by Life*. Please contact her at judea777@msn.com or www.wearysouls.com.

Holly Engel-Smothers, the author of ten books and numerous articles, has a Master's Degree in Teaching Reading. Although the world extends far beyond her backyard, Holly is content to set the picnic table with plastic dishes and serve Beanie Weenies to her husband, identical twin girls and their younger sister. holly.smothers@gmail.com.

Delores Fraga-Carvalho has been married to Luis for 33 years and is mother to Lisa-Marie, 31, and Luis, Jr., 25. She is a member of The Red Hat Society local chapters in Moses Lake, WA, Rebel Reds and Desert Reds. She crochets and enjoys water aerobics. Please e-mail her at divinedamedee@accima.com.

Kathleen Gerard is the author of *Still Life*, a spiritual memoir. Her writing has been widely published, featured on National Public Radio (NPR), awarded the Perillo Prize for Italian American Writing and nominated for "Best New American Voices," a national prize in literature. E-mail her at katgerard@aol.com.

Ellen C.K. Giangiordano graduated from Temple University School of Law in 1990 and was a litigator for eight years in Philadelphia before returning home to raise her five children. Ellen enjoys cooking, sewing, weight lifting, yoga, spending time with her family, and reading the works of John Paul II. Ellen and her family now live in Georgia.

Susan M. Goldberg has been a registered nurse for more than thirty years—most of them spent in the operating room—as a staff nurse and an educator. She has enjoyed writing and publishing for the past fifteen years. Susan continues to work, write, travel, and play with her grandson. Harmony51480@aol.com.

Blair P. Grubb is a Professor of Medicine and Pediatrics at the University of Toledo School of Medicine in Toledo, Ohio. His hobbies include writing and fountain pen collecting. He lives with his wife, Barbara, and children, Helen and Alex.

Therese Guy is an owner/operator of a martial arts studio. She has been teaching martial arts in the Midwest for twenty-six years. She enjoys horses, reading, and writing. She has a non-fiction book in progress about life as a Baby Boomer. Please e-mail her at: Therese-tkd@juno.com.

Floriana Hall, born 1927, Pittsburgh PA, Distinguished Alumna of Cuyahoga Falls High School, attended Akron University, author and poet, ten nonfiction and inspirational poetry books, founder and coordinator of THE POET'S NOOK, poetry teacher. Married Robert Hall sixty years, five children, nine grandchildren, one great-grandchild. Many winning poems. Contact: HAFLORIA@sbcglobal.net, website: http://www.alongstoryshort.net/FlorianaHall.html.

Cynthia Hamond has numerous stories in the *Chicken Soup for the Soul* series and other major publications, including *Woman's World* magazine and *King Features Syndication*. She received two awards and was feature writer in *Anthology Today*. Two stories have been made for TV. She enjoys school visits and group talks.

Paulette L. Harris is a freelance author/speaker in Colorado. She has completed the CWG Apprenticeship Program. She taught for several years before retiring. She enjoys her grandchildren and her husband of thirty-nine years. Her hobbies include golfing, gardening, animals, and writing novels. coloradopolly@yahoo.com.

Jonny Hawkins is a fulltime cartoonist from Sherwood, Michigan. Thousands of his cartoons have appeared in more than 400 publications over the last twenty-three years. His Cartoon-a-Day calendars are available annually, as well as his many books including *Laughter From the Pearly Gates* and *A Joke A Day Keeps the Doctor Away*. E-mail Jonny at jonnyhawkins2nz@yahoo.com.

Jeanne Hill is an author, an inspirational speaker and a contributing editor to *Guidepost* magazine. Her award-winning short stories and articles are often chosen for anthologies. She has published two books, *Daily Breath*, Word Books and *Secrets of Prayer Joy*, Judson Press.

Pamela Hackett Hobson, a wife and mother of two sons, is a banker and author of *The Bronxville Book Club* and *The Silent Auction*. Pam's debut novel, *The Bronxville Book Club* was featured in *The New York Times*. To learn more about the author, visit www.pamelahobson.com or send an e-mail to author@pamelahobson.com.

Dawn Holt received a Bachelor of Science degree, a Master of Education degree, and a Ph.D. in Educational Leadership. She is currently a counselor at Fuller Performance Learning Center in Fayetteville, NC. This is her third contribution to *Chicken Soup for the Soul*. Please e-mail her at dawnholt@yahoo.com.

Dave Huebsch has a Bachelor of Science degree in Education with a degree in Language Arts. He has been working doing human development in Guatemala for the past twenty-four years. Dave and his wife Bina are the founders of two non-profits: Rising Villages, Inc. (www.risingvillages.org) and Common Hope, Inc.

Taryn R. Hutchinson served on staff with Campus Crusade for Christ for twenty-one years, serving ten of those years in Eastern Europe. Currently, she works at Golden Gate Seminary and lives in Marin County, California, with her husband, Steve. Taryn enjoys people and travel. Please e-mail her at terenahutchison@hotmail.com.

Ellen Javernick is a graduate of DePauw University. She lives in Loveland, Colorado. She loves teaching, tennis and spending time with her seven grandchildren. She is the author of *What If Everybody Did That* and numerous other children's books. You can e-mail her at javernicke@aol.com.

Sally Kelly-Engeman is a freelance writer who has had numerous short stories and articles published. In addition to writing, she enjoys reading and researching. She also enjoys ballroom dancing and traveling the world with her husband. She can be reached at sallyfk@juno.com.

Carol Kenny's family came to Maryland in the 1600s, fleeing religious persecution. She wrote her first poem at age seven and recently wrote the forthcoming book, *Whispers from St. Mary's Well*, a 19th century historical novel with a touch of mystery and mysticism. She'd love to hear from you at ck@carolkenny.com.

Eileen Knockenhauer is a retired school secretary. Married for thirty-seven years, she has three daughters and four grandaughters. Eileen earned a Bachelor of Arts in 2005 and enjoys writing for children. Eileen loves Long Island beaches, likes to bike ride, fish, and entertain friends and family. E-mail her at eirishnana@optonline.net.

Cathy Kruse lives with her husband and two teenage children in Minnesota. A former public relations professional, Cathy is working on a nonfiction book and enjoys interior design, volunteering, scrapbooking, gardening, and travel. She is grateful for the powerful intercession of the rosary which sustained her family through her father's illness and death.

Ben Lager holds a Masters degree in Sacred Scripture from St. John's University in Collegeville, MN. He is a lifelong environmentalist and dedicated bicyclist. He continues to reach out to the homeless of Juarez through his non-profit, The St. Jerome Mission. Contact him at lagerb@earthlink.net.

Dorothy LaMantia writes stories of everyday faith and redemption. Wife of Joe, mother of Andy, Jon, and Kate, and teacher of English, she serves her church as a reader, choir member, and a volunteer of the Society of Saint Vincent de Paul. E-mail her at dotelama@aol.com.

Jeremy Langford is an award-winning author whose books include *Seeds of Faith* and *The Spirit of Notre Dame*. He is the Communications Director for the Chicago Province of the Jesuits and runs the Langford Literary Agency. He lives in Evanston, IL, with his wife and their three children. E-mail: jereditor@aol.com.

Marianne LaValle-Vincent, a first generation Italian-American, is an author, poet and humorist. She has achieved worldwide publication and is the author of three full-length poetry collections and hundreds of short stories and essays. She works and lives in Syracuse, NY, with her seventeen-year-old daughter, Jess.

John J. Lesjack, has been published in *Chicken Soup for the Chocolate Lover's Soul*, *Chicken Soup for the Father & Son Soul*, *San Francisco Chronicle* magazine, *Grit*, *Reminisce*, and many other publications. He is a retired grade school teacher who lives to play tennis in northern California. Jlesjack@gmail.com.

Jaye Lewis is an award-winning inspirational writer and frequent contributing author to *Chicken Soup for the Soul*. She lives with her family in the beautiful Appalachian Mountains of Virginia, which Jaye insists is the most romantic place on earth. Visit Jaye's website at www.entertainingangels.org or e-mail Jaye at jayelewis@comcast.net.

Eileen Love is a writer, speaker and teacher and has worked in parish ministry for more than twenty-five years. She is a master catechist, a graduate of the Catholic Biblical School and has her Master's Degree in Theological Studies. She is currently an editor for ENDOW. She and her husband, Mike, have four boys.

Donna Lowich lives in New Jersey with husband and three cats. She works as an Information Specialist providing information on spinal cord injury and paralysis. Her hobbies include her cats, cross stitching and writing about her life experiences. Please e-mail her at donnalowich@aol.com.

Natalia Lusinski created her first "newspaper," *Nat's Neat News Notes*, at the age of ten. Since then, she has worked as a writers' assistant on several TV shows, most recently *Desperate Housewives*. She also writes film and TV scripts, as well as short stories. E-mail her at: writenataliainla@yahoo.com.

Linda Mainard has lived in Milwaukie, Oregon, for thirty-three years. Linda and her husband have four children and have three grandchildren. She has had an amazing life. There is nothing that she cares about more then her family and her faith. This story is a record of that love.

Sister Mammaw C.W. is a Consecrated Widow in the Catholic Church. Married thirty-nine years, five children, thirteen grandchildren and two great-grandaughters. Her husband, Harry, was ill for twelve years before dying August 1, 1998. She is a Director of Religious Education in Cordova, TN. She writes about Spirituality in Life. E-mail her at terry.harvey@SFAchurch.cdom.org.

Joanne Mancuso spent her early childhood in Chicago, IL. At age ten, her family moved to Arizona where she graduated high school and attened the University of Arizona. Joanne currently resides in nothern California where she works as a Library Aide. She is married and has three children.

In 2001, **Miriam Mas** started Canines with a Cause, a charity dedicated to training assistance dogs for people with disabilities. She left the high-tech world to better focus on helping others. By sharing this story, she hopes others will also take the time to share hope with others in need. You can reach Miriam at miriam.mas@gmail.com.

Julienne Mascitti is a writer, public speaker, wish granter, and Mrs. Claus for Make-A-Wish Foundation and children's hospitals. She received the Stellar Achievement and the North Star Award from MAW and the President's Award for HRA. She recently completed children's books about Santa. Jules lives in Naperville, Illinois, with husband, Ron, and puppies "Baci and Porsha." juleslentz@msn.com.

Kathy McGovern holds Masters degrees in both Liturgical Studies and Sacred Scripture. She has published numerous articles on Scripture and spirituality, and is the composer of the popular Christmas song "Mary had a Baby." She and her husband Ben Lager live in Denver, Colorado. Reach her at mcgovern.kathy@yahoo.com.

Rosemary McLaughlin taught English and creative writing for thirty-five years and especially enjoyed coaching her writing students. She wrote a column for a local paper for eight years and still writes short pieces and poetry. Rosemary enjoys traveling worldwide with her husband and returning home to Pittsburgh, her children, and grandchildren.

Marie-Therese Miller lives in New York with her husband and five children. She is the author of *Distinguished Dogs, Helping Dogs, Hunting and Herding Dogs, Police Dogs*, and *Search and Rescue Dogs* (Chelsea House, 2007). Her stories appeared in *Chicken Soup for the Preteen Soul 2* and *Chicken Soup for the Soul: Love Stories*. Contact her via e-mail at thisisthelife@hvc.rr.com.

Maryjo Faith Morgan, freelance writer, is grateful to the IHM sisters at Our Lady of Grace, Somerdale, NJ. She now understands her grasp of sentence structure is due to countless sentences diagramed for being such a chatterbox in class! Maryjo's husband Fred (of www.FredsUsedWebsites.com) is the skilled webmaster behind www.MaryjoFaithMorgan.com.

Richard J. Mueller, an award-winning itinerant teller of tales, roving pizza entrepreneur, and consultant, is currently holding court in San Antonio, Texas. Please reach him via e-mail at polermodude@yahoo.com.

Nancy Noonan is a funny, high-content motivational speaker, trainer and author. A former Miss Maryland, Master-Teacher-awarded college instructor, business owner and tap dancer, Nancy helps people and organizations live and work at their highest, Masterpiece levels. Nancy lives in Colorado with husband of thirty-one years, Richard. Reach Nancy at www.nancynoonanspeaks.com.

Sherry O'Boyle is a writer living in Eugene, Oregon, and has been published in several magazines including *Oregon Coast, Northwest Travel, E/The Environmental Magazine*, and the *Catholic Sentinel*. In 2008, she received her Master's degree in Adult & Higher Education Leadership from Oregon State University. Sherry enjoys camping, fishing, traveling, and visiting with family.

Sally O'Brien, the mother of four girls and a priest, is retired and lives in Iowa. She writes mostly articles, with a few short stories, plus she recently completed a novel. She is active in her church and spends as much time as possible reading. Please e-mail her at sobrien95@msn.com.

Linda O'Connell has been a preschool teacher in St. Louis, MO, for thirty-one years and she also teaches an adult writing class. She is a widely-published, multi-genre writer. Her essays have appeared in several *Chicken Soup for the Soul* books. Linda enjoys traveling and long walks on the beach. Billin7@juno.com.

Linda L. Osmundson has written for art, children, parents, grand-parents, travel, newspaper, religious, teacher, *Chicken Soup for the Soul* and *Family Circle* publications. She enjoys her grandchildren, crafts, golf, reading, writing, Dixieland jazz and traveling. She lives with her husband in Fort Collins, Colorado. You may contact her at LLO1413@msn.com.

Mark Parisi's "off the mark" comic, syndicated since 1987, is dis-tributed by United Media. Mark's humor also graces greeting cards, T-shirts, calendars, magazines, newsletters and books. Check out: offthemark.com. Lynn is his wife/business partner. Their daughter, Jen, contributes with inspiration (as do three cats).

Diane C. Perrone writes between babies—sixteen grandchildren so far. Her articles have appeared in *Chicken Soup for the Soul* (*Writer's*, *Wine Lover's*, *Mother's*) and periodicals (*Redbook*, *Catholic Digest*, *Our Family* and aviation magazines). Diane speaks to seasoned citizens and companies that market to them. E-mail her at Grandma1Di@AOL.com.

Bruce R. Porter, D.Div, has ministered in over forty nations, respond-ing as a Chaplain crisis counselor to such high-profile disasters as the Columbine, Red Lake, Erfurt-Germany, Beslan-Russia, and Amish school massacres, as well as the 9/11 Islamic terror attack in New York and the tsunami disaster in Sri Lanka. www.torchgrab.org.

John R. Powers is a playwright of the Broadway musical, *Do Black Patent Leather Shoes Really Reflect Up?* as well as four best-selling books. He is also a professional speaker for business, educational and community groups. www.johnpowers.com. E-mail him at johnpowerspmi@aol.com.

Kate Prado is the youngest daughter of well-known writer, the late Martin Buxbaum. She left a career in property management in 2005 to move to Hagerstown, Maryland, to write. Her heart's desire is to feed children and help the elderly. She can be reached at kateprado@aol.com or www.pradospen.com.

Tom Reilly is author of *Next of Kin: A Brother's Journey to Wartime Vietnam* (Potomac Books, Inc., Washington, DC) He is finishing a second novel, *August Pearl*, based on an actual event that took place in 1968 during the Cold War in Europe. Please e-mail him at thomaslreilly@aol.com.

Christina Robertson received her Bachelor of Science with honors from Bethel College in 2000 and her Masters Degree in Education from Cumberland University in 2006. She teaches 7th and 8th grades in Middle Tennessee. Christina enjoys reading, singing, drama, and working with children. She hopes to become a published author in the near future.

Elizabeth Schmeidler is happily married and a mother to three wonderful sons. She is an author of children's stories, novels, short stories, and poetry and has also recorded three CDs of original Christian music. Elizabeth is an inspirational speaker and anxiously awaits the upcoming recording of her 4th CD. www.elizabethshop.org.

Debra Scipioni teaches fourth grade and fifth grade writing/grammar, and is a Reading Specialist. She holds certifications in reading, elementary, and special education. Debra received her Master's Degree with Distinction in 2003. She enjoys reading, writing poetry, and the Yankees. Debra plans to teach college courses for those studying education.

Terri Scott graduated with a BA in Rhetoric and Communications. She is a freelance writer for *The Prairie Messenger*, a Catholic newspaper; *The New Wine Press*, and the *Winnipeg Archdiocesan Newspaper*. Terri was awarded Life Membership in The Catholic Women's League of Canada. She loves to travel to Europe and enjoys scrapbooking.

Joyce Seabolt has been a nurse for forty-five years and a writer for five. Her work appears in two other *Chicken Soup for the Soul* books as well as numerous nursing magazines. She and her husband, Hal, live in Red Lion, Pennsylvania. E-mail her at joyceseabolt@hotmail.com.

When **Mary Z. Smith** is not writing for *Angels on Earth* and *Guideposts*, she is volunteering with Social Services, helping needy families. She and her husband have two biological daughters, Autumn and Amber, and two adopted, Adi and Ronen. Mary resides in Richmond, VA, with husband, Barry, mother-in-law, Flora, and their rat terrier, Frankie.

Joan Stamm received her M.F.A. in Writing and Literature from Bennington College in 1998. She has recently moved to a small island off the coast of Washington State where she continues to write and practice Ikebana. Since her experience finding the white rosary she has discovered a meditative practice in the Catholic tradition.

Stephanie Staples is an international motivational speaker, coach and author. Her business, Your Life Unlimited, uses radio, print and speaking to inspire, educate and encourage people to make small choices that lead to big life changes. Her greatest sources of pride are her successful twenty-year marriage to Randy and their three great teens. Visit her website at www.yourlifeunlimited.ca.

Judy Stoddart, formerly the Editorial and Advertising Assistant for *Style Manitoba* magazine is a freelance writer, published poet, songwriter and storyteller. Born in Grandview MB, Ms. Stoddart attributes a considerable portion of her literary flair to the inspiration of growing up in a rural community. Currently, she is composing a collection of poems entitled *Crossing the Tracks*.

Carol Strazer received her BS degree in speech and English education and MA in counseling psychology. She was editor of a community newsletter, spearheaded a local writers group, and is working on a non-fiction biography of WWII refugee camps. Her husband Bob and she celebrated their 46th anniversary.

Craig A. Strickland attends Corpus Christi, in Aliso Viejo, California (avcatholics.org). Craig has seen the publication of many short stories in both magazines and anthologies, plus—so far—two nationally distributed fiction books. For more information or to contact Craig, go to CraigStrickland.net.

Joyce Sudbeck received her Associate's Degree, with honors, in 1986. She recently left her Marketing Department position at Liguori Publications to pursue new challenges. Joyce enjoys choir, composing, piano, poetry, crocheting, knitting, sewing, cooking and writing. Joyce plans to continue writing poetry, short stories and perhaps a novel.

Annmarie B. Tait lives in Conshohocken, PA, with her husband Joe and Sammy the "Wonder Yorkie." In addition to writing stories about life in a large Irish Catholic family, Annmarie also enjoys singing and recording American and Irish folk songs which reflect her heritage. She can be reached at irishbloom@aol.com.

Christine M. Trollinger is a freelance writer whose stories have been published in several anthologies and magazines. She is a widow, mother of three, and enjoys working with the local animal rescue groups. Please e-mail her at trollys_2@yahoo.com.

Connie (Milardovich) Vagg retired in 2000, as secretary with the 652nd Combat Logistics Support Squadron (CLSS), McClellan AFB CA. Mother of two daughters, grandmother of four, and a parishoner at St. Rose Catholic Church. She collects teapots, but time with family is cherished most. You can e-mail her at cvagg@netzero.net.

Karen Adragna Walsh, received a BS degree in nursing from D'Youville College. Wanting to keep people in "stitches," she's an operating nurse by day and writes humorous articles by night. Author of *Good Crazy: Essays of a Mad Housewife*, Karen can be reached via e-mail at humormeso@aol.com.

Emily Weaver is a freelance writer/stay-at-home mom in Springfield, Missouri. She enjoys spending time with her three young children and husband. Her work has appeared in *Chicken Soup for the New Mom's Soul*, *Chicken Soup for the American Idol Soul* and *Chicken Soup for Soul: Empty Nesters*. She can be reached by e-mail at emily-weaver@sbcglobal.net.

Kerrie Weitzel lives in Fort Collins, Colorado, where she writes poems, prayers, blessings, short stories, kids' stories, and is working on her first novel.

Rev. Mr. Thomas J. Winninger ignites passion whether he is delivering a homily, launching an annual convention, helping a business repurpose itself, or counseling someone individually. He is a Permanent Catholic Deacon, father of seven children, a business journalist who has written five books, and a master's student in Catholic Studies. thomas@winninger.com

Who Is
Jack Canfield?

*J*ack Canfield is the co-creator and editor of the Chicken Soup for the Soul series, which Time magazine has called "the publishing phenomenon of the decade." Jack is also the co-author of eight other bestselling books including *The Success Principles™: How to Get from Where You Are to Where You Want to Be*, *Dare to Win*, *The Aladdin Factor*, *You've Got to Read This Book*, and *The Power of Focus: How to Hit Your Business and Personal and Financial Targets with Absolute Certainty*.

Jack is the CEO of the Canfield Training Group in Santa Barbara, California, and founder of the Foundation for Self-Esteem in Culver City, California. He has conducted intensive personal and professional development seminars on the principles of success for over a million people in twenty-three countries. Jack is a dynamic keynote speaker and he has spoken to hundreds of thousands of others at more than 1,000 corporations, universities, professional conferences and conventions, and has been seen by millions more on national television shows such as *The Today Show*, *Fox and Friends*, *Inside Edition*, *Hard Copy*, CNN's *Talk Back Live*, *20/20*, *Eye to Eye*, and the *NBC Nightly News* and the *CBS Evening News*.

Jack is the recipient of many awards and honors, including three honorary doctorates and a Guinness World Records Certificate for having seven books from the *Chicken Soup for the Soul* series appearing on the New York Times bestseller list on May 24, 1998.

You can reach Jack at:

Jack Canfield
The Canfield Companies
P. O. Box 30880 • Santa Barbara, CA 93130
phone: 805-563-2935 • fax: 805-563-2945
www.jackcanfield.com

Who Is
Mark Victor Hansen?

*M*ark Victor Hansen is the co-founder of Chicken Soup for the Soul, along with Jack Canfield. He is also a sought-after keynote speaker, bestselling author, and marketing maven. For more than thirty years, Mark's powerful messages of possibility, opportunity, and action have created powerful change in thousands of organizations and millions of individuals worldwide.

Mark's credentials include a lifetime of entrepreneurial success. He is a prolific writer with many bestselling books, such as *The One Minute Millionaire*, *Cracking the Millionaire Code*, *How to Make the Rest of Your Life the Best of Your Life*, *The Power of Focus*, *The Aladdin Factor*, and *Dare to Win*, in addition to the Chicken Soup for the Soul series. Mark has had a profound influence in the field of human potential through his library of audios, videos, and articles in the areas of big thinking, sales achievement, wealth building, publishing success, and personal and professional development. Mark is also the founder of the MEGA Seminar Series.

He has appeared on *Oprah*, CNN, and *The Today Show*. He has been quoted in *Time*, *U.S. News & World Report*, *USA Today*, *The New York Times*, and *Entrepreneur* and has given countless radio interviews, assuring our planet's people that "You can easily create the life you deserve."

Mark is the recipient of numerous awards that honor his entrepreneurial spirit, philanthropic heart, and business acumen. He is a lifetime member of the Horatio Alger Association of Distinguished Americans, an organization that honored Mark with the prestigious Horatio Alger Award for his extraordinary life achievements.

You can reach Mark at:

Mark Victor Hansen & Associates, Inc.
P. O. Box 7665 • Newport Beach, CA 92658
phone: 949-764-2640 • fax: 949-722-6912
www.markvictorhansen.com

Who Is
LeAnn Thieman?

*L*eAnn Thieman is a nationally acclaimed professional speaker, author, and nurse who was "accidentally" caught up in the Vietnam Orphan Airlift in 1975. Her book, *This Must Be My Brother*, details her daring adventure of helping to rescue 300 babies as Saigon was falling to the Communists. LeAnn and her incredible story have been featured in *Newsweek Magazine's Voices of the Century* issue, FOX News, CNN, PBS, BBC, PAX-TV's *It's A Miracle*, and countless radio and TV programs.

Today, as a renowned motivational speaker, LeAnn inspires audiences to balance their lives, truly live their priorities, and make a difference in the world.

After her story was featured in *Chicken Soup for the Mother's Soul*, LeAnn became one of Chicken Soup's most prolific writers. That, and her devotion to thirty years of nursing, made her the ideal co-author of *Chicken Soup for the Nurse's Soul*. She went on to co-author *Chicken Soup for the Caregiver's Soul*, *Chicken Soup for the Father and Daughter Soul*, *Chicken Soup for the Grandma's Soul*, *Chicken Soup for the Christian Woman's Soul*, *Chicken Soup for the Christian Soul 2*, *Chicken Soup for the Nurse's Soul, Second Dose*, and *Chicken Soup for the Adopted Soul*. Her life-long practice of her Catholic faith led her to co-author *Chicken Soup for the Soul: Living Catholic Faith*. LeAnn is one of about ten percent of speakers worldwide to have earned the Certified Speaking Professional Designation award and in 2008 she was inducted into the Speakers Hall of Fame.

She and Mark, her husband of thirty-eight years, reside in Colorado.

For more information about LeAnn's books and tapes, or to schedule her for a presentation, please contact her at:

LeAnn Thieman, CSP, CPAE
6600 Thompson Drive
Fort Collins, CO 80526
1-970-223-1574
www.LeAnnThieman.com

380   About the Authors: *Who Is LeAnn Thieman?*

Thank You!

We wish to express our heartfelt gratitude to the following people who helped make this book possible:

Our families, who have been chicken soup for our souls!

LeAnn's devoted, loving, supportive family: Mark, LeAnn's husband, who has traveled her faith journey for thirty-eight years, strengthening her faith, her love of God, and love for him, and Angela, Brian, Dante, Lia, Christie, Dave, Dagny and Mitch. May your great faith be empowered by the stories shared here.

LeAnn's mother, Berniece, who for ninety years has role modeled for the world, the ideal Catholic faith-filled woman of God we all strive to be.

A special thanks to Amy Williams who trusts LeAnn's faith and her own as she manages LeAnn's speaking business.

Our glorious panel of readers who helped us make the final selections: Catherine Barczyk, Bobbie Bonk, Denise Carr, Caryll Cram, Joan Demma, Deborah Duello, Richard Duello, Shirley Dino, Holly Engel-Smothers, Jackie Fleming, Pierrett Guidry, Renee King, D. LaMantia, Grace Larralde, Julie Lentz, Eileen Love, Maryjo Faith Morgan, Christie Rogers, Mary Streit, Carol Strazer, Mark Thieman, Karen Adragna Walsh and Jeanie Winstrom.

We also want to thank Amy Newmark, D'ette Corona, Barbara LoMonaco, Kristiana Glavin, Bill Rouhana, and Bob Jacobs at Chicken Soup for the Soul for supporting this project. Brian Taylor at Pneuma Books also deserves thanks for his brilliant vision for our cover and interior.

Most of all, thank you to everyone who submitted their heartfelt stories, poems, quotes and cartoons for possible inclusion in this book. While we were not able to use everything you sent, we love and appreciate you for sharing them. They blessed us. Because of the size of this project, we may have left out the names of some people who contributed along the way. If so, we are sorry; please know we appreciate you very much.

And to God, for His divine guidance and abundant blessings.

Chicken Soup for the Soul

Improving Your Life Every Day

Real people sharing real stories—for fifteen years. Now, Chicken Soup for the Soul has gone beyond the bookstore to become a world leader in life improvement. Through books, movies, DVDs, online resources and other partnerships, we bring hope, courage, inspiration and love to hundreds of millions of people around the world. Chicken Soup for the Soul's writers and readers belong to a one-of-a-kind global community, sharing advice, support, guidance, comfort, and knowledge.

Chicken Soup for the Soul stories have been translated into more than forty languages and can be found in more than one hundred countries. Every day, millions of people experience a Chicken Soup for the Soul story in a book, magazine, newspaper or online. As we share our life experiences through these stories, we offer hope, comfort and inspiration to one another. The stories travel from person to person, and from country to country, helping to improve lives everywhere.

Share with Us

We all have had Chicken Soup for the Soul moments in our lives. If you would like to share your story or poem with millions of people around the world, go to www.chickensoup.com and click on "Submit Your Story." You may be able to help another reader, and become a published author at the same time. Some of our past contributors have launched writing and speaking careers from the publication of their stories in our books!

Your stories have the best chance of being used if you submit them through our website, at

www.chickensoup.com

If you do not have access to the Internet, you may submit your stories by mail or by facsimile. Please do not send us any book manuscripts, unless through a literary agent, as these will be automatically discarded.

Chicken Soup for the Soul
P.O. Box 700
Cos Cob, CT 06807-0700
Fax 203-861-7194

Chicken Soup for the Soul

www.chickensoup.com